AFRICAN ISSUES

Africa Rising?

T0341277

AFRICAN ISSUES

AFRICAN ISSUES

Africa Rising?

BRICS
– Diversifying
Dependency

IAN TAYLOR
Professor in International
Relations & African Politics
University of St Andrews

JAMES CURREY

James Currey
is an imprint of
Boydell & Brewer Ltd
PO Box 9, Woodbridge
Suffolk IP12 3DF (GB)
www.jamescurrey.com
and of
Boydell & Brewer Inc.
668 Mt Hope Avenue
Rochester, NY 14620-2731 (US)
www.boydellandbrewer.com

© Ian Taylor 2014

First published 2014

1 2 3 4 5 17 16 15 14

British Library Cataloguing in Publication Data
A catalogue record for this book is available on request from the British Library

ISBN 978-1-84701-096-4 (James Currey paper)

The publisher has no responsibility for the continued existence or accuracy of URLs for
external or third-party internet websites referred to in this book, and does not guarantee
that any content on such websites is, or will remain, accurate or appropriate.

This book is printed on acid-free paper

Typeset in 9/11 Melior with Optima display
by Avocet Typeset, Somerton, Somerset

DEDICATION

This book is dedicated to
Professor Philip Nel of the University of Otago;
past supervisor and mentor,
and to whose academic qualities
I have always aspired

CONTENTS

LIST OF TABLES

ACKNOWLEDGEMENTS

In the course of my research I have had the privilege of visiting a number of institutions, in Africa, in the BRICS countries and elsewhere. In particular, I would like to acknowledge, in Brazil: the comments, criticisms and advice provided by staff and students at the BRICS Policy Center, Rio de Janeiro; the Institute of International Relations at PUC-Rio; and the Department of International Relations, PUC-Minas; in India: the Centre for African Studies, Jawaharlal Nehru University; the Department of African Studies, University of Delhi; the India International Centre; the Institute for Defence Studies and Analyses; and the Open Research Foundation; in China: the Centre for African Studies, University of Peking; School of International Studies, Renmin University of China; Carnegie-Tsinghua Center for Global Policy, Tsinghua University; the Institute of African Studies, Zhejiang Normal University; and the Institute of West Asian and African Studies, Chinese Academy of Social Sciences; in South Africa: the University of Cape Town; the University of Stellenbosch; the Centre for Chinese Studies; and the Trade Law Centre for Southern Africa (TRALAC). In Russia, Aleksandra Arkhangelskaya and Vladimir Shubin, both of the Institute for African Studies, Russian Academy of Sciences, have been very helpful in enabling me to shape my ideas about Russo-African relations.

I am very grateful to the following funders who supported this work: Marco Polo Santander Award, Saferworld, Chiang Ching-kuo Foundation for International Scholarly Exchange, the Chinese Ministry of Education, the Carnegie Trust for the Universities of Scotland and the Kemp Family.

Pádraig Carmody of Trinity College, Dublin, gave extensive and very helpful insights and comments on an earlier draft – *buíochas a lán Pádraig!*

Finally, I would like to thank Jo, Blythe and Archie for both accompanying me on extended visits to China and different parts of Africa and for also allowing me to disappear (all too frequently) to the continent.

Ian Taylor

LIST OF ACRONYMS

ABC	*Agência Brasileira de Cooperação* (Brazilian Cooperation Agency)
ACBF	Africa Capacity Building Foundation
ACSA	Airports Company South Africa
ADB	African Development Bank
AERC	African Economic Research Consortium
AGOA	African Growth and Opportunities Act
ASSOCHAM	Associated Chambers of Commerce and Industry of India
ANC	African National Congress
AU	African Union
BNDES	*Banco Nacional de Desenvolvimento Econômico e Social* (Brazilian Development Bank)
BRIC	Brazil, Russia, India and China
BRICS	Brazil, Russia, India, China and South Africa
BRICSAM	BRICS plus Mexico
BRIICKS	BRICS plus Indonesia and South Korea
BWIs	Bretton Woods Institutions
CAFTA	Central American Free Trade Area
CEO	Chief executive officer
CIVETS	Colombia, Indonesia, Vietnam, Egypt, Turkey and South Africa
CNOOC	China National Offshore Oil Corporation
COMESA	Common Market for Eastern and Southern Africa
COMPLANT	China National Complete Plant Import & Export Corporation
CPC	Communist Party of China
CPLP	*Comunidade dos Países de Língua Portuguesa* (Community of Portuguese Language Countries)
DAC	Development Assistance Committee of the OECD
DRC	Democratic Republic of Congo
ECOSOC	United Nations Economic and Social Council
ECOWAS	Economic Community of West African States

EMBRAPA	*Empresa Brasileira de Pesquisa Agropecuária* (Brazilian Agricultural Research Corporation)
EMs	Emerging markets
EU	European Union
EXIM	Export-Import Bank of India
FDI	Foreign direct investment
FICCI	Federation of Indian Chambers of Commerce and Industry
FOCAC	Forum on China-Africa Cooperation
G-7	Canada, France, Germany, Italy, Japan, United Kingdom and United States
G-8	Canada, France, Germany, Italy, Japan, Russia, United Kingdom and United States
G-15	Algeria, Argentina, Brazil, Chile, Egypt, India, Indonesia, Jamaica, Kenya, Nigeria, Malaysia, Mexico, Peru, Senegal, Sri Lanka, Venezuela and Zimbabwe
G-20	Argentina, Australia, Brazil, Canada, China, European Union, France, Germany, India, Indonesia, Italy, Japan, Mexico, Russia, Saudi Arabia, South Africa, South Korea, Turkey, United Kingdom and United States
G-20+	Argentina, Bolivia, Brazil, Chile, China, Colombia, Costa Rica, Cuba, Ecuador, El Salvador, Guatemala, India, Mexico, Pakistan, Paraguay, Peru, the Philippines, South Africa, Thailand and Venezuela
G-24	Algeria, Argentina, Brazil, Colombia, Democratic Republic of Congo, Egypt, Ethiopia, Gabon, Ghana, Guatemala, India, Iran, Ivory Coast, Lebanon, Mexico, Nigeria, Pakistan, Philippines, Peru, South Africa, Sri Lanka, Syria, Trinidad and Tobago, and Venezuela
G-77	A loose coalition of developing countries at the UN, founded in 1964: 77 founding members, since expanded to 132 member countries
GATT	General Agreement on Tariffs and Trade
GDP	Gross domestic product
GNI	Gross national income
GNP	Gross national product
GNPC	Ghana National Petroleum Corporation
GS	Genuine saving
HABITAT	United Nations Human Settlements Programme
HIPC	Heavily Indebted Poor Countries
IBRD	International Bank for Reconstruction and Development
IBSA	India-Brazil-South Africa Dialogue Forum
IDA	International Development Association
IFC	International Finance Corporation
IFIs	International financial institutions
IMF	International Monetary Fund
IOC	Indian Oil Corporation

ITEC	Indian Technical and Economic Cooperation Programme
LDCs	Least developed countries
LEDCs	Less economically developed countries
LICs	Low Income Countries
LTO	Light tight oil
MAP	Millennium Africa Recovery Plan
MDRI	Multilateral Debt Relief Initiative
MFA	Multifibre Arrangement
MFA	Ministry of Foreign Affairs (China)
MINT	Mexico, Indonesia, Nigeria and Turkey
MOFTEC	Ministry of Foreign Trade and Economic Cooperation (China)
MPLA	*Movimento Popular de Libertação de Angola* (People's Movement for the Liberation of Angola)
MVA	Manufacturing value added
NAI	New Africa Initiative
NAM	Non-Aligned Movement
NATO	North Atlantic Treaty Organisation
NEPAD	New Partnership for Africa's Development
NIEO	New International Economic Order
NNPC	Nigerian National Petroleum Corporation
NSIC	(NEPAD) Heads of State and Government Implementation Committee
OAU	Organisation of African Unity
OECD	Organisation for Economic Co-operation and Development
OFC	Offshore financial centre
OFDI	Outward foreign direct investment
ONGC	Oil and Natural Gas Corporation Limited
OPEC	Organisation of the Petroleum Exporting Countries
OVL	ONGC Videsh Limited
PALOP	*Países Africanos de Língua Oficial Portuguesa* (African Countries of Portuguese Official Language)
PIO	People of Indian Origin
PPP	Purchasing power parity
PRC	People's Republic of China
PT	*Partido dos Trabalhadores* (Workers' Party)
SADC	Southern African Development Community
SAPs	Structural Adjustment Programmes
SCAAP	Special Commonwealth Assistance for Africa Programme
SSA	Sub-Saharan Africa
TIMBI	Turkey, India, Mexico, Brazil and Indonesia
UN	United Nations
UNAMSIL	United Nations Mission in Sierra Leone
UNCTAD	United Nations Conference on Trade and Development
UNDESA	United Nations Development Policy and Analysis Division
UNDP	United Nations Development Programme

UNECA	United Nations Economic Commission for Africa
UNGA	United Nations General Assembly
UNICA	*União da Indústria de Cana-de-Açúcar* (Brazilian Sugarcane Industry Association)
UNSC	United Nations Security Council
UPA	United Progressive Alliance (India)
WTO	World Trade Organization

Introduction

The African continent is currently encountering interesting dynamics. African per capita growth figures (if taken at face value) are relatively high and have been sustained for a decade or so. This has been constructed on the back of 'a commodity price boom that was unprecedented in its magnitude and duration. The real prices of energy and metals more than doubled in five years from 2003 to 2008, while the real price of food commodities increased 75%' (Erten and Ocampo, 2013: 14). To a large degree, this was intimately linked to new trading geographies and the emergence of 'non-traditional' actors in Africa. The commodity price hike of the first decade of the twenty-first century has been credited to the robust growth performance by emerging economies (particularly China). Indeed, China was a central driver of high prices in a significant number of commodities (Akyüz, 2012). The increase in the activities of emerging economies across Africa are then said to be reshaping Africa's international relations. Analyses thus far have had a strong evangelical aspect to them, suggesting that Africa has turned a corner and that the emerging economies have been decisive in propelling this actuality.

Barely a week passes without some new official report, media article or conference eulogising Africa and its growth figures, this then being automatically and uncritically extended to announcements about the unlimited potential for capital accumulation and profit to be made in this new frontier. This is natural given the ongoing dominant social system and its normative values where the underlying logic and driving force of capitalism and capital is the accumulation of profits; in the words of Marx, the 'boundless drive for enrichment' and the 'passionate chase after value' (Marx, 1867/1976: 254). It is this 'dynamic of endless accumulation' and quest for 'accumulation for its own sake' (Brenner, 2006: 80) that makes capitalism such a pioneering and productive economic system, albeit intrinsically and pitilessly exploitative. Played out in Africa, 'Business conferences are filled with frothy talk of African lions overtaking Asian tigers. Bob Geldof, the founder of Live Aid, is leading the pack in his new incarnation as head of an investment group' (*The Economist*, 2 March 2013).

Obviously, Geldof is *not* 'leading the pack'. He is, however, boldly stating that 'I'm a PE [private equity] whore' (*Daily Mail*, 26 May 2012) and as chairman of a £125 million private equity firm, 8 Miles, is just one of those talking up the continent. What is interesting about this – and Geldof is by no means alone – is that on the one hand a bullish portrayal of Africa is painted, with the explicit goal of attracting investors, and on the other it is admitted by more sober analysis that 'the present growth is socially unsustainable' (Africa Progress Panel, 2012: 8). Such inconvenient facts however are generally crowded out by narratives that Africa is on a 'steady journey from subsistence towards unprecedented prosperity and political pluralism now enjoyed by the world's most advanced countries' (*African Business*, January 2013: 17).

In the context of depressed or stagnating economies in the core, at face value Africa's growth *does* look comparatively healthy, setting aside for one moment the flattening out of over 50 variable countries into one entity known as 'Africa'. But this in itself raises an interesting ontological problem. As Mentan (2010: xi) notes:

> To understand Africa in global capitalism we may view it from two perspectives. That is, there are two ways of picturing Africa in the context of global capitalism. One is from the point of view of the people living and hoping to improve their lot in Africa's fifty-four nation states with a considerable variety of kinds of 'insertion' into the global capitalist economy, and a corresponding range of experiences of development (or lack of it). The other is from the point of view of capital, for which Africa is not so much a system of states, still less a continent of people in need of a better life, as simply a geographic – or geological – terrain, offering this or that opportunity for global capital to make money.

As this book makes clear, the tropes surrounding a notional 'Africa Rising' fully reflects this latter understanding, one based on the point of view of capital, where poles of accumulation and sites of investment have been identified by various actors as spaces offering this or that opportunity. In both the core and some emerging economies, a declining rate of profit means new markets have been sought after: the 'need of a constantly expanding market for its products chase the bourgeoisie over the whole surface of the globe. It must nestle everywhere, settle everywhere, establish connections everywhere' (Marx and Engels, 1888/2004: 37).

Regarding the 'Africa Rising' narrative, what is interesting is that many of the stellar economic indicators have been possibly exaggerated so as to lure investors, emblematically revealed by the fact that whilst 'the United Nations Conference on Trade and Development reckons that foreign investment in Africa was $42.7 bn. in 2011 … the accountants Ernst & Young put it at more than $75 bn' (*Africa Confidential*, 2013: 1). Coincidentally, at the same time, Ernst & Young opened their new 'Africa Global

Tax Desk' in Beijing which 'offers Chinese companies a helping hand' in their investments in Africa (Ernst & Young, 2013). This involvement by speculators 'has had a pernicious effect on distorting perceptions about Africa'. As one analysis notes, 'financial investors used the recent surges in commodity prices as a way to hedge against potential risks in portfolio management. The new commodity indexes developed by financial corporations have not only become profitable investment vehicles, but [have] also fuelled demand in commodity markets', which then drives the 'Africa Rising' mantra (Erten and Ocampo, 2013: 14).

The ongoing dynamics however deepen Africa's dependent position in the global economy. Indeed, the current process 'deepens and intensifies Africa's inveterate and deleterious terms of (mal)integration within the global political economy – terms which continue to be characterised by external dominance and socially-damaging and extraverted forms of accumulation' (Bracking and Harrison, 2003: 9). This is why the Kenyan writer and investigative journalist, Parselelo Kantai, refers to the 'Africa Rising' trope as an 'insidious little fiction manufactured by global corporate finance' (quoted in Rickett, 2013), whilst *Africa Confidential* (2014) notes: 'Much of the [Africa]-boosting, local and international, will serve [only] political and financial interests.' Elsewhere in the world, concern has already been expressed in detailed form about the effects of the emerging economies on other parts of the developing world (e.g. Gallagher and Porzecanski, 2010).

What is interesting however is the way in which the discourse about 'Africa Rising' reflects – and is an extension of – the wider narrative surrounding emerging economies, mostly emblematically captured in the acronym BRICS (Brazil, Russia, India, China and South Africa). The BRICS term has become a neologism symbolising a putative changing world order where the normative principles associated with the capitalist core are allegedly threatened by a new set of alternatives. As this book makes clear, such an understanding of the BRICS is spectacularly wrong. The acronym was coined from the asset management world and was formulated by Jim O'Neill of Goldman Sachs (O'Neill, 2011). 'The inclusion of emerging economies reflects a pragmatic acknowledgement that the task of stabilizing the global economy could not be achieved without them. It also reflects an integrative strategy towards these countries' (Vezirgiannidou, 2013: 644). After all, 'as an adventure of hegemony building, capitalist development relies on regional and global power networks' (Lin Chun, 2013: 10).

As a consequence, 'a new growth regime' has developed through integrating 'emerging markets' into the extant capitalist structures (Aglietta, 2008). This has serious implications for those who place hope on the BRICS as centres of resistance to the dominant neoliberal system. This is particularly (but not exclusively) so with regard to Africa, where numerous elites and intellectuals have greeted the BRICS as the heralds of a new dawn.

It is a contention of this book that the BRICS concept and the 'Africa Rising' trope reflect different spatial impulses of the same phenomenon. The BRICS hypothesis is, as Desai (2007: 785) points out, 'more than a narrative about the sources of new growth in the world economy: it was a directive to first world political and corporate leaders about where new opportunities lay and another to third world political and corporate leaders about the conditions – mainly consistency of neoliberal policy – they must secure if the fruits foreseen were to be theirs'. The 'Africa Rising' narrative is a precise reproduction of this sentiment.

On the BRICS side there are articulations which aim to smooth out difficulties in the world order. This translates into stances that may at times delegitimise the dominant global (state) powers – in particular their hypocritical behaviour on trading matters. But these are firmly reformist and problem-solving. In fact, the BRICS' multilateral diplomacy is largely restricted to pragmatically exposing occasions where the rhetoric of free trade is not actually implemented by the powerful. As Amin has put it, 'governments of the South still seem to fight for a 'true' neoliberalism, whose partners of the North, like those of the South, would agree 'to play the game" (quoted in Herrera, 2005: 553). On the Africa side, the most that has been seen thus far is a clamouring for investment and claims that the BRICS are somehow going to change the world (and Africa's place in it) for the better.

Clearly, the ever-increasing role of emerging economies in Africa *has* been of importance to the continent. According to the United Nations Economic Commission for Africa 'trade with the BRICS has grown faster than with any other region in the world, doubling since 2007 to $340 billion in 2012, and projected to reach $500 billion by 2015' (UNECA, 2013a: 1). What has accompanied such developments is the apparent sudden realisation that Africa is *not* marginal to the world. Sub-Saharan Africa is in fact very well integrated into the global system and has been for decades. It is the pundits, as well as diverse speculators and opportunists, who have abruptly discovered that Africa's foreign trade represents 45 per cent of its Gross National Product (compared to 30 per cent for Asia and Latin America and 15 per cent for the core countries). Quantitatively, the continent is 'more', not 'less', globally integrated. However, the problem, which will be expounded as this work progresses, is the terms of this integration.

Obviously the situation depends on national context, but broadly, 'As a result of their colonial legacy, the present-day economies of the African countries are characterised by a lop-sided dependence on the export of raw materials, and the import of manufactured goods' (Harris, 1975: 12). That this assessment was written nearly 40 years ago and there has not been any radical departure from such a milieu for most countries, reflects the tragedy of much of Africa's post-colonial trajectories. Set in motion by colonialism and the insertion of Africa into the global political economy, the status quo has been ably assisted by the African elite political class

– 'the policemen of ... multinational corporations' (Nkrumah, 1970: 63).

Any analysis of Africa's relations with the BRICS (or any other external actors) needs to be grounded in the above understanding of the dialectical relationships engendered. This necessarily recognises that 'governments serve as the foreman to keep civil society producing a surplus to be accumulated by foreign finance capital and parasitic native social classes that enjoy almost absolutist power' (Mentan, 2010: xii). Despite the celebration of 'democratisation' across the continent and the attempts to link this to Africa's recent growth spurt, there is little evidence that overall the quality of Africa's democracies are improving or that governance is dramatically improving across the continent. The composite Mo Ibrahim Index of African Governance had a continental average of 47/100 in 2000 – by 2013 it had increased to 51.6/100 – hardly seismic and in fact, less than half (43 per cent) of people living in Africa live in a country which has shown overall governance improvement since 2010 (Mo Ibrahim, 2013: 24). This then brings us to a fundamental issue *vis-à-vis* the BRICS engagement in Africa: African agency.

The state-society complex in Africa

Due to the manner in which colonialism created states in Africa and the nature of the independence process in most African countries, the ruling classes lack hegemony over society (Gramsci, 1971). By the ruling class, we mean the senior political elites and bureaucrats, the leading members of the liberal professions, the nascent bourgeoisie and the top members of the security arms of the state (Markovitz, 1987: 8). The early years of post-colonial nationalism in Africa were, broadly speaking, an attempt to build an hegemonic project which bound society together around more issues than simply discontent with the imperial powers. This project quickly collapsed into autocracy and failure, a process accelerated by dynamics linked to the Cold War and to the failure by the new political leaders to make a decisive break from the past: 'the nationalist movement which arose from the contradictions of the colonial economy achieved political independence, not economic independence' (Ake, 1981: 93). Consequently, 'unlike the ascending bourgeoisie of Europe, which transformed all political and economic institutions into its own image and became socially hegemonic, the petit-bourgeoisie in Africa has no criteria of its own, it merely inherited colonial institutions with which the mass of the people did not identify' (Nabudere, 2011: 58).

Of course, 'Africa's leaders are neither autonomous nor robots; they reflect diverse class and fractional interests located within the continent but separable from their extra-continental connections' (Shaw, 1985: 5). These interests vary from state to state and within each state too: 'state power rests in the hands of a local class or classes which constitute the ruling class. This class or classes have their own class interests arising from the place they occupy in social production' (Shivji, 1980: 740). How the centralised organs of the state relate to external interests depends on the positions of various domestic classes *and* the balance of forces between the external and the internal. Indeed, 'African interests can expel and exclude external interests should they wish to do so. In practice they rarely exercise this option, preferring to modify the 'balance of power' over time through almost continuous negotiation' (ibid.: 11). Whilst '[c]ondemnation there must be; but compassion too, for those who talked so boldly about freedom but had so little room for manoeuvre' (First, 1970: 465), this dialectic is central to any analysis of Africa's international relations and the agency of African governments.

Within the realm of the superstructure, moral and political modes that rise above notions of economic-corporate interests and instead reflect broader ethico-political ones have remained missing. Consequently, because the ruling classes have been unable to preside over a hegemonic project that is viewed as legitimate, they have been forced to revert to modalities of governance that seek to dominate. These are commonly expressed through both the threat and actual use of violence *and* the immediate disbursal of material benefits to supporters within the context of neopatrimonial regimes. Without these twin strategies the ruling elites in much of Africa cannot maintain order. After all, 'the state [in Africa], unlike the bourgeois state, is not entrenched in the society as a whole. It is ... a bureaucratic connivance' (Mafeje, 1992: 31). Legitimacy, 'in the sense of a theoretical legitimation of the status quo ... is expressed in the concept of "development", which is "that which we are all in favour of" and given statistical respectability in figures measuring the growth of commodity production' (Williams, 1980: 40). Beyond such rhetoric however, the substance of this belief in 'development' is pretty thin.

The sort of political culture that has matured has had important consequences for Africa, further adding to underdevelopment. Here, a brief definition of what we mean is required. The orthodox criterion is the per capita measurement of national income, used in a rather formalised comparative fashion. This study follows Tamás Szentes' objection to such quantitative indices as 'they do not point out qualitative sameness and differences' (1971: 25). Underdevelopment is a much too multifaceted phenomenon, irreducible to mere quantitative portrayals. Instead, 'there are two aspects, two sides of underdevelopment: the basically external, international aspect, which, from the historical point of view of the emergence of the present state, is the primary aspect; and the internal aspect, which from the point of view of future development, is increasingly important' (ibid.: 163). In short, 'poverty [is] not the result of some historical game of chance in which [Africa] happened to be the losers; it [is] the result of a set of economic relationships, rooted in the colonial era, that [has] served to enrich a minority by impoverishing the majority' (Adamson, 2013: 12).

In general, the modes of governance in Africa have encouraged despotism and unpredictability. As a result, for most of the post-colonial period, much of Africa has been trapped in cycles of crises, which have stimulated societal conflict. Although Africa's elites undoubtedly command the state apparatus, with varying levels of intensity their own practices often undermine and subvert the state's institutions on a daily basis. The relative autonomy of the state is absent and their rule is intrinsically unstable, even though many manage to tenaciously cling to power (Fatton, 1999). There is very little political space to allow reform. Instead of a stable hegemonic project that binds different levels of society together, what exist are intrinsically *unstable* personalised systems of domination. Corruption is the cement that binds the system together and links the patron and their predatory ruling class together. If political elites do ever articulate a vision for the country, 'their notion of emerging out of economic backwardness amounts essentially to Westernisation', where 'the general trend is to try and stimulate economic growth within the context of the existing neocolonial economic structure' (Ake, 1981: 139). This is indeed an accurate appraisal of the contemporary 'development strategies' which characterise much of Africa, only now with the BRICS included, furthering the continent's underdevelopment.

Underdevelopment is a dynamic – not static – condition: it is a relationship and 'expresses a particular relationship of exploitation: namely, the exploitation of one country by another. All of the countries named as 'underdeveloped' in the world are exploited by others; and the underdevelopment with which the world is now pre-occupied is a product of capitalist, imperialist and colonialist exploitation' (Rodney, 2012: 14). The external domination of Africa's economies and the pathologies of dependency that this engenders, constructed during the colonial period, have proven markedly resilient. 'The root dilemma of Africa's economic development has been the asymmetry between the role of the continent in the world and the degree to which that world ... has penetrated Africa' (Austen, 1987: 271). Broadly speaking, '[t]he rigidity of the international division of labour has not allowed African economies to break out of the role of primary producers, for reasons which include lack of access to technology, the comparative advantage of the industrialised nations in manufacturing, and the constraints of the domestic market' (Ake, 1981: 92). Indeed, African economies are integrated into the very economies of the developed economies in a way that is unfavourable to Africa and ensures structural dependence. In short: 'The geo-economy of [Africa] depends on two production systems that determine its structures and define its place in the global system: 1) the export of 'tropical' agricultural products: coffee, cocoa, cotton, peanuts, fruits, oil palm, etc.; and 2) hydrocarbons and minerals – copper, gold, rare metals, diamonds, etc.' (Amin, 2010: 30). This has not radically changed since independence and is overlooked in the excitement to both anoint Africa as the new frontier of opportunity for speculators *and* exaggerate the role of emerging economies as potential redeemers.

'Africa rising'

Currently a great deal of noise is circulating that Africa's time has come and that the continent is embarking on a radically different (and better) stage in its history. This has been connected by many to the growing interest by emerging economies in Africa. Growth in GDP has been the central focus of such commentaries and talk of the 'the hopeless continent' as *The Economist* had it in 2000 has been spectacularly dropped in various circles. Now, it is 'A hopeful continent' (*The Economist*, 2 March 2013). The mood swing about Africa is 'due, directly or indirectly, to the increasing global demand for the continent's resources: notably for oil, but also for gas, minerals, and other energy sources. This was driven, above all, by the sudden appearance of China as a world economic actor, whose dramatic burst of late industrialisation fuelled a global upswing' (ibid.). Yet this has been missed by the 'Africa Rising' mantra. As Patrick Bond (2011: 31) notes:

> Ongoing resource extraction by Western firms was joined, and in some cases overtaken, by China [and others] ... Still, Africa's subordinate position did not change, and aside from greater amounts of overseas development aid flowing into fewer than 15 'fragile states', the North–South flows were not to Africans' advantage. One would not know this from reading reports by the elite multilateral institutions in 2011, which celebrated the continent's national economies as among the world's leading cases of post-meltdown economic recovery.

The flip-flop regarding the continent has, to a certain extent, refuted the familiar media images of fly-blown children that so dominates much discussion of Africa. This *is* a good thing. Yet equally, the narrative has swung almost entirely in the opposite direction, with little critical reflection. Growths in GDP and opportunities for investors are the new intonations in a crude binary construction of Africa that has shifted overnight from basket case to bonanza.

The 'Africa Rising' discourse neglects a most fundamental context: 'only for nine of the forty three [Sub-Saharan] countries were growth rates during 1980–2008 high enough to double per capita income in less than thirty years, and only sixteen in less than one hundred years. Performance would have been considerably worse had it not been for the brief years of relatively rapid growth in the mid-2000s' (Weeks, 2010: 3). Africa needs to grow at least 7 per cent a year for the next 20 or 30 years if any serious tackling of continental poverty is to be realised. However, growth induced by commodity prices increases, new discoveries of natural resources or increase in sources of foreign capital 'is simply not sustainable' (Amoako, 2011: 24).

To the extent that GDP growth has occurred, it 'is overwhelmingly characterised by the deployment and inflow of capital intensive investment for the extraction and exportation of African natural resources. There is a distinct lack of value added on the African side. The principal focus of this activity is in oil which not only offers limited opportunities for local employment, but also deliberately and actively seeks to avoid the hiring of African labour for fear of encountering resistance and the costs of appeasing affected local communities' (Southall, 2008: 148). Problematically, 'while the hope of the development literature has been that higher rates of inflow of capital investment will have downstream effects on African employment (through increased government revenues and spending alongside an injection of consumer wealth into local economies), there is little evidence that this will take place on a substantial scale. The fundamental reason for this is that the [growth] rests heavily on the engagements of foreign governments and corporations with African elites' (ibid.: 149). In *most* neopatrimonial administrations, sustainable and broad-based development is unlikely to occur (cf. Kelsall, 2013).

In late 2012 the Deputy Executive Secretary of the Economic Commission for Africa noted that Africa's relatively good economic growth performance over the past decade had been driven mostly by non-renewable natural resources and high commodity prices. Alongside this, he noted, deindustrialisation had been a key feature, with the share of manufacturing in Africa's GDP falling from 15 per cent in 1990 to 10 per cent in 2008, going hand-in-hand with an increase in unemployment (*Addis Tribune*, 8 December 2012). McMillan and Rodrik (2011) in fact show that since 1990, Africa has experienced a relative shift in the composition of employment toward sectors that create too few high productivity jobs. Manufacturing growth has been near the bottom in twelve growth sectors – only public administration lagged behind.

This of course is not to write off the recent growth as devoid of any value at all. At the minimum, improved fiscal space is being generated. Retail sectors are growing, with revenue increasing by around 4 per cent per year, and there is growing investment in infrastructure (McKinsey Global Institute, 2010). Given that there is a correlation 'between infrastructure and export diversification, and the current low levels and distorted composition of exports from SSA [Sub-Saharan Africa] are partly due to poor trade infrastructure', it can be stated that the improvement in infrastructure 'has *per se* a positive impact on SSA growth and trade capacity' (Sindzingre, 2013: 44). Africa's debts have fallen, partly thanks to the Heavily Indebted Poor Countries Initiative (HIPC) and the Multilateral Debt Relief Initiative (MDRI), and partly due to improved management, although note that 'in spite of the HIPC initiative, only half of SSA countries have witnessed a temporary reduction of their annual debt service' (Petithomme, 2013: 119). In social sectors, performance is varied but increases in the years of schooling are reported across the continent, albeit unevenly. Health outcomes, particularly life expectancy at birth, have also generally improved, in some countries substantially. These are all obviously to be welcomed.

However, it is a contention of this book that there is a desperate need to convert natural resources and high commodity prices into structural change, 'defined as an increase in the share of industry or services in the economy, or as the diversification and sophistication of exports ... or as the shift of workers from sectors with low labour productivity to those with high labour productivity' (Sindzingre, 2013: 26). This is not happening. Instead, with the arrival of emerging economies in Africa alongside traditional trade associates, the historical process of underdevelopment is in danger of being further entrenched.

The new saviours?

Comprehension of the extent of the challenges facing the continent, as well as the actual nature of Africa's insertion into the global order is vitally needed, as is a more critical look at some of the 'new' actors engaging in Africa (see Carmody, 2013). These have been held up in some quarters as the new saviours of Africa – the latest cargo cult to latch onto. In the process, the huge variation in each economic and social profile is flattened out and all are collapsed together as the BRICS, as if they somehow constitute a unified bloc of similar-status nations. A quick glance at some figures demonstrates that this is wholly inaccurate:

Table 1 BRICS Socio-economic indicators

	Population (millions)	Total GDP in US$ (2011)	GDP Growth rate (2011)	Per capita GDP in US$ (2011)	Share in world GDP (per cent)	Ease of doing business rank
Brazil	197	2.4 trillion	2.7%	12,594	2.9	126
Russia	143	1.8 trillion	4.3%	12,995	3	120
India	1.2 billion	1.8 trillion	6.3%	1,509	5.4	132
China	1.3 billion	7.3 trillion	9.3%	5,445	13.6	91
South Africa	52	408 billion	3.1%	8,070	0.7	35

(Source: World Bank, 2013)

It is true that the emergence of new or 'non-traditional' actors in Africa has opened up varying degrees of space for African elites to manoeuvre. Problematically however, this has been seized on as evidence of a new and emerging set of dynamics in international politics, one that creates room for alternatives to neoliberal capitalism. Walter Mignolo, for example, asserts that 'The economic success of the BRICS countries comes from the fact that the leadership is engaged in epistemic economic disobedience *vis-à-vis* the IMF and World Bank' (2012: 43). Martyn Davies of Frontier

Advisory (a research, strategy and investment advisory firm) similarly asserts about the BRICS: 'After the onset of the (Western) financial crisis of 2008, there has been a deep questioning of the free market ideology' (*Financial Times*, 25 March 2013). This naïveté really does need challenging.

Such jubilation is somewhat redolent of Bill Warren's thesis (1973) in which he argued that the Third World, under the effect of local industrial development, was storming ahead, playing a progressive role in reducing the gap between the core and the developing world. Yet just then as now, such predictions were based on growth per capita figures which seemed to suggest a noteworthy redistribution of world industrial power. However, as McMichael et al. (1974) wrote in their rebuttal of Warren's argument:

> To measure distribution of world industrial power by 'growth rates' of industry, which include economies starting from the barest minimum of industrial production and cover a generation, is delightful simplicity. The volume of production, the level of technology, the research capabilities, the allocation of resources, the development of education and the use of manpower, are equally or more relevant to measuring the historic capacity of a country to become a significant industrial power. Warren wishes to prove a 'redistribution' of industrial power, but can only scrape up a one per cent difference in the industrial growth rate between the imperial centres and the Third World: a very slender reed upon which to hang such a weighty claim!

This might be reflected upon today. Whilst per capita growth rates are most relevant with regard to standards of living, from the evaluation of any notional distribution of industrial power and the growth of the market globally, industrial production rates are key. Aggregating figures from the *World Factbook* suggests that whilst the BRICS are doing well, they are not doing *that* much better than the capitalist core. Whilst in 2010, the average industrial production growth rate for the BRICS was 8.7 per cent and for the G-7, 5.6 per cent, in 2011 estimates were that the BRICS average was 5.24 per cent, whilst the G-7 was 1.96 per cent. This sounds substantial. However, if one leaves out Japan's negative rates (distorted by the earthquake and tsunami), then the G-7 (minus Japan) have an average industrial production growth rate of 5.7 per cent. This might well indeed be 'a very slender reed' upon which to announce the replacement of the West by the BRICS.

Besides, the cost to the global ecology is never factored: 'all eyes are on the so-called emerging powers. Why? Because they have rocked the global economy with their stunning GDP growth rates. Never mind, of course, the cost in terms of ecological degradation and social impoverishments that the achievement of this status has implied' (Fioramonti, 2013: 154). Indeed, 'According to the International Energy Agency (IEA), the four BRIC economies alone account for over a third of global carbon emissions caused by land use and deforestation' (International Energy

Agency, 2012a). Of course the status of the BRICS nations as poster children for gross inequality is equally ignored: 'Data from household statistics reveal that income inequalities in all BRICS countries have remained well above the ... OECD average. From the early 1990s to the late 2000s, China, India, the Russian Federation and South Africa all saw steep increases in income inequality. In the same period, Brazil's Gini indicator was almost twice as large as the OECD average' (Ivins, 2013: 3).

Background noise about South–South solidarity aside, none of the BRICS have any serious agenda to change the world. There is no ideal world order that the BRICS wish to promote. Rather, increasing the bargaining power of the elites from the BRICS with the core is the sum total of any 'vision':

> BRIC states, while officially denouncing US-originated neoliberalism are implementing neoliberal economic policies to boost their own economic growth ... The rise of the BRIC states will not bring the new economic world-order [or] bring the redistribution of economic power through the existing system, since the BRIC states have in general accepted (not all of them in the same degree) the neoliberal economic ideology and applied neoliberal economic policies or some of its aspects. (Kurečić and Bandov, 2011: 30)

This is an important point to make. During the period of economic growth in emerging economies, a variety of non-academic commentators emerged, to gloat that the core was finished and that the future belonged elsewhere. Deploying a rather crude Occidentalism to castigate the West for every evil, an unprocessed form of Asian triumphalism (in particular) momentarily took stage. Unformed but provocative statements were temporarily listened to during a time when the core appeared to be in irrecoverable crisis (see e.g. Mahbubani, 2008). Analysis like this now seems rather embarrassing. As Sharma (2014: 52) notes, such media pundits 'stopped looking at emerging markets as individual stories and started lumping them into faceless packs' and objectified spatial entities (such as in Mahbubani's *The New Asian Hemisphere*). 'They listened too closely to political leaders in the emerging world who took credit for the boom and ignored the other global forces, such as easy money coming out of the United States and Europe, that helped power growth'. Some 'experts' even 'cited the seventeenth-century economic might of China and India as evidence that they would dominate the coming decade, even the coming century' (ibid.: 53). Emblematically: 'From year 1 to 1820, China and India provided the world's two largest economies. By 2050, we will return to the historical norm' (Mahbubani, 2011: 132). This supremacism however was merely a celebration of elitism, hierarchy, inequality and local imperialism; after all, 'China and India dominated merely based on the size of their populations, and economic production was largely driven by the need to produce enough food for the masses to survive and for the small elite to preserve their higher standards of living' (Lin and Rosenblatt, 2012: 173). As one source caustically notes:

> The future is seen in terms of a historical continuity ruptured temporarily by a couple of hundred years of decline … Celebration of thousands of years of historical glory, punctured only by attacks by hostile forces from without and disunity within, takes the place of the emancipatory, progressive liberatory impulse of anticolonial or revolutionary nationalisms. The source of pride is the emergent nation, but one which is merely a modern expression of an ancient civilisational entity. There is limited tolerance of dissent from this picture of centuries of glory upset by decades of humiliation that are over now and will soon be followed by a regaining of rightful place as a great power in the scheme of things (Anand, 2012: 75).

Interestingly, the relative rise in profile of these emerging economies has gone hand in hand with internal developments within Africa where, under strong pressure from the international financial institutions and Western donors, many African states have opened up their economies through deregulation, privatisation, etc. In a number of African countries, the elites have bought into the neoliberal message and now actively seek to attract foreign investment. These two factors have served to facilitate the expansion of foreign capital in Africa more broadly, and from emerging economies in particular.

Yet alongside some new developments, a lot of continuities remain the same. There has been a huge rise in commodity prices and this has contributed in a big way to Africa's impressive growth figures, if taken as an increase in GDP per capita, but the benefit to African economies in terms of providing a sustained platform for development is far more muted. After all, growth is 'a quantitative process, involving principally the extension of an already established structure of production, whereas development suggests qualitative changes, the creation of new economic and non-economic structures' (Dowd, 1967: 153). Pertinent to the notion of an 'Africa Rising' are the words of Amin (2014: 139):

> Emergence is not measured by a rising rate of GDP growth (or exports) … nor the fact that the society in question has obtained a higher level of GDP per capita, as defined by the World Bank, aid institutions controlled by Western powers, and conventional economists. Emergence involves much more: a sustained growth in industrial production in the state [or region] in question and a strengthening of the capacity of these industries to be competitive on a global scale.

A key question about the role of emerging economies in Africa is whether routine collusion between exploitative foreign actors and dysfunctional regimes – a depressing and undeniable feature of Africa's international relations – may be simply reproduced. This is precisely what Mallam Sanusi Lamido Sanusi, the Governor of the Central Bank of Nigeria warned against in March 2013 when, specifically speaking about Sino-Nigerian ties, he asserted that 'China takes from us primary goods and sells us manufactured ones. This was also the essence of colonialism. China is no longer a fellow underdeveloped economy. China is the second biggest economy in the world, an economic giant capable of the same forms of exploitation as the West. China is a major contributor to the de-industrialisation of Africa and thus African underdevelopment' (*This Day*, 13 March 2013). Talking more broadly of the BRICS, the United Nations Economic Commission for Africa (UNECA) notes:

> [BRICS–Africa] trade is in primary commodities with few linkages to the rest of the economy and with most export earnings going to foreigners, and so Africa's development and employment receive few gains. Also, the growth of the BRICS suggests it will become harder for African exporters to break into new (non-commodity) sectors – and their home country producers (as in footwear or clothing) may be hurt by the BRICS' low-cost output. (UNECA, 2013a: 1)

Some proponents of the 'Africa Rising' trope have argued that improved governance and modes of doing business have facilitated the upsurge in African GDP. In a detailed study, Scott Taylor (2012) argues that a 'hospitable climate for business' has been spurred by institutional change and political and economic reform. This is one of the central arguments around which much of the new-found optimism about Africa has been built. For instance, the *Oxford Companion to the Economics of Africa* claims that 'improved macroeconomic frameworks and political governance in a majority of countries were key drivers for the improved economic performance' (Aryeetey et al., 2012: 8). *The Economist* cannot resist its own spin on the story, claiming that 'Africa's retreat from socialist economic models has generally made everyone better off' (*The Economist*, 2 March 2013). In fact however,

> If one disaggregates the countries into conflict-affected, and those not affected by conflict into petroleum exporters and others, the recovery during 2004–2008 appears less impressive. For the twenty-nine countries that did not export petroleum and were not burdened by severe conflict, the average growth rate in the second half of the 2000s was hardly different from the average ten years before. (Weeks, 2010: 6)

Already, what one representative from the African Development Bank has referred to as export-led jobless growth in Africa characterises the current situation, where job creation at 3 per cent per annum has trailed far behind GDP growth (5.4 per cent per annum) and way behind export growth, which stands at 18.5 per cent growth per annum (Ancharaz, 2011). Indeed, the UN Development Policy and Analysis Division noted that Africa's economic growth will 'continue to be driven by expanding economic ties with Asia, fiscal spending on infrastructure projects and oil-exporting countries. Whilst income per capita is anticipated to grow, this will not be at a sufficient pace to accelerate poverty reduction' (UNDESA, 2013). This makes nonsense of strident claims that:

> What took the UK centuries can now be a matter of decades, even years ... Today Africa has the greatest room to boom on the back of two centuries of global progress ... In other words, Africa is ideally poised to leapfrog centuries of industrial development ... It has an added advantage in that it does not have to carry baggage from the past. (*African Business*, January 2013: 19)

Thus (yet another) commodity-driven boom in Africa, this time propelled by emerging economies, wipes the historical slate clean, makes dependent relationships and unequal terms of trade vanish instantaneously, and positions the continent to reach OECD status virtually overnight! Much of this is said to be hinged on the BRICS as the new saviours.

Plus ça change, plus c'est la même chose

It hardly needs repeating that most commodity-rich African countries, which are the main partners of the emerging economies on the continent, have poor records in terms of inequality, human development indices, etc. With a few exceptions, such as Botswana (which is however an extremely unequal society – see Taylor, 2003), many are corrupt entities managed by leaders at the apex of neopatrimonial systems. These elites have been previously quite happy to extract rent from Western corporations wishing to exploit their country's resources. What is perhaps now new in Africa is the range of competitors vying for attention. As Rampa et al. (2012: 248) note, 'It is clear that [emerging economies'] growing presence on the continent brings trade, massive investment in infrastructure and resources development. Politically it helps Africa become more assertive in the world and increases development aid and technical assistance'. This should not however be seen in terms of India vs. China or France vs. the USA but is rather an expression of inter-capitalist competition, something which has long been integral to the global system. What the emerging economies bring are more competitors and at times, different business practices, but the broad pattern remains the same. Yet, we are told confidently that '[T]he Africa-pessimists have got it wrong' (presumably including *The Economist* a few years ago) as 'the engines of development are still going strong. Democratic governance, political participation and economic management look set to improve further' (*The Economist*, 2 March 2013).

The patterns of continuity are of course taking place within the context of global capitalism, which historically has generated growth in the centres and peripheries but in different ways. 'Whereas at the centre growth is development – that is, it has an integrating effect – in the periphery growth is not development, for its effect is to disarticulate.

Strictly speaking, growth in the periphery, based on integration into the world market, is the development of underdevelopment' (Amin, 1974:18–19). What is remarkable about the 'Africa Rising' discourse is that this is generally ignored: growth is fetishised and taken as a Good Thing in its own right. There is no acknowledgment that what is occurring reflects an ongoing trend of polarisation, where there is 'the concurrent construction of dominant centres and dominated peripheries, and their reproduction deepening in each state' and continent (Amin, 2004: 13).

Exploitation by capitalist productive relationships and the appropriation of Africa's economic surpluses characterises the continent's political economies. Such a milieu encourages visionless African elites to focus on the static comparative advantages of the spaces which they control. Given the weak levels of diversification and strong concentrations in specific export sectors, it is remarkable that a narrative has been built that claims that Africa is 'rising' in the absence of any indication of a widening domestic manufacturing base or actual industrialisation. This is problematic given that a task ahead for Africa is to develop an industrial base that can assist the agricultural sector in its growth and transformation. Both of these sectors could potentially compose the engines of development, but only under conditions where the exigencies of global capital were not paramount, but rather domestic and internal requirements of various social formations were prioritised. A rebalancing away from allowing global capitalism to dictate the pace, rather than the logic of domestic development, is absolutely central.

Yet in the context of the new trading geographies being crafted, many extant pathologies are being reproduced, even reified. As one commentator puts it, the 'BRIC's trading approach towards Africa, while favouring bilateral trade, does not encourage a ... necessary African coherence and regional integration. Rather, such an approach that is based on mutual benefits, and thus not necessarily need-based, marginalises countries with lower income, while favouring resource rich countries' (Mbaye, 2011: 3). Such dynamics also reproduce dependency.

Due to the colonial experience, Africa was inserted into the global division of labour in a particular fashion. This is well known and the effect has been to generate and reproduce underdevelopment. As noted, a central characteristic of capitalism is 'development at one pole and underdevelopment at the other' (Smith, 1990: 188) and this may be graphically witnessed in Africa. As James Ferguson (2006: 38) has noted:

> Capital does not 'flow' from New York to Angola's oil fields, or from London to Ghana's gold mines; it hops, neatly skipping over most of what is in between. Second, where capital has been coming to Africa at all, it has largely been concentrated in spatially segregated, socially 'thin' mineral-extraction enclaves. Again, the 'movement of capital' here does not cover the globe; it connects discrete points on it.

Replace New York with Brasília or London with Beijing and the same logic of spatially uneven investment applies to the dynamics of the BRICS in Africa. Of course, the extraction of economic surplus by global corporations, without reinvesting it to transform agriculture and industry, has been a key feature of Africa's political economy since independence, with compliant elites collaborating in this venture (Amin, 2002). A key concern of this book is to interrogate as to whether or not the engagement by actors from the BRICS is likely to change matters.

Where is South Africa?

Observant readers will notice that though this book claims to be about the BRICS, there is no chapter on South Africa. This can be explained. As Gerardo Rodriguez, former Mexican Under-Secretary of Finance, noted, Jim O'Neill 'never imagined the economic and political impact he would trigger just by coining the term BRICS ... He was mainly trying to make a point about China but needed a broader packaging of countries in order to make for a better sell. But it appears that the country selection of the original BRICs group was rather an accident of size, demographics and, more importantly, of words' (*Financial Times*, 22 February 2013). Following Rodriguez, South Africa's inclusion into the BRICs (to make the BRICS) was more an accident of geography rather than any considered analysis as to whether South Africa really fitted, although it has, since the demise of apartheid, consciously positioned itself as some sort of middle power promoting global capitalism and hoping to stabilise and legitimise the neoliberal world order (Taylor, 2001).

Eager to have a representative from all of the 'developing' continents, China reacted positively to the calls from Pretoria as to their inclusion (Cornelissen, 2009). But this is where it becomes interesting. Though Pretoria would bristle at such a notion, is it the case that their membership of BRICS is a token inclusion at the behest of China? Does South Africa's membership serve China's interests in Africa, demonstrating Beijing's munificence to the continent? More importantly, was admitting non-threatening South Africa into the BRICS club, rather than *actual* emerging powers (such as South Korea or Turkey) a tactic to preserve the self-appointed pre-eminence of China and India as embodying 'the future', which both countries so ostentatiously flaunt?

Membership of the BRICS has of course indubitably excited the South African commentariat, as it reinforces a long-standing trope in their country – its exceptionalism. This often plays out in open arrogance towards the rest of the continent, splendidly captured in the statement that 'We [South Africa] are the default choice representing the African continent' (Davies, 2013: 1). This hubris is a reflection of elitist fantasies, exemplified by Jacob Zuma's assertion that 'We (i.e. South Africa] are now equal co-architects of a new equitable international system' (quoted in Shubin, 2011: 6). *Equal? Co-architects?*

When asked whether South Africa should be included in the BRICS Jim O'Neill's reply was a firm 'no', because in his opinion, 'South Africa, at a population of less than 50 million people, was just too small to join the BRIC ranks and he regarded Nigeria a better candidate' (quoted in *Business Report*, 14 December 2010). He went on to later state that 'South Africa's inclusion has somewhat weakened the group's power' (*Mail & Guardian*, 23 March 2012). Beyond the self-congratulatory rhetoric, there is little substance behind Pretoria's membership: South Africa's economy is smaller than that of Belgium's, and if it was a province of China, South Africa would be ranked 6th largest in terms of GDP.

It is true that until recently the South African economy was growing by an average of 3.5 per cent a year, but this has now slowed: in 2012 growth declined to 2.5 per cent and the first quarter of 2013, South African GDP grew by only 0.9 per cent, with the rand depreciating by 12 per cent in the same period. The South African Reserve Bank Governor, Gill Marcus, observed that these developments are not temporary, but rather 'an indicator of deep-rooted structural problems which [are] manifested in high levels of unemployment and inequality ... These in turn are caused by weak competitiveness, a poor skills profile and an educational system that is dysfunctional, low domestic savings ... and spatial distortions' (quoted in *Mail & Guardian*, 6 June 2013). The claim therefore that 'BRICS has become the global ranking standard for the first tier of emerging markets' (Davies, 2013: 1), when it does not include Mexico, South Korea, Turkey, Indonesia or Argentina but *does* somehow include South Africa is rather problematic. Notably, the influential *Foreign Affairs* magazine recently ran a story 'to survey ... up-and-comers: countries and regions whose combination of size, recent performance, and economic potential will make them particularly interesting to watch and attractive to investors over the next half decade' (Rose and Tepperman, 2014: 2). The magazine's choices? Mexico, South Korea, Poland, Turkey, Indonesia and the Philippines, and the Mekong region. No South Africa.

Certainly, South Africa has added nothing qualitatively new to the BRICS agenda, fitting with ease into being another emerging economy pushing for neoliberalism and the benefits of globalisation (Taylor, 2001). Campbell (2012: 2) notes: 'When South Africa became a full member there were a number of choices before the South Africans, either reproducing realist ideas that South Africa was the strongest economy in Africa, a regional hegemon and hence logically entered the club of the "emerging powers", or pushing for BRICS to engage questions of peace, health and the environment to break the preoccupation with "trade and development"'. Pretoria's elites most certainly chose the former option, opting to exploit their membership of the BRICS to position themselves as the "natural partners" for international capital investing in Africa. This is why South Africa is now assiduously promoting itself as the "gateway" to Africa – the entry point for capitalism. Membership has also been a useful device to advance the interests of South African capital into the continent, and particularly the southern African region. South Africa's renewed ambition to drive forward greater regional integration is an after-effect of it being admitted into the BRICS, as there is now greater pressure to enlarge its market depth by means of incorporating the Southern African Development Community (SADC) economy into Pretoria's, what Bond (2004) has described as "sub-imperialism". Whilst the *political* project has faced obstacles, the *economic* drive has been relentless (Taylor, 2011a). Pretoria's support for the putative BRICS Development Bank can be explained by the hope that it would be 'be used for increased state-driven infrastructure spend around prioritised regional corridors in SADC' which would 'draw in its BRICS partners into South Africa's foreign policy design for the region' (Davies, 2013: 5). That these 'development corridors' have been explicitly based on neoliberal policy frameworks which have strengthened the hand of South African capital, is important to note in this regard (see Söderbaum and Taylor, 2003).

However, why South Africa is excluded from this study is that the book's main aim is to discuss both the 'Africa Rising' narrative and the role of emerging economies in this – how they are part of the process through their commodity demands and what dynamics are being reproduced and why. The rationale behind this volume is that the emerging economies have been identified as being major drivers of Africa's GDP figures of late *and* that they are held up in certain quarters as being the potential saviours of the continent. The focus on the BRICS is not because they are seen as a united bloc (far from it) or even that they are likely to remain a permanent fixture of international relations (ditto). Rather, it is in the symbolic weight they hold as being emblematically representative of the role of emerging economies in the global political economy and in Africa. As much ink has been spilled on the apparent differences that these new actors bring to both Africa and the international system, it is imperative that a study be conducted on just how different they are and just what have been their effects on the continent. The deployment of the BRICS then as a focus of study *vis-à-vis* Africa is really a heuristic device rather than any qualitative judgment on their cohesiveness or unique properties. In short, this book is a study of how emerging economies have driven the 'Africa Rising' trope and what have been some of the effects on the continent in terms of continuing (possibly deepening) extant tendencies.

Structure of the book

The book proceeds as follows. Chapter 1 critically examines the 'Africa Rising' narrative and the role of the BRICS as emblematic emerging economies in these processes. It is suggested that whilst there are some differences from the continent's traditional partners, there are a great deal of continuities – in fact often a re-inscribing of Africa's dependent status in the global economy and the concomitant underdevelopment that this engenders. It is also suggested that there is little evidence for the ecstatic reception that some of the BRICS countries have received in some of the presidential palaces across Africa, certainly from the perspective of the normal citizen and certainly not from any assessment with regard to the possibilities of Africa's structural transformation as a prerequisite for sustainable and broad-based development.

The following four chapters then individually examine and analyse the political and economic relations of the individual BRIC countries with Africa: Brazil, Russia, India and China respectively. Through this treatment, some of the nuances of the relationships are brought out in a systematic comparative fashion. Finally, the book ends with concluding thoughts on where the ongoing processes leave Africa. The book's overall aim is to contribute to current debates on the state of Africa's international relations, the condition of the continent's economies at a time of great hype, and the role of emerging economies (captured as the BRICS) in Africa's contemporary political economies.

1
The BRICS
& 'Africa Rising'

Until recently, Africa was depicted as the 'hopeless continent' (*The Economist*, 13 May 2000), a spatial entity supposedly in 'the limbo of the international system, existing only at the outer limits of the planet which we inhabit' (Bayart, 2000: 217). Studies have concentrated on how and why the continent has been in a state of 'permanent crisis' (Van de Walle, 2001) or exists in a milieu dominated by conflict, poverty, disease and criminality. From this it has been easy to move to the next step of believing that the continent does not have any significant politics, only humanitarian disasters (for counter arguments, see Dunn and Shaw 2001; Taylor and Williams 2004).

Given Africa's recent strong growth figures, a perceptible shift has now moved in the opposite direction. Africa has now moved from one extreme to another and is now the 'rising star' (*The Economist*, 3 December 2011). In late 2012, *Time* magazine's 3 December edition was emblazoned with the headline, 'Africa Rising', capturing a certain *l'esprit du temps* in some quarters. Other observers now argue that we are living in 'Africa's moment' (Severino and Ray, 2011), where it is 'Africa's turn' (Miguel, 2009). In this new world, 'Africa emerges' (Rotberg, 2013), moving from 'darkness to destiny' (Clarke, 2012), where it is 'leading the way' (Radelet, 2010). In fact, we are told, 'The Next Asia is Africa' (French, 2012: 3), based on an 'African Growth Miracle' (Young, 2012). In its more excitable moments, we are even told 'Why Africa will rule the 21st century' (*African Business*, January 2013: 16). Previous studies on the political economy of Africa are now dismissed as 'Afro-pessimism', to be swept away by this new Africa: 'The Ultimate Frontier Market' (Matean, 2012). A recent book on 'the story behind Africa's economic revolution' even has a quasi-Superman springing from Africa on its front cover (see Robertson, 2012). In short, 'It's time for Africa' (Ernst & Young, 2011).

Of course, asset managers need to set a drumbeat to attract investors' and searching out The Next Big Thing is integral to the system. That is why after BRICS, we were presented with a shameless free-for-all that resulted in, among others, BRICSAM, BRIICKS, CIVETS, TIMBI, MINT, etc. *ad nauseam*. The epistemic community of investment management corporations consciously aims to form and 'create' new capital markets through shaping judgments based on how information is presented and sold. Enthusiasm and over-selling is to be expected – as the CEO of Ernst & Young Africa has openly admitted, 'we are optimists ... our perspective is deliberately a glass half full rather than half empty one. This is mainly because we believe that it takes a positive mind-set to succeed in Africa' (Ernst & Young, 2012: 1). Succeeding in Africa for Ernst & Young means optimising capital from investors, and telling a good story is essential. Such actors 'do not care too much about distinguishing between evidence and rumours. If they believe that enough investors will believe the rumour [e.g. 'Africa Rising'], then the latter becomes evidence – enough that is, to switch investment plans' (Fioramonti, 2014: 61).

As part of such dynamics, there are claims that huge improvements in governance across Africa have occurred, no doubt to reassure nervous investors. Emblematically, Yvonne Mhango of Renaissance Capital confidently claims that 'Governments [in Africa] have got policy spectacularly right and created the low-debt, low-inflation, much-improved macro conditions that have enabled growth to take off' (cited in *African Business*, January 2013: 18). It is not just asset managers spinning this story though. Recently, Ellen Johnson Sirleaf, President of Liberia, stated that 'In ten years [a] rapidly transforming Africa will move into the industrial age' (*New African*, May 2013: 41).

However, 'the empirical evidence on growth and policy related indicators is consistent with the null hypothesis that more than twenty years of so-called policy reform had limited impact on strengthening the potential for rapid and sustainable growth in the sub-Saharan region. The drivers of the brief recovery during the second half of the 2000s appear to have been a commodity price boom, debt relief and a decline in domestic conflicts' (Weeks, 2010: 10). World Bank figures with regard to the annual percentage growth rate of GDP at market prices, based on constant local currency (for all income levels, rounded up), compared to the movement of the Commodity Price Index reveals this intimate link (see below).

The years when SSA's growth figures surpassed 1996 levels (2004–2008) can be demonstrably linked to the period when China and India (and other emerging economies) began to hugely demand commodities, as reflected in the CPI. In the energy realm, concern over predicted declines in petroleum reserves, apprehensions over the so-called 'peak oil' scenario, instability in the Middle East and oil price speculation placed further pressure upwards on prices, peaking in 2008 (only to tumble after the core underwent the worst recession in a century). This reality is qualitatively different from the picture Goldman Sachs, Renaissance Capital et al. portray, where 'spectacularly right' policies have driven growth. Official reports from international organisations have at times bolstered this

Table 2 Correlation between GDP growth for SSA and the Commodity Price Index (CPI)

Year	GDP growth	Commodity Price Index
1990	1.3	
1991	0.9	
1992	−0.9	52.6
1993	0.4	52.5
1994	1.8	50.06
1995	3.7	58.6
1996	4.9	58.7
1997	3.7	64.6
1998	2.3	51
1999	2.4	43.3
2000	3.7	59.4
2001	3.7	61.9
2002	3.5	50.1
2003	4.4	66.3
2004	6.4	69.1
2005	5.8	86.7
2006	6.1	113.1
2007	6.9	112.9
2008	5	162.4
2009	1.9	102.4
2010	4.9	146.1
2011	4.5	182.1
2012	4.2	188.4

(Sources: World Bank, IMF data)

latter interpretation, postulating Africa's 'economic resurgence' as being hinged on the ability of the continent to recover from the global crisis relatively quicker than other areas of the world (World Economic Forum et al, 2011: v). Whilst true in and of itself, Africa's growth record over the last ten years or so has occurred within the context of *overall* global growth. In this regard, Africa's growth has only been around 1 per cent higher than the world average: credible, but not fantastic (African Development Bank, 2012). An interesting by-product of the 'Africa Rising' narrative are the wild claims about Africa's middle class, with assertions that it now amounts to over a third of Africa's population. It emerges that this figure was arrived at by calculating the number of people *estimated* (using dubious statistics) to have a per capita consumption between $2 and $4 per day (see African Development Bank, 2011b). This criteria itself sets the bar at an incredibly low level, but of course then allows the African Development Bank to add its voice to the narrative that the dawn has arrived and that the corner has been turned, etc. In fact, currently only 4 per cent of Africans have an income in excess of $10 a day (Africa Progress Panel, 2012: 17).

Before progressing, it is worth however discussing the accuracy of Africa's statistics (see Jerven, 2013). Shanta Devarajan, Chief Economist for the Africa Region of the World Bank, has noted Africa's 'statistical tragedy', where published figures are suspect (Devarajan, 2013: 1). In fact, 'only half the countries (housing 68 per cent of Africa's population) use the 1993 UN System of National Accounts; the others use earlier systems, some dating back to the 1960s' (ibid.), meaning that 'in presenting GDP per capita for many African countries, we cannot be sure of either the numerator or the denominator' (ibid.: 3). Indeed, 'basic underlying data to construct national accounts are often missing or estimated, weights are outdated, and price information is missing or subject to poor quality'. Consequently, 'there are serious questions about the reliability of GDP estimates' (Harttgen et al., 2013: 2).

In a detailed cross-national study of data between 1965 and 1995, it was concluded that the 'study of accuracy in growth reporting for these countries shows that trusting any source at face value is unwise. In terms of a growth rate of any given year the data can indeed be described as random' (Jerven, 2010a: 291). As Blades (1975: 8) noted earlier, 'it is not possible to make intelligent use of the published statistics without knowing the estimation procedures used and the assumptions on which they are based'. Jerven (2010a: 292) caustically adds: 'It follows literally that since such care has not been taken, most academic work on economic growth in Africa has been unintelligent'. This sums up much of the 'Africa Rising' narrative.

We have heard all this noise about Africa's immanent renaissance before – on multiple occasions. It is ironic that *Time* magazine's late 2012 edition celebrated 'Africa Rising', given that fourteen years earlier (30 March 1998, to be precise), *Time* ran a story with the *exact* same title! Then, we were told that 'Hope is Africa's rarest commodity. Yet buried though it is amid the despair that haunts the continent, there is more optimism today than in decades'. Better times are always coming tomorrow, as Easterly (2003: 35–36) notes, citing passages from various World Bank reports:

From a 1981 World Bank report, *Accelerated Development in Sub-Saharan Africa* (p. 133): 'Policy action and foreign assistance…will surely work together to build a continent that shows real gains in both development and income in the near future'. From a 1984 World Bank report, *Toward Sustained Development in Sub-Saharan Africa* (p. 2): 'This optimism can be justified by recent experience in Africa ... some countries are introducing policy and institutional reforms'. From a 1986 World Bank report, *Financing Growth with Adjustment in Sub-Saharan Africa* (p. 15): 'Progress is clearly under way. Especially in the past two years, more countries have started to act, and the changes they are making go deeper than before'. From a 1989 World Bank report, *Sub-Saharan Africa: From Crisis to Sustainable Growth* (p. 35): 'Since the mid-1980s Africa has seen important changes in policies and in economic performance'. From a 1994 World Bank report, *Adjustment in Africa* (p. 3): 'African countries have made great strides in improving policies and restoring growth'. From a 2000 World Bank report, *Can Africa Claim the 21st Century?:* 'Since the mid-1990s, there have been signs that better economic management has started to pay off'. From a 2002 World Bank press release on *African Development Indicators*, 'Africa's leaders ... have recognised the need to improve their policies, spelled out in the New Partnership for African Development'.

In 2008 Africa was at a 'Turning Point' (Delfin and Page, 2008), restated in 2011 with the assertion that the continent was 'on the brink of ... economic take-off, much like China was 30 years ago' (World Bank, 2011).

The real story as it pertains to contemporary excitement about Africa seems to be in the upsurge of interest in Africa by formerly non-traditional actors. High economic growth in Africa must be understood in the context of the rise in importance of various 'emerging powers' within the global political economy (Cornelissen, 2009). The relationship that these 'new' powers have with Africa *has* elevated the continent in the strategic thinking of the extant 'traditional' (largely ex-colonial) partners. As one French minister was quoted as saying: 'Thanks to the Chinese, we [have] rediscovered that Africa is not a continent of crises and misery, but one of 800-million consumers' (*Business Day*, 19 October 2007). Though this comment was directed at the 'rise' of China in Africa (see Taylor, 2009a), it might be equally applied to relatively new sets of economic and political linkages. Embedded in 'a fluid period of transition in the global balance of power and the international state system characterised by traditional and emerging powers', the continent now plays a more prominent role in international politics (Kornegay and Landsberg, 2009: 171). Obviously, of fundamental importance to Africa is what this development actually means.

An alternative?

Since around 2000, there has been greater engagement between Africa and the global North, reflected in various initiatives largely focused on the issue of poverty with a strong emphasis on 'good governance' (Cargill 2011). With this, conditionalities have been applied, often in a fairly static and dogmatic fashion – a continuation of a longstanding pattern. This has oftentimes been bitterly resented by African elites, even though Africa's own New Partnership for Africa's Development (NEPAD) placed standard liberal definitions of governance at the centre of its project (see Taylor, 2005). What is interesting with regard to the BRICS is that they provide options outside the traditional North–South axes. An emphasis on developing infrastructure has been notable in this new set of relations, in themselves issues that have been neglected by traditional actors (World Economic Forum et al., 2011: 108). Politically, this has also introduced new competitive dynamics into Africa's international relations: Africa has 'never been in such a strong bargaining position' than at the present, with numerous 'suitors' (Cargill, 2011: viii). The growing diversity of partners potentially offers a 'tremendous opportunity', 'as each country brings with it an array of capital goods, developmental experience, products and technology as well as new opportunities to trade goods, knowledge and models' (World Economic Forum et al., 2011: 105). Trade with – and investment from – emerging economies potentially reduces the North's political leverage and economic dominance in Africa (Southall, 2009: 31), which may 'increase the negotiating power enjoyed by [African] governments seeking to maximise local benefits' (Prichard, 2009: 254).

These developments may be interpreted in alternative ways. It may be put forward that these new actors now emerging are merely exploitive and self-interested, overall just as damaging to Africa as the extant and well-established set of relations with the traditional powers. Alternatively, these new relationships may be seen as somehow reflecting South–South values (whatever that may mean) and contributing to Africa's developmental goals. This appears to be what many African elites believe. Yet it seems obvious that Africa is the weaker partner in these new relationships. Specifically regarding the BRICS, actors from those states are in Africa not because of some notional love of Africa or Africans, but for reasons based on capitalist logics. Interest in gaining access to natural resources in Africa is often central (Naidu et al., 2009: 3). As Kimenyi and Lewis (2011: 20) put it, the attention of emerging economies towards Africa 'is not based on an altruistic goal to improve the economic well-being of Africans' but rather, *just like most other external actors*, actors from emerging economies are 'trying to maximise their own strategic economic and political interests by engaging with African countries'.

Their relationships with Sub-Saharan Africa (SSA) do not exhibit any notable 'exceptionalism', displaying patterns that are 'broadly similar to those of SSA 'traditional' partners and mostly reinforce existing commodity-based export structures' (Sindzingre, 2013: 45). This contrasts with the diplomatic claims made by the emerging economies that their engagement with Africa is qualitatively different – and *better* – than that of the North, with relentless incantations about 'South–South' ties, 'solidarity', 'mutual benefits', 'win-win relations' and 'partnerships'.

Given the 'growing expectations among the citizens' in countries targeted by the emerging economies 'of the immediate upswings in their livelihoods and improvements in quality of life' (Aryeetey and Asmah, 2011: 22), the solidarity rhetoric may backfire. It is obvious that the quality of a country's governance institutions are crucial determinants in development and growth and though there have been *some* improvements in governance in Africa of late, the incidence of corruption and general pathologies of maldevelopment remains high. Possibly compounding this situation is the 'non-interference' practised by some of the new partners. What this means in practical terms is that until and unless the elites in Africa themselves promote pro-development policies, no such standards will be adopted. In such a milieu, the perpetual question will then be: how might Africa engage with and exploit the increased engagement by new partners in order to benefit ordinary people and promote development?

Institutions, Africa and the BRICS

Recently, a revitalised diplomacy has been initiated towards Africa. With regards to the emerging economies specifically, various summits, institutions and agreements have been established which have witnessed an outpouring of enthusiasm for the Korea-Africa Forum, the Turkey-Africa Partnership, the Africa-Singapore Business Forum, the Malaysia-Africa Business Forum, the Taiwan-Africa Summit, Brazil-Africa Forum and so on. All of these have (consciously or not) replicated the Chinese example set by the Forum on China-Africa Cooperation (FOCAC), established in 2000.

The background to FOCAC can be traced to the visit by Chinese Premier Jiang Zemin to Africa in 1996, when he publicly unveiled a new Chinese approach to Africa. According to a Chinese report, '[t]he guiding principle that China follows in developing relations with African countries in the new situation is: "to treat each other as equals, develop sincere friendship, strengthen solidarity and cooperation, and seek common development"' (*Xinhua*, 22 May 1996). During a keynote speech to the Organisation of African Unity (OAU), entitled 'Toward a New Historical Milestone of Sino-African Friendship', Jiang advanced a five-point proposal for a new relationship between China and Africa:

1. fostering a sincere friendship between China and Africa and both sides becoming each other's reliable 'all-weather friends';
2. treating each other as equals and respecting each other's sovereignty and non-interference in each other's internal affairs;
3. seeking common development on the basis of mutual benefit;
4. enhancing consultation and cooperation in international affairs;
5. looking into the future and creating a better world. (ibid.)

Jiang's proposal was warmly received by the OAU and may be seen as laying the foundation for current Sino-African relations. FOCAC has subsequently been the official vehicle to realise these ambitions.

In October 2000 a Forum on China-Africa Cooperation Ministerial Conference in Beijing was held that culminated in the formation of FOCAC. Previously, in October 1999 President Jiang Zemin had written to all heads of African states, as well as the Secretary-General of the OAU, to propose the convening of a Sino-Africa forum. When this was greeted with a favourable reception, the Chinese established a preparatory committee comprised of eighteen ministries, with the Ministry of Foreign Affairs and Ministry of Foreign Trade and Economic Cooperation (MOFTEC) assigned the roles of anchormen. Interestingly, Chinese sources claim that it was African leaders who initiated and asked for a summit. He Wenping (2007: 147) asserts: 'At the end of the 1990s, some African countries proposed that as the US, Britain, France, Japan and Europe had established mechanisms for contact with Africa, it was necessary for China and Africa to establish a similar mechanism to fit in with the need to strengthen relations. After earnest study, China decided to echo the suggestions of African countries, and proposed to hold the Forum in 2000'. Whether or not it was Beijing or African states that called for and initiated the summit, FOCAC has quickly proved to be a major feature in Africa's international relations.

The meeting in October 2000 was attended by 80 ministers charged with foreign affairs and international trade and economic development, from 45 African states. Representatives of international and regional organisations also attended, as did delegates from two African countries that did not then have diplomatic ties with China (Liberia and Malawi). Discussions were organised into four separate sessions: trade; economic reform (with China's programme being showcased as a possible model); poverty eradication and sustainable development; and cooperation in education, science technology and health care.

At the meeting, Jiang Zemin gave the keynote speech, starting off with the implicit claim that China was the leader of the developing world, with the oft-reported refrain that 'China is the largest developing country in the world and Africa is the continent with the largest number of developing countries' (*Peoples' Daily*, 11 October 2000). This 'Third Worldism' was then made explicit by Jiang's claim that the meeting was a tangible example of South–South linkages: 'closer South–South

co-operation and the establishment of an equitable and just new international political and economic order' was needed (ibid.). Notably,
Jiang cast Sino-African relations within an international context that
'is moving towards multi-polarity and [where] the international situation is on the whole easing off' (ibid.). This was seen as providing new
opportunities for trade and co-operation. These favourable conditions
however were potentially threatened as 'Hegemonism and power politics still exist' (ibid.). Conflict and instability in the developing world
was squarely blamed on the 'many irrational and inequitable factors
in the current international political and economic order [which] are
detrimental not only to world peace and development, but also to the
stability and development of the vast number of developing countries'
(ibid.).

Jiang then went on to outline four key ways that China and Africa
could, working together, help establish a new global order:

1. 'Strengthen solidarity and promote South–South cooperation'.
   South–South cooperation was seen as the main way developing
   countries could 'give full play to their advantages in natural and
   human resources, tap to the full their respective productive and
   technological potential, take advantage of the others' strengths to
   make up for their own weaknesses, and achieve common improvement' (*Peoples' Daily*, 11 October 2000).
2. 'Enhance dialogue and improve North–South relations'. According
   to Jiang, '[d]eveloped countries should take full account and care of
   the interests of the less privileged developing countries and increase
   financial investment and technology transfer to them to help build
   up their capacity for development'. Intrinsic to this point was the
   assertion by Jiang that a 'smaller development gap and better political and economic relations between the North and the South is
   an important foundation for a just and equitable new international
   political and economic order' (ibid.).
3. 'Take part in international affairs on the basis of equality and in an
   enterprising spirit'. According to Jiang, China and Africa needed
   to increase consultation and cooperation on both 'the bilateral
   and multilateral fronts' and vigorously participate in international
   affairs and the formulation of international rules. Central to this
   was the promotion of reform of the international economic system
   as through this, 'a fair international environment will be created
   and the legitimate rights and interests of developing countries will
   be effectively safeguarded' (ibid.).
4. 'Look forward into the future and establish a new long-term stable
   partnership of equality and mutual benefit'. Jiang stated that
   increased exchanges, 'especially direct contacts between top leaders
   of both China and African countries', would be pursued as central to
   this goal (ibid.).

FOCAC now meets every three years (alternately in Africa and China) and is a formalisation of China's engagement with Africa. Its model has been copied by others.

India, for example, instigated the India-Africa Forum Summit in 2008, which 'marked the culmination of India's renewed focus on Africa' (Kragelund, 2011: 596). Fourteen African countries attended the summit, which gave rise to two declaratory documents: the *India–Africa Framework for Cooperation Forum* and the *Delhi Declaration*. Both documents stressed South–South cooperation, capacity building and mutual interests. A plan of action was launched, a clear replication of FOCAC's own institutional framework (see Taylor, 2011b). Subsequent to the summit, New Delhi committed a $5.4 billion credit line over the next five years (rising from $2.15 billion in the past five years), grants worth $500 million and a unilateral opening of the Indian domestic economy to exports from all least developing countries (LDCs). Similarly, the inaugural Brazil–Africa Forum met in Forteleza, Brazil in June 2003'.

This growing interest in Africa has arguably also been reflected by a changing attitude towards a greater inclusion of African voices in international financial institutions. Though ultimately unsuccessful, the very fact that Ngozi Okonjo-Iweala led a credible campaign to become president of the World Bank speaks volumes. Setting aside her decidedly orthodox neoliberal position and status as a World Bank insider, along with former Colombian finance minister Jose Antonio Ocampo, Okonjo-Iweala helped create the bank's first-ever competitive race for the presidency. That an African was one of the candidates – *and was taken seriously* – is noteworthy. Previously, the World Bank Group's Annual Meeting in 2008 agreed on reforms that created an additional Chair for Africa on the World Bank Board. The continent has become 'increasingly assertive in international forums and aware of its influence' as a region making up nearly 25 per cent of the world's countries and thus is a potentially influential bloc (Cargill, 2011: 43).

For its part, the IMF has been discussing reforming its voting structure in order to better reflect the contemporary world, rather than the world as it was when the IMF was founded. As part of this, it was proposed that emerging economies would be granted increasing voting weight. Of interest, African countries 'reacted furiously' to such proposals and argued that this would give undue priority to emerging countries 'while delaying action to give the world's poorest countries greater influence over the body that often dictates their economic policies' (Elliot, 2006: 8). Rather than endorse the proposal in the spirit of South–South solidarity, African elites argued that such plans would leave them in an even weaker and dependent position than ever. Although they ultimately stalled (the US Congress refused to ratify the quota increase), such discussions do reflect a changing global reality: the plan is to make China the third-largest voting member and revise the IMF's board to reduce Europe's dominance, 'part of a broader plan by the IMF to recognise within the organisation the growing economic clout of emerging economies' (*Reuters*, 8 October 2012).

However, the reforms, supposed to be introduced in late 2012, were, at the time of writing, held up by interminable wrangling over the formula used to decide voting weight. What such developments indicate however is that emerging economies' elites are more and more pressing for some reform of global relations, albeit in problem-solving terms. Africa's support in such questions is actively sought, although there remains no common African position and the African Union continues to have no serious strategy for managing the continent's burgeoning relationships.

Towards the African century?

As noted, Africa's generalised robust economic performance (in terms of growth) has coincided with increasing engagement with emerging economies. The diversification of Africa's international relations has been increasingly influenced by the shift in relative capabilities to emerging economies. The financial crisis of 2008 had potentially significant repercussions for the international system in that a shift in material capabilities from traditional to emerging powers appeared evident, not least in the absolute need by the guardians of the global liberal order to incorporate new partners from the South to legitimise the overall system. The debate over IMF quota shares and a reliance on emerging actors to provide capital injections in order to stabilise the global economy reflects this (Kose and Prasad, 2010: 7). The very decision to expand the G-8 to the G-20 as the key international institution to discuss future economic global governance was a further manifestation of these processes.

Until the turn of the century, it would be fair to say that many African economies were dependent on the Northern-based international financial institutions (IFIs) for establishing key ideas and approaches to their development models *and* for access to capital and policy advice. This has now changed somewhat. The emerging economies' rise in material capabilities and their incorporation into the key global governance architecture has given rise to the notion that Africa's international relations are in a process of change, perhaps away from the North and towards the South, with attendant debates over the possibility of alternative models of development. Certainly, the potential ability to access different methodologies and new ideas concerning developmental thinking could possibly lessen Africa's dependence on the IFIs and their conditionalities (Cargill 2011: vii). Whilst these can be seen as reflecting neocolonial impulses – and the policy advice has been rigidly doctrinaire in its application of neoliberal prescriptions – it is uncertain that shifting to *no* conditions is better, given the governance modalities of many African states. Equally, the environmental and social models on which the emerging economies base their rise (intensified labour and environmental exploitation and a free rein to capital) are hardly a superior alternative.

As Africa is routinely ranked the most corrupt region of the world, a hands-off approach by the BRICS over matters related to governance is not helpful. Furthermore, a set of new relationships based on the intensification of natural resource extraction will be equally problematic. One of the key lessons for Africa from the financial crisis was that those countries that were more diversified generally tended to be more resilient than those that were highly dependent on a few primary commodities (Mutenyo, 2011: 29). Re-inscribing African dependence on commodities hardly offers any novel framework to emerging relationships with Africa and undermines the BRICS claims to be somehow 'different'. Even if the emphasis placed by some of the BRICS on addressing structural bottlenecks in Africa has been beneficial for the continent, in the absence of serious reforms new roads and railways will hardly make a sustainable and long-term contribution.

This returns us to the question as to whether emerging economies' increasing engagement with Africa is exploitive or benign. This question can only be answered in a contextual manner, dependent upon which actors from which emerging economy and in which sector of which country in Africa is being discussed. But it is important to remember that actors such as the BRICS have increased engagement with Africa as a means to achieve their own economic and political goals and that, overall, Africa remains the weaker partner. The weakness is usually ascribed to the continent's dependent relationship in the international system and Africa's historic insertion into the global capitalist economy. However, dependence is 'a historical process, a matrix of action', that permits the prospect of alteration stemming from changes in the dynamics, processes and organisation of the international system and the fundamental tendencies within Africa's political economy (Bayart, 2000: 234). Current emergent trends, such as robust economic growth and an increasing diversification of the continent's international relations may play important roles in this regard, yet massive challenges remain. Africa's world market share in processing industries is extraordinarily low: SSA exports just 0.9 and 0.3 per cent of world light and heavy manufacturing exports respectively (World Economic Forum et al., 2011: 15). The bulk of the growth in African exports in the last decade or more has been heavily underpinned by mining-related commodities, deeply problematic in terms of development. After all, the export growth that the Asian economies used to leapfrog development was based on an increasing list of manufactures. Africa is nowhere near that position.

Yet it is true that actors from both the global North and South are now actively pursuing closer engagement with Africa. This provides the elites of the continent opportunities to extract leverage in return for access. This may or may not be a good thing, depending on the conjectural circumstances in each state formation and the nature of the external partners. It cannot be taken for granted that actors such as the BRICS are interested in furthering Africa's developmental priorities. Though Africa has possibly never been in a stronger bargaining position than at present, the key question remains: how can African leaders take advantage for the benefit of the ordinary citizen. Currently, this does not seem to be happening. A recent Afrobarometer survey revealed that despite a decade of strong GDP growth and the incessant narrative of an 'Africa Rising', there is 'a wide gap in perceptions between ordinary Africans and the global economic community', where 'a majority (53%) rate the current condition of their national economy as "fairly" or "very bad"' and only 'one in three Africans (31%) think the condition of their national economies has improved in the past year, compared to 38% who say things have gotten worse'. Notably, when it came to their own elites, 'Africans give their governments failing marks for economic management (56% say they are doing "fairly" or "very badly"), improving the living standards of the poor (69% fairly/very badly), creating jobs (71% fairly/very badly), and narrowing income gaps (76% fairly/very badly)' (*AfricaFocus Bulletin*, 2013). As Hofmeyr (2013: 1) notes, 'popular opinion is thus increasingly out of sync with the "Africa Rising" narrative that has been gaining traction among government officials and international investors'.

The question of levels of agency is something that needs to be at the forefront of any discussion on the role of the BRICS in Africa and the potentialities of these emerging relationships in fostering development. This is highly contingent on a variety of contextual factors and it is these dynamics that need to be borne in mind when reviewing each BRICS member's interaction with the continent, as the rest of the book makes clear.

2
Brazil in Africa

Since around 2000, Brazil has enjoyed a sustained period of economic growth which has translated into the impulse by Brazilian elites to claim – and then push for – a loftier global position. Brazil has been recognised as not only an emerging power but also an emerging provider and actor in the development assistance community (White, 2010: 227). This is important for the country's elites, who are ever-anxious to be accepted as important continental and global players. Until fairly recently associated in the global mind as a country with severe economic and social challenges, its elites wish to see public opinion accept that 'it has transformed itself into a model for successful development' (Stolte, 2012: 19). The focus on the international has been a key way in which Brasília has sought to facilitate this process.

Economically, in 2006 foreign direct investment (FDI) flowing out of Brazil for the first time matched inbound FDI, making Brazilian capital increasingly internationalised. Such dynamics have led to some hubris: the former President of Brazil Luiz Inácio 'Lula' da Silva comment that 'the 21st century will be Brazil's century' (Webb, 2010) is emblematic of this, uneasily sitting alongside equally assertive claims that this century will be Africa's, India's, China's, etc. The self-confidence behind Lula's statement stemmed from a sustained period of economic growth and a concomitant increasing international presence, leading to *The Economist* asserting that the country was currently experiencing the 'best moment in the entire history of Brazil' (*The Economist*, 2010).

Africa's place in Brasília's diplomacy became elevated after Lula's election victory in 2002 and when analysing Brazil's current diplomacy it is clear that its 'desire to cultivate close relations with African states constitutes one of the top priorities of the country's current foreign policy agenda' (Kragelund, 2010: 13). Lula presided over a period of extraordinary political and economic engagement between Brazil and Africa, building on the concept of South–South cooperation and towards renewed and innovative efforts in Africa. Between 2000 and 2011, Brazil–Africa trade increased more than six-fold, from $4.2 billion to $27.6 billion. 'After suffering an interim drop in 2009 owing to the global financial and economic crisis, trade ... resumed its upward trend the following year. Since 1990 trade between Brazil and Africa has registered impressive growth rates of 16 per cent p.a. Compared with its BRICS partners, Brazil has seen the second highest increase in trade with Africa after China' (Freemantle and Stevens, 2009: 10).

Brazil's aims in Africa have been multi-layered: to diversify and expand its role as an emerging market while seeking piecemeal political reform of institutions associated with global governance. Though Brazil also pursues the encouragement of social development across the under-developed world, this cannot be said to be a main priority and is deployed to provide a degree of legitimisation for Brazilian activities. Brazil also feels some level of competition with the other BRICS and this is played out in terms of vying for political influence and seeking to be accepted as a notional head of the Global South, rather than through comparisons of economic size in which Brazil is obviously bettered by both China and India.

Current Brazilian foreign policy

Brazilian foreign policy underwent a major change at the turn of the century (Burges, 2009). Formerly, policy was based on protecting the country's boundaries, consolidating and strengthening the state, avoiding conflicts with neighbours and maintaining a cordial relationship with the United States. The preservation of autonomy to pursue domestic policies and total respect for state sovereignty underpinned this (Vigevani and Cepaluni, 2009). Brazil avoided a leadership role in Latin America and rather projected itself as an aloof non-aligned country, only occasionally partnering with Washington during the Cold War. In the 1990s this reclu-siveness came to an end. Major domestic change and shifts in global poli-tics and economics propelled this as Brazil embraced the image of being an emerging power (Sweig, 2010).

Under Fernando Henrique Cardoso's presidency (1995–2003), Brasília sought to promote a multilateral, institutionalised world order, with economic cooperation at the fore. Cardoso's neoliberal convictions meant that Brazil's interests were seen to be congruent with economic and commercial projection. Military and strategic issues, long a concern of former Brazilian leaders, were put to one side. Under Cardoso, an 'emphasis [on] monetary stability and external constraints, even at the expense of growth, increased employment, and the redistribution of income' was pursued, with a focus on seeking approval from the IFIs and support for multilateral trade negotiations that sought to embed neoliber-alism globally (de Castro and de Carvalho, 2003: 481). In short, Cardoso's foreign policy 'sought to internalise, absorb, and consolidate the liberal changes that globalisation brought to international society during the 1990s, in contrast with the failure of the Collor de Mello administration and the hesitancy of the Itamar Franco administration in this regard' (Vigevani and Cepaluni, 2009: 53). These moves were enthusiastically supported by those sectors of the Brazilian economy with external experience and interests. As part of Cardoso's foreign policy, the primacy of Washington as the hegemonic guardian of the world order was accepted, although friction at times did exist, leading to one of Cardoso's foreign ministers, Luiz Felipe Lampreia, describing Brasília's foreign policy as being a form of 'critical convergence' – acceptance of the neoliberal normative order, but cautious with regard to asymmetries in global power (quoted in Vigevani and Cepaluni, 2009: 58).

Although Lula's credentials as leader of the Workers' Party (*Partido dos Trabalhadores*) were historic and the source of much criticism and suspicion by the United States, upon accession to the presidency in 2003 previous criticisms and a rejection of imperialism and the role of the international financial institutions, as well as the policies of the United States, were quietly dropped. 'Lula and his Workers' Party (PT) [had] been the harshest critics of Cardoso's policy of concession to financial interests. However, once in power ... he ... followed with enthusiasm the road already taken, not only following an ultraconservative macroeconomic policy, but intensifying the financial opening of the economy' (Prates and Paulani, 2007: 34). This has been described as the 'normalisation of an anomaly', whereby once in office, the PT – through the hope of re-election – was incentivised to weaken its programmatic positions whilst forging opportunistic alliances (Hunter, 2007). At best, 'neoliberal reforms were implemented in the 1990s, and eventually acquired a somewhat social democratic facet ... after Lula's administration since 2003' (Boschi, 2014: 124).

'Lula retained the orthodox economic policies of his predecessor, paying off an IMF loan early and maintaining good relations with the business community, especially key financial and business interests based in São Paulo'. However, to be fair to Lula, 'this economic continuity was complemented by a commitment to boost the living standards and opportunities of the poor (Pereira, 2012: 778). This resulted in Ban (2012) arguing that Brazilian economic policy was a 'a hybrid made out of economically *liberal* policy goals and instruments associated with the [Washington] Consensus and policy goals and instruments that can be traced to the *developmentalist* tradition'. Ban dubs this set of policies 'liberal neo-developmentalism' (Ban, 2012: 2), or neoliberalism with a 'somewhat social democratic facet', which springs from the current domestic compromise of combining statism with corporatism under market conditions (Boschi, 2014: 139).

Yet such developmentalism was only at the domestic level and had its limitations. Lula was quintessentially 'a candidate with a populist base, but one who was also broadly acceptable to global financial capital' (Foster, 2007: 15). Burges argues that 'Lula [pushed] Brazilian foreign policy far to the left along idealized humanist grounds in order to satisfy the ambitions of his political base in the Workers' Party and to distract supporters from his decision to stick with the liberal economic policies of the centre-right government of Fernando Henrique Cardoso that had preceded his' (2013: 580). Indeed, a Wikileaks cable revealed the true state of mind of Lula *vis-à-vis* foreign policy, especially as he became more secure (and arguably more distant from his core constituencies). In a meeting between the American ambassador and Gilberto Carvalho, Lula's chief of personal staff, the following conversation was reported:

> Carvalho ... underscored again that the second Lula mandate will see a closer approximation to the US, including on the trade front. Carvalho – who has been Lula's confidante and advisor for more than 30 years – explained that Lula's first term had been a balancing act between maintaining credibility with the conservative market and keeping the far left of Lula's base content by assuring them Lula, as president, was not surrendering their traditional banners. In the second term, Lula is better positioned to take issues on pragmatically, including trade, Carvalho said ... and reiterated that the GOB [Government of Brazil] is focused on working with us. (Wikileaks, 2011)

During the 2006 presidential election campaign, Lula was interviewed at length by the *Financial Times*. 'The interview touched on many topics but mainly concentrated on Lula's adherence in his first term of office to the global neoliberal policies of monopoly-finance capital, particularly repayment of debt and "fiscal responsibility". At two points in the interview the *Financial Times* bluntly asked whether Lula was looking toward a "radical change in the model" i.e. whether he and his Workers' Party intended to break with financial capital and neoliberalism in his second term of office. Lula gave them the answer they wanted: "There is no radical change in the model ... What we need now, in economics and in politics, is to strengthen Brazil's internal and external security"' (Foster, 2007: 15).

As mentioned, implicit in Brazilian foreign policy is the ambition to be treated as a global player (de Lima and Hirst, 2010). For Seibert (2011: 14), 'The main political goal of strengthening relations with African countries is the support of African governments for Brazil's global political ambitions, particularly playing a greater role in international politics and having a permanent seat in the UN Security Council'. As part of this, Brazil has increasingly made efforts to develop close ties with other developing countries (Taylor, 2010: 20). Through the encouragement of outward investment, this fits with a broader goal of 'channelling most of the capital harnessed in the country to promote the international competitiveness and ... globalisation of the largest Brazilian corporations' (Kröger, 2012: 896).

One analyst has commented that 'Brazil is a big country and Brazilian business people have "big country" ideas. They think big and act like Portuguese-speaking Texans' (Seeber, 2001: 27). This description applies not only to the Brazilian business community, but to the Brazilian administration, especially its external relations ministry, members of whom exude a secure self-confidence in the promise of Brazil as the natural leader of Latin America (Klom, 2003: 351). Beyond the region, Brazilian claims to be taken seriously as a leading voice of the South are no less imperative. This 'big country' self-perception is an important aspect of understanding the country's policies towards Africa. When asked whether Brazil should join the OECD, an academic at the University of São Paulo rather arrogantly replied that 'Brazil does not really have to join the OECD; it is not worth the cost of trying to pass all levels of evaluation. A country that would appreciate OECD membership would be Argentina. Argentina would like to be recognised as a "normal" country, like Mexico was. But we all know Brazil as it is. Brazil is not a small country' (ibid.: 352).

It is true that Brazil's economy is now in the world's top ten. Its inclusion by Goldman Sachs in the BRIC grouping in 2003 reflected a degree of excitement by finance capital with the country. Like other members of this putative club, Brazil welcomed this recognition enthusiastically and actively and repeatedly used Goldman Sachs appellation to promote Brasília's leadership on various global issues (Sweig, 2010). With this has come a push to alter the membership structures of key global governance institutions so as to reflect changing global dynamics – which in Brazilian terms equates to Brazil joining the top table of global affairs. In order to pursue this aim, Brazil needs to develop a support constituency and Africa is an important element of this strategy: 'Brazil's recent assertiveness around South–South cooperation and rebalancing of representation in international organisations constitutes a bid for greater global influence' (Armijo and Burges, 2010: 15).

However, some context is required here before assigning Brazil the role as a champion of the South. After Lula's accession to power, he was assiduous in signalling various messages to diverse constituencies. For 'the market' (domestic and international) he appointed conservative neoliberals to the ministries such as Agriculture, Finance and Industry, Trade and Development, as well as the Central Bank. *Itamaraty* (the Ministry of External Relations) went to leftists from the PT such as 'nationalist' Foreign Minister Celso Amorim and 'anti-American' Secretary General (Deputy Foreign Minister) Samuel Pinheiro Guimarães. As Burges (2009: 160) noted, 'electoral victory had only been achieved because he [Lula] was able to assuage the fears of the Brazilian middle class and business elite that he would responsibly manage the economy. Yet his party faithful and core political constituency demanded the sort of radical nationalist policies that had come to mark the rhetoric of the Chavez presidency in Venezuela'. Hence the balancing act.

It was in the realm of foreign policy that Lula and his government were permitted to posture a leftist inclination, one grounded in rhetorical South–South solidarity, aimed at satisfying his core constituents. Africa was obviously an area where this was exercised. Meanwhile on the economic front, neoliberalism was advanced domestically and Brazilian companies were encouraged to seek out new markets, hardly surprising given that Lula 'had the best connections to the export orienting elite of any recent Brazilian government' (Cason and Power, 2009: 129). The end result was that for the Brazilian elite, 'core public policy instincts embrace familiar "Northern" preferences: liberal, and mixed-capitalist, democracy' (Armijo and Burges, 2010: 14).

Brazil–Africa: some history

The shared history, culture and language between Brazil and parts of Africa is seen by many policymakers in Brazil as granting Brasília a comparative advantage, with wild claims about how Brazil is somehow an African country and that its history impels Brazil to be the natural friend of the continent: 'Brazil has its body in America but its soul in Africa' (Rodrigues, 1965: 1). Much of this sentiment is used to justify Brazil's claim to a normative and qualitative superiority over the North's links with Africa. Yet until relatively recently, engagement that did occur was bilateral in nature and limited to selected countries based on 'cultural affiliation and strategic interest' (White, 2010: 222). According to Nieto (2012: 165) and citing Ambassador José Vicente de Sá Pimentel, Brazilian thought on Africa has long been divided between the *nostalgicos* 'who argue that Brazil has "historical responsibilities" regarding Africa' and who 'wish to see a role for Brazil in African affairs like in the 1970s', and the *catastrofistas* who claim that Brazil should have nothing to do with Africa, 'in view of the numerous conflicts and human catastrophes that the continent experiences'.

Brazil's cultural ties with Africa are well-known and barely need repeating. Between the 16th and 19th centuries, an estimated three million African slaves arrived involuntarily in Brazil. Today, as Skidmore (2010: 5) notes, 'more than 50 per cent of Brazilians are of African ancestry – the largest population of African descent outside Nigeria'. Portuguese coastal colonies in the Gulf of Guinea reflected the 'complete subordination of the [African] colon[ies] to the slave interests of Brazil' (Rodrigues, 1965: 18) and even after Brazilian independence in 1822, Brazil's elites saw their country's future as being slave-based, actively resisting British attempts to end slavery. The last slaves to arrive in Brazil were as late as 1860; slavery was only finally abolished in Brazil in 1888. From that point on, other than ad hoc individualistic efforts, Brazil–African links were basically cut. It was the demographic and cultural legacy that influenced Brazil, not direct connections with the continent, contributing to 'the forging of the new cultural and social identities in the New World' (Skidmore, 2010: 40).

Yet despite such richness in cultural and historical ties, the African link was not particularly valued until the time of Lula. Certainly, 'during the Cardoso administration, Brazil lost interest in Africa' (Nieto, 2012: 165). Until Lula, the (false) notion of a 'racial-democracy' was energetically put forward by Brazilian elites. In this, deep-rooted disadvantages faced by Afro-Brazilians were denied in favour of a positive image of a Brazil where 'all' had equal opportunities, irrespective of colour or background. In fact, Brazil has long endured alarming levels of racism and inequality, with Afro-Brazilians earning less than half of the average Brazilian wage and suffering the highest homicide, poverty and illiteracy rates in the country. Brazilians who flourish and hold positions of political influence are rarely – if ever – of African descent and Lula's appointment of four Afro-Brazilians to his cabinet in 2009 was a noteworthy and remarkable event.

Attempts by Lula to address Brazil's racist experience was one of the most important tropes employed by the Lula administration in its re-engagement with Africa, leading to assertions – however questionable – that 'Afro-Brazilian equality is central to its domestic *and* international efforts' (Captain, 2010: 195). Certainly Lula was quite public in his claim that Brazil owed Africa, remarking at a banquet in Mozambique, that Brazilian society was 'built on the work, the sweat and the blood of Africans' (Harsch, 2004: 4). Lula consistently held that Brazil–Africa relations had a deeper meaning than purely business and as part of this Brasília actively defined itself as being different from other actors, with a tone in Brazilian diplomacy focused on messages of cultural similarities and political solidarity. This was used to both justify and enhance Brazilian relations with Africa, which usefully connected back to domestic politics. Lula sought to craft an agenda that questioned the division between 'developed' and 'developing' countries and aimed at reframing the dichotomy (Burges, 2005: 1134). This stimulated conservative domestic criticism, which framed the revival of South–South diplomacy as a step backwards towards a 'Third World' mentality (Vigevani and Cepaluni, 2007: 1315).

As noted, prior to Lula Brazilian interactions with Africa were limited. Competition with the continent in global markets over similar commodities, notably coffee and cocoa, marked one aspect. Indeed it was the fact that major African exporters such as Uganda (cotton) and Ghana (cocoa) were allowed to benefit from low or tariff-free access to European markets through the Yaoundé Convention which led to the sentiment in Brazil that Brazilian interests were being 'sacrificed for European unity and African prosperity' (Rodrigues, 1965: 241).

However, South Africa dominated the pre-Lula relationship with the continent: 'in the first half of the 20th century 90 per cent of Brazil's trade with the continent was concentrated exclusively in South Africa' (Visentini and Pereira, 2008: 2). Post-1945 this situation remained (despite apartheid), with South African mining companies investing in Brazil. The largest of these, Anglo American, 'drew other South African investors from a diversity of sectors to Brazil ... It also pioneered the way for deeper political and cultural relations between South Africa and Brazil post-1994' (White, 2010: 224). Whilst Brasília was more than happy to deal with apartheid South Africa, sanctions and other measures actually facilitated a greater entry into Africa by Brazilian companies as, 'in geopolitical terms there [was] a real sense in which the exclusion of South African capital and goods from African markets [was] to Brazil's advantage' (Forrest, 1982: 17). It was only with the demise of apartheid that Brazil could rid itself of the hypocrisy of condemning Pretoria in international forums whilst at the same time maintaining strong economic links with South Africa. Staying with the same theme, it should be pointed out that Brazil was the only developing country at the United Nations General Assembly that voted *against* resolutions condemning Portugal's colonial policies.

After the 1973 oil crisis, Brazil adjusted its Africa policies, spurred on by the fear that a potential oil boycott would seriously damage its domestic economy. Consequently interest in African oil, especially in Nigeria, became important (Carlsson, 1982: 31), cemented in 1974 by cooperation between the Nigerian National Petroleum Corporation and Brazil's state-owned oil company, Petrobras (Hoffmann, 1982: 58). Equally, Brazilian corporations' interest in Africa's commodities and new export markets prompted the military regime to undertake new initiatives in Africa as part of a so-called policy of 'ecumenical pragmatism'. What is interesting is that already, in the 1970s, Brazilian elites were attempting to posture their country as an emerging power. Thus then-Foreign Minister, Antonio Azeredo da Silveira, asserted in a speech in 1976 that as 'an emergent power, with a wide range of interests in many fields [Brazil] cannot allow rigid alignments, rooted in the past, to limit her action on the world stage' (Gall, 1977: 2). Carlos de Meira Mattos, a key intellectual in geopolitics at the time infused his writings with the theme of Brazil on the cusp of attaining great power status (see Kelly, 1984). Yet, after the Carnation Revolution in Portugal in 1974, Brasília sought closer ties with the Lusophone states in Africa and consciously portrayed itself as a developing nation, *not an aspiring world power*, asserting Brazil's identity within the G-77. In July 1974 Brazil recognised Guinea-Bissau's independence even before Lisbon did and was the first country to recognise Angola. The last military dictator ruler, João Figueiredo (1979–1985), was the first Brazilian president to make an official state visit to Africa, visiting the five Lusophone countries in 1983.

In short – and this has continued to the present day – Brazil's diplomatic identity has been Janus-faced, even contradictory. On the one hand, when it is deemed advantageous Brasília asserts Brazil's 'African identity' and the country's developing world status. Garnering political support, leveraging economic ties and contracts to satisfy the Brazilian capitalist class, etc. stimulates this aspect of Brazilian foreign policy. On the other hand, a longstanding claim to great power status and membership in the highest level clubs of global politics remains extant (Christensen, 2013). How Brazilian policymakers have brought these two strands together is through pursuing a typical middle power bridge building role. Brazil is developing and 'feels the pain' of other members of the majority world whilst simultaneously it is an emerging great power seeking the ear of world powers. Endorsing the BRICS concept is a concrete crystallisation of this position, however incoherent it may be.

Contemporary relations

As mentioned, a key impulse behind the deepening relationship between Africa and Brazil was the presidency of Lula (2003–2010). Under Lula, the number of Brazilian embassies in Africa more than doubled to 35 (At the time of writing, Brazil has more embassies in Africa than the United Kingdom). Trade between Brazil and Africa grew in ten years to $27.6 billion (from $4.3 billion in 2002) (*New York Times*, 7 August 2012). Overall, Lula made twelve trips to the continent during his presidency, visiting 21 individual countries and, during his inaugural speech for the second term in 2007, Lula described Africa as one of the 'cradles' of Brazilian civilisation (de Almeida, 2007). But clearly, Brazil's new found drive for Africa was based on something more tangible than romantic cultural ties.

Historically, Brazil's foreign policy has always maintained two prominent principles: economic development and preservation of autonomy in an asymmetric international system (White, 2010). Although Lula's approach to Africa was perpetually sketched out with solidaristic rhetoric, material interests always dominated. Regarding the international system, Brazilian elites are highly sensitive to the dominance of the North in international affairs and world trade and so Brazilian foreign policy has a strong element within it aimed at working towards reforming and balancing out unequal trading relations. One way this is pursued is through 'autonomy through diversification' (Vigevani and Cepaluni, 2007), which in simple terms is based on constructing a nascent bloc from the South to pursue multilateralism.

A firm commitment to multilateralism and the pursuit of middle-power diplomacy is a defining feature of current Brazilian foreign policy and can be observed not least in Brazilian interaction with the continent and with the other BRICS nations. 'Brazilian diplomacy firmly sustains the belief that the solutions to the problems Brazil faces in several fields, from disarmament to the environment, must be universal. The challenge is not to abandon the UN, but rather to strengthen it and to ensure that partial movements converge toward the universal forum. More than ever, there is a need for countries that know how to build bridges in a world' (Fonseca, 2011: 395). Consequently, 'Brazil has become an effective political entrepreneur at the global level, initiating and participating in multilateral fora' (Armijo and Burges, 2010: 14). This serves the ultimate purpose to promote Brasília's demands for 'reform to international institutions that could accommodate Brazil's great power aspirations' (Haslam and Barreto, 2009: 10).

Whilst the focus on 'South–South' solidarity was a most visible aspect of Lula's presidency, it should not be exaggerated. Maintaining a friendly set of policies towards the North was equally crucial. As Hurrell (2010: 6) noted, Lula's position sought 'to be both the favoured son of Wall Street and to claim to speak for the progressive Global South'. This is important to note as it reflected *both* elements of Brazilian foreign policy. Based on the assertion that 'Brazil is not a small country ... It does not, and cannot have, a small-country foreign policy' (Foreign Minister Amorim quoted in Pecequilo, 2009: 8), it was decided that the country would pursue 'high profile diplomacy with a sense of pride' (Visentini, quoted in Pecequilo, 2009: 8).

At least rhetorically, Brazil continues to look South in a much more tangible manner than previously. Here the discourse of the 'Africanness' of Brazil has been employed to link together domestic and international policies. With an aim to stabilise, diversify and expand its trade partners to ensure future economic growth, Brazilian corporations have been active in pursuing contracts in Africa (Brazil's closest economic partners on the continent, Angola, South Africa and Nigeria, represent half of this commercial activity) (Visentini, 2010: 8). The economic justification for the push into Africa has been that it further diversifies Brasília's global insertion, which is of great interest to the large Brazilian corporations involved in construction, mining and oil.

This diversification of trade links was a significant component to Lula's discourse regarding new international trade geographies. This had clear material roots as Brazilian producers increasingly complained about their inability to penetrate either European or North American markets for value-added exports such as capital goods, consumer durables or other manufactured products. On this score, Lula was active in denouncing the North for its hypocrisy: 'We shall seek to eliminate the outrageous agricultural subsidies practiced in the developed countries that harm our farmers by denying them their comparative advantages. With the same ardour, we shall take pains to remove unjustifiable barriers to our exports of industrial goods' (da Silva, 2008). Alongside Latin America, Africa was seen as an alternative market whilst such barriers remained. However, what the policymakers in Brazil neglected to consider was the level of competition for these markets from China, India and others.

While Brazil cannot hope to compete with the economic might of other BRICS countries such as China and India, Brasília *has* been keen to carve out its own spheres of trade and political influence, particularly in what are seen as reliable trade ties with Africa. Both Brazilian parastatals and private companies are going into Africa, but the nature of the state corporations means that they have an added motivation in contributing to the national goal of cutting Brazil's current account deficit towards Africa due to the volume of oil imports.

The formalisation of broad Brazil–Africa ties was cemented in 2003 by the formation of the Brazil-Africa Forum, which demonstrated an 'unprecedented willingness to make a firm commitment to Africa' (Doelling, 2008: 6). Lula's visit to the continent soon after (in November 2003) was framed as a 'rediscovery' of Africa and Brazil's African roots. This discourse of fraternity was enunciated by Lula in his first speech in São Tomé and Príncipe when he spoke of how enslaved Africans had left for Brazil, creating bonds that remained (*Mail & Guardian* (Johannesburg), 7 November 2003). However, 'even though Brazilian officials resorted to a "cultural discourse" or "cultural diplomacy" recalling Brazil's African heritage ... new actions were necessary in order to convince African states of Brasília's intentions' (Lechini, 2005: 6). Though some Brazilian academics and commentators are assertive in their claim that Brazil is qualitatively different from other actors (due to the racial dimension), this can be largely dismissed. Captain's claim that the reasons for Brazil's 'greater dialogue with Africa [are] the renewed dialogue among South–South nations and the domestic issue within Brazil concerning long-overdue racial equality for Afro-Brazilians' (Captain, 2010: 194) are overly romantic.

In fact, trade and market diversification, agribusiness development and the insertion of Brazilian multinational companies into Africa are the motors behind Brazil's current engagement with the continent. The upsurge in interest in Africa has a 'pragmatic commercial nature due to the interest in diversifying trading partners' (Lechini, 2005: 6). As Hopewell has demonstrated, rather than challenging the neoliberal agenda of the World Trade Organization (WTO), Brazil has emerged as one of the most enthusiastic advocates of free market globalisation. This has been driven by the rise of Brazil's export-oriented agribusiness sector, who are now significant new protagonists in advancing – not challenging – the WTO and its neoliberal discourse (Hopewell, 2013). Whilst Brazilian elites may talk the talk of repaying the country's 'debt' to Africa, it in this quest for markets and commercial insertion that Brazil prioritises lie, applied even to those African members of the *Comunidade dos Países de Língua Portuguesa* (CPLP) (Angola, Cape Verde, Guinea-Bissau, Mozambique and São Tomé and Príncipe).

Of note, Brazil was, together with Portugal, a founding member of this organisation and one of the main engines behind its formation in 1996. Interestingly, the CPLP in itself sprang from an African initiative. In 1992, the five Lusophone African countries formed an organisation entitled *Países Africanos de Língua Oficial Portuguesa* (PALOP). The PALOP countries signed official agreements with Portugal, the EU and the UN and sought to work together in the cultural and educational realms (Vilela, 2002). These five countries currently receive over half of all Brazilian technical cooperation, with agricultural and vocational training the two most popular project topics (Cabral and Weinstock, 2010).

Demonstrating both the leadership role Brasília has within CPLP as well as Brazil's wider policies of engagement with Africa, in May 2013, Brazil announced that it was ready to support the admission of Equatorial Guinea to the CPLP as a full member (having held observer status since 2008). Described by Human Rights Watch as 'a brutal and corrupt dictator' (Human Rights Watch, 2010), Equatorial Guinea's president, Teodoro Obiang Nguema, visited Lula in February 2008. Obiang then received the Brazilian president in July 2010 with a joint declaration being issued extolling the 'excellent relationship' of friendship and brotherhood which united the two countries (Keating, 2010). Similarly reflecting Brazilian 'realism', Blaise Campaoré's Burkina Faso has received Brazilian support in the areas of agriculture and biofuels following Lula's 2007 visit, which interestingly coincided with the twentieth anniversary of Campaoré's coup and subsequent murder of Thomas Sankara.

What these examples illustrate is that Brazilian relations with African states are driven by a 'business is business' approach (Foreign Minister Amorim, quoted in Uchoa, 2010), similar to China's in principle, but not in scale (Chapter 5). There is clearly an incentive for Brasília's friendliness towards regimes of all stripes and if Brazil is serious in promoting long-term involvement in the continent, only picking the savoury governments is not going to go too far. This is particularly so given a focus on developing ties with regional and pan-continental bodies, where all sorts of regime types co-exist. In July 2009 Lula was the guest of honour at the African Union (AU)'s Summit in Libya, where he also signed a Partnership Agreement with the AU (African Union, 2009), with Brazil's ambassador to Libya announcing: 'It is a sign for the entire world to see that Brazil is regarded as an important player in Africa' (Rocha, 2009). Bearing in mind the nature of most African governments, Brazil's policy is hardly unexpected and of course all other external actors practice the same pragmatism (or, alternatively, cynicism). Brazilian pronouncements about qualitative difference and an implied superiority does ring somewhat hollow however in the light of day.

Economic relations

Economics is central to understanding Brazil's new engagement in Africa. As an emerging economy, Brazil is still very dependent on global markets (Vieira et al., 2010: 148) and one strategy to diminish this vulnerability is by export diversification:

The desire to diversify Brazilian trade linkages was a critical element of the underlying rationale for Lula's talk of a new international economic geography. From the Brazilian point of view, the challenge was the tremendous difficulty of gaining entry to either European or North American markets for value-added products such as capital goods, consumer durables or simple manufactured goods. Africa and the rest of Latin America were the obvious alternative markets. (Burges, 2013: 583)

Currently, Brazilian exports focus mainly on basic and manufactured goods, including beef, sugar, cereals, vehicles, agricultural equipment and iron. Commodity trade in foodstuffs and simple technologies are important Brazilian industries.

Though some Brazilian companies have had an interest in Lusophone Africa for a long period, most of the contemporary exchanges are of recent provenance. The dynamics behind this stem not only from Lula's activism but are also a *reaction* to the 'New Scramble for Africa'. Yet, as with the other 'scramblers', mineral resources – and particularly hydrocarbons – are central. In terms of total trade the major African trading partners with Brazil are Nigeria, Angola, Algeria, South Africa and Libya, whilst the top import products from Africa to Brazil in 2011 were mineral products (83 per cent) (Fundira, 2012a: 4). Much of this is led by Petrobras.

State-owned Petrobras, the fourteenth largest oil and gas company in the world, with operations in 23 countries, has been present in Africa since the 1970s. It currently has exploration or production programmes in Angola, Equatorial Guinea, Libya, Mozambique, Nigeria, Senegal and Tanzania (Taylor, 2010: 20). Brazil, so far, has depended heavily on Angola and Nigeria for oil, but this is likely to change as Brazil's new reserves cause it to become a major exporter. How this affects links with the oil-rich African nations will be of great interest. Currently, Petrobras presides over six blocks in Angola for exploitation and production; in 2005, Brazil opened an oil-backed loan credit line with Angola for almost $600 million over three years with 20,000 barrels of oil a day (Frynas and Paulo, 2007). Consequently, oil and other natural resources make up almost 90 per cent of Brazil's imports from Africa. 'Its most important trade partners on the continent also seem to fit neatly into the pattern of a resource-hungry BRICS country coming to Africa: its major trade partners Nigeria, Angola, South Africa and Libya are all rich in resources' (Stolte, 2012: 9).

Yet, a crucial difference between China, India and others is that Brazil has been self-sufficient in oil since 2006 (Guan, 2010: 85). Furthermore, new discoveries have been made recently which should cover the increase in domestic consumption and, in fact, turn Brazil into an oil exporter. Brazil then is ideally placed to take advantage of the simple fact that 'cheap oil will be hard to find in 2030' (Almeida, 2009: 117). Since 2007, when one of the world's largest oil discoveries in twenty years was made in Brazil, it has become increasingly evident that Brasília will no longer be dependent on foreign oil and that its demand for oil from Africa will decline. Such realities are already being revealed in Petrobras' business plans. Whereas its old 2007–2011 plan predicted a doubling of the corporation's investment into Africa, the current plan (2012–15) foresees 95 per cent of total investment from the company going into Brazil, with a concentration on pre-salt reserves found off the Brazilian coast (Petrobras, 2006; 2011). These new domestic fields mean that the current domination of oil in Brazil's relationship with Africa will necessarily wane, meaning that agriculture and the development of the biofuels industry (see below) will likely dominate future economic relations with Africa.

Outside of such activities, *Companhia Vale do Rio Doce* (Vale) is the world's second-largest mining company and a global leader in the production and exportation of iron and an important producer of copper, bauxite, aluminium, potassium, gold, manganese and nickel. Vale maintains a presence in Angola, Democratic Republic of Congo, Gabon, Guinea, Mozambique and South Africa. In 2009 it launched a $1.3 billion coal-mining project in Mozambique, intended to produce eleven million tonnes of coal each year to be exported to Brazil, Europe, Asia and the Middle East. If the project realises its ambitions, Vale will play a key role in transforming Mozambique into Africa's second-largest coal producer, after South Africa. Vale plans to produce 4.6 million tonnes of coal at the Moatize mine to meet growing demand from Asia and is investing heavily to increase the mine's capacity to 22 million tonnes by 2017. At present, production is constrained by the limited capacity at Beira port and the Sena railway line, although Vale is investing $4.5 billion to rehabilitate another railway line and the northern port of Nacala to carry coal (*Reuters*, 30 August 2012). Vale also has a joint venture with South African group African Rainbow Minerals in Lubambe, part of the Konkola North copper project in Zambia, which produced its first copper concentrate in late 2012. Of note, in 2008, the company placed an $85 billion bid to take over Anglo-Swiss rival, Xstrata, demonstrating the strength of Brazilian business prospects (Vieira et al., 2010: 130).

Much like India and South Africa – but in contrast to Russia and China – the private sector tends to lead Brazilian economic engagement with the continent. In infrastructure, firms such as *Odebrecht Sociedade Anônima* (Odebrecht) and the *Grupo Camargo Corrêa* (GCC) have developed considerable interests. For example, Odebrecht, a Brazilian conglomerate in the engineering, construction, chemicals and petrochemicals fields, has embarked on an aggressive foray into Africa, completing various projects including new terminals for Tripoli's international airport, dams, airports, railways and roads in Angola, an outdoor coal mine for Vale in Mozambique, and Pietermaritzburg's water system. For its part, GCC operates in construction and engineering, doubling in size between 2005 and 2007, with international capital flows driving a huge growth in the company's revenue. A $3.2 billion hydroelectric plant in Zambia and a

51 per cent stake in a cement plant in Mozambique are some of GCC's key investments. Finally, *Construtora Andrade Gutierrez* (Andrade) is among the largest heavy construction companies in Latin America and among the top three largest Brazilian construction companies, generating more than half of its overall engineering and construction revenues outside Brazil. Andrade is involved in motorway construction in Angola, Congo-Brazzaville, Libya, Guinea and Mauritania and is currently constructing the Mongomeyen International Airport in Equatorial Guinea (Freemantle and Stevens, 2010).

The Brazilian Development Bank (*Banco Nacional de Desenvolvimento Econômico e Social* (BNDES)) and the Brazilian Agricultural Research Corporation (*Empresa Brasileira de Pesquisa Agropecuária.* (EMBRAPA)) both play important roles in this commercial expansion across the continent, providing incentives to Brazilian firms in areas of agriculture, construction and biofuels. For example BNDES has contributed $1.75 billion to Angola to be used for infrastructure construction, using Brazilian contractors. Since 2005 the number of Brazilian companies operating in Angola has increased by 70 per cent, but here Brazil faces the same criticism that the Chinese do: employment opportunities are not going to locals. Unlike China, Brazil has largely avoided negative media coverage. Indeed, unlike some of the other 'new' actors in the continent, Brazil appears to have a positive image, especially in Angola (White, 2010). This may perhaps be explained by the Lusophone connection as well as Lula's positive representation when he was president, something which continues even after he has left office. In part, this has been stimulated and maintained by an activist aid policy.

Aid to Africa

Brazil is still officially a developing country and receives developmental assistance from the international community. Yet Brazil is rapidly emerging as one of the world's biggest providers of aid. Official figures do not reflect this, as officially the Brazilian Cooperation Agency (*Agência Brasileira de Cooperação* (ABC) has a budget of around only $30 million. As *The Economist* put it:

> [S]tudies by Britain's Overseas Development Institute and Canada's International Development Research Centre estimate that other Brazilian institutions spend 15 times more than ABC's budget on their own technical-assistance programmes. The country's contribution to the United Nations Development Programme (UNDP) is $20m–25m a year, but the true value of the goods and services it provides, thinks the UNDP's head in Brazil, is $100m. Add the $300m Brazil gives in kind to the World Food Programme; a $350m commitment to Haiti; bits and bobs for Gaza; and the $3.3 billion in commercial loans that Brazilian

firms have got in poor countries since 2008 from the state development bank (BNDES, akin to China's state-backed loans), and the value of all Brazilian development aid broadly defined could reach $4 billion a year ... That is less than China, but similar to generous donors such as Sweden and Canada. (*The Economist*, 15 July 2010)

Obviously, aid is not disbursed for unselfish motives. Brazilian aid has a strategic motive to firmly establish Brasília on the world stage and win allies and the BNDES is no exception, with a strategic goal 'to increase the export of Brazilian high-value industrial equipment, such as electrical and agriculture machinery' (Marcondes, 2013: 2–3). As one commentator has noted, there is a 'seamless link between Brazil's active diplomatic agenda in Africa, development cooperation and its commercial interests' (White, 2013: 133).

Of Brazilian assistance to Africa, debt forgiveness was prominent under Lula and often accompanied (with much fanfare) Lula's many state visits to Africa. In 2004, 95 per cent of Mozambique's debts ($332 million) owed to Brazil were cancelled, whilst Nigeria had $83 million forgiven in 2005. Over $246 million worth of Tanzanian debt was waived in July 2010 (de Lima and Hirst, 2010). Behind these grand gestures was often a desire to ensure access to resources or to pave the way for major commercial contracts for Brazilian companies, with an 'emphasis [on] Brazilian cooperation [in] supplying technical, not financial, assistance' (Cabral and Weinstock, 2010: 29). Brazilian officials do not use the word 'aid' but instead prefer 'technical assistance' to stress notions of partnership and mutual interest (in much the same way as the Chinese and Indians do). Programmes have been exported in what has been termed a transfer of 'social technology' and ABC has greatly increased its activities in Africa with the 'majority of the projects target[ing] agriculture, education and health' (Kragelund, 2010: 15). EMBRAPA plays a crucial role in this regard, providing 'specialised technical expertise' (Cabral and Weinstock, 2010: 12) in biotechnology and agribusiness, with an emphasis on food security. Having produced impressive results domestically, EMBRAPA began exporting its expertise to Africa, opening its Africa office in Accra, Ghana, in 2006.

In 2010, Brazil announced the Africa–Brazil Agriculture Innovation Marketplace, intended to strengthen agricultural collaboration between Africa and Brazil. Partners with the Marketplace include the World Bank, the International Fund for Agricultural Development, the United Kingdom's Department for International Development, EMBRAPA, the Forum for Agricultural Research in Africa, and African national and sub-national agricultural research and development organisations. The Marketplace's ostensible aim is to transfer knowledge and technology and stimulate policy dialogue between Brazil and Africa. Monty Jones, co-chair of the Marketplace and executive director of the Forum for Agriculture Research in Africa, has asserted that 'Africa has the potential to be the world's food basket, but poor technology and innovation adoption remain a constraint. This would be greatly improved with better exchange of science and technology' (Busani, 2010). The idea behind the Marketplace appears to be that researchers find partners that fit their interests and then apply for collaborative research funding. Given that a lack of funding or poor dissemination of information often prevents or undermines the development of African science, the Marketplace may be seen as a positive step.

Having said this, a substantial amount of Brazilian assistance is geared towards helping the production of biofuels (Lima, 2012: 35). Biofuels are liquid fuels extracted from biomass and which can replace or be blended with petroleum-based fuels, such as gasoline and diesel. Petrol/gasoline is replaced by ethanol, normally produced from starch- or sugar-rich crops (e.g., corn, sugarcane), and diesel is replaced by biodiesel, produced from vegetable oils or animal fats. Brazil, along with the USA, is the world leader in the biofuel industry, with its production quadrupling between 2003 and 2009 (UNICA, 2010). Brazil's 'ethanol diplomacy' (Almeida, 2009: 121) has been prominent and Lula himself was given the name *garoto propaganda do etanol* ('the ethanol advertisement boy'). Lula framed the issue of biofuels in terms of Brazil defending the 'democratisation of energy production' (quoted in 'Bush, Lula Sign Co-op Agreement for Biofuels', *Xinhua*, 3 October 2007) with a logic that argued that biofuels would transform poor countries. This was then linked to the claim that 'rich countries have an obligation to stop using pollutant fuel … soon they will have to face reality and open up to *our* ethanol' (*Investnews*, 2010, emphasis added).

Yet biofuels raise a number of ethical questions about Brazilian policy towards Africa. According to officials at EMBRAPA, by viewing Brazil as a 'partner' with Africa and not a donor, this controversy is somehow avoided with claims that EMBRAPA is not forcing an unwelcomed technology, but is rather sharing development experience to aid economic growth and energy autonomy. With ample arable land and a suitable climate, Brazil has identified Africa as a place where biofuels may be a solution to climate change-related distortions and a relatively cheap source of fuel. The argument has been put that oil-importing nations will no longer have to depend on this expensive commodity. As Brazil is one of the leading producers and users of ethanol technology however, is there a danger that African nations swap one form of economic dependency for another? As one of the world's most efficient ethanol producers, Brazil needs a global market for its renewable energy and this may explain the importance of biofuels in EMBRAPA's activities in Africa and certainly, by encouraging ethanol technology in Africa, new suppliers are created which generates business for Brazilian firms.

Clearly, there is a strong economic incentive for Brazil to develop biofuel technology in Africa, despite this somewhat damaging Brazilian reputation. Criticism tends to hinge on the ethics of promoting large-scale ethanol production on a continent where food security is tenuous, with related concerns that biofuel production may escalate food prices as land needed for crops is turned over. The ability (or willingness) of African states to enforce environmental regulations is also deemed problematic, with concerns that biofuel production may 'lead to even more degradation of vulnerable ecosystems in some of the world's poorest places' (Dauvergne and Neville, 2009: 1097–98). It seems clear that 'new production bases in Africa could benefit Brazilian biofuel producers' ('EU, Brazil, Mozambique to Sign Bioenergy Pact', *Reuters*, 12 July 2010) and unlike Brazilian bioethanol, which faces high import tariffs into the EU market, African-produced biofuel avoids this with minimal tariff rates. Thus 'developing a competitive food and biofuel energy supply chain across the south Atlantic carries enormous commercial potential for Brazil and particularly those holders of Brazilian technology' (White, 2010: 234).

What is of note, however, is that the biofuel controversy highlights the implications of the BRICS giving aid on terms of their own choosing outside OECD Development Assistance Committee (DAC) standards (Woods, 2008). DAC members have emphasised the risk that emerging donors put their economic ambitions before the concerns of the recipient countries (presumably unlike the OECD). True, Brazil offers African elites more choice and, potential increased agency; like the others, it also distances itself from hard conditionalities. Yet support for Brazilian foreign policy is in fact a *de facto* requirement for being granted assistance from Brasília and the lack of economic and political conditionalities are hardly likely to improve governance (Kragelund, 2010). Of course, it is problematic to picture the BRICS as being unique in this regard and we should avoid 'overestimate[ing] the extent to which [neoliberal] goals have been furthered by direct conditionalities imposed by OECD DAC donors' (Woods, 2008: 7). In fact, technology, advice and professional assistance from a country such as Brazil that already practises policies domestically in a developmental setting may be more useful to recipient countries needs than that offered by the traditional donors.

South Africa

Though the Lusophone countries obviously have a special relationship with Brazil, Brasília has been quite explicit in its desire to foster a special relationship with South Africa. Both are states that practise middle power diplomacy and occupy a 'Janus-like' position in the world economy, facing pressure from Northern capital while exporting similar pressures to their surrounding regions (Martin, 2008: 352). When South Africa was admitted to the BRICS, Brazil asserted that 'The addition of South Africa will expand the geographic representation of the mechanism at a time that we are looking, on the international level, to reform the financial system and increase democratisation of global governance' (*Xinhua*

(Brasília) 1 January 2012). Previously, the then-vice-president of Brazil, had remarked that, together, Brazil and South Africa should 'strengthen the cooperation among the sub-regional group to which we are associated, that is Mercosur and the Development Community of South Africa' [sic] (Maciel, 1996: 15).

Holding dominant positions within their respective regions, both Brazil and South Africa practise a diplomacy recognising that on their own they do not have significant heft at the international level but, by alliance-building, influence may be gained. Alliance-building and middle power diplomacy thus dominates. This is 'because Brazil still faces, and will continue to face, a relative deficit of economic and military might', thus Brasília's elites have 'resorted to a strategy commonly used by "middle powers", countries that rely on multilateralism, coalition-building, and other such methods to achieve systemic influence' (Brands, 2010: 3–4).

A clear example of this was the launch of the India–Brazil–South Africa Dialogue Forum (IBSA) in 2003, which was ostensibly 'determined to contribute to the construction of a new international architecture, to bring their voice together on global issues and to deepen their ties in various areas' (India–Brazil–South Africa Dialogue Forum, 2012). IBSA promotes themes of mutual interest in the global governance agenda, as well as promoting increased trade and investment between and among the three states (Taylor, 2009b). Yet when analysing the *actual* policies that the countries practise, there have been fears that IBSA are little more than 'neoliberals in disguise' (Senona, 2010), talking about common issues of the South but actually promoting their own externally-oriented factions. As Armijo and Burges (2010: 27) noted, 'there is not a great deal of difference between the United States' approach and Brazil's essentially pro-globalisation stance ... Where difference emerges is in how the doctrine of the liberal economic agenda is to be advanced and who is to lead and manage it'. That the creation of IBSA coincided with Lula's African emphasis, ties in with the obvious desire to assert political influence in the international arena through such alliances.

The established institutions of global governance have continuously failed to address most of the concerns of the leading emerging powers and in this context, IBSA may be seen as a step towards legitimisation through the increased engagement and cooperation of leading elites from the South: IBSA, after all, has been validated by the United States. Washington has publicly praised IBSA for their commitment to global governance issues. Having 'intentionally promoted themselves as advocates for an emerging developing world' (Taylor, 2010: 86), the IBSA states in fact promote the need for liberalised trade regimes, something which jars with traditional postures emanating from the South, but to which the core can happily subscribe. It is no coincidence that both South Africa and Brazil are highly dependent upon the North for much of their trade. Trade liberalisation is a strategy aimed at helping their key exporters.

Yet this in itself highlights the potential differences between Brazil and South Africa and the overworked notion that the BRICS countries complement each other or have similar interests in Africa. The dispute in 2012 between Brazil and South Africa over their respective poultry industries exemplified these tensions. Close to 60 per cent of all poultry imports into South Africa came from Brazil in 2011, a 40 per cent year-on-year increase of Brazilian imports. Claiming that Brazil was dumping chickens onto the South African market at 'unfair' prices, Pretoria imposed additional import duties on chicken from Brazil. The import tariff expired in September 2012, at which point Brazil insisted that the WTO should rule on whether Pretoria was wrong to impose the tariff in the first place. This may sound arcane, but it reflects a tangible reality: the BRICS states are competitors and South–South solidarity is very fragile when material interests are at stake: 'Both countries are emerging economies [but] Brazil has got to look for new markets because the traditional markets have problems and that may hit South Africa where it hurts the most ... it is about taking competitive advantage where you have it' (Fihlani, 2012). In other words, setting aside the rhetoric associated with IBSA, competitive advantage trumps all else and each side looks after its own. Hardly radical, or different from other actors. What in fact is behind Brazil's claim to promote South–South dialogue is Brazil's self-interested prioritisation of national objectives. The expansion of economic interests is central to this (see Dauvergne and Farias, 2012).

Conclusion

Whether the rhetoric of partnership and reciprocity will fade if or when Brazil attains its hoped-for global status will only be revealed in years to come. Brazil's adherence to multilateralism and a middle power-type posture are strategic moves which seek strengthened economic and political relationships in the South whilst offering Brazil more bargaining power *vis-à-vis* global governance issues. In this sense, Brazil is partially dependent on Africa for achieving its much-vaunted status. Regarding the BRICS, this places Brazil up against China and India, as Brazil must strive to appear an attractive partner given that both Beijing and New Delhi have substantially more material bargaining power. Perhaps in recognition of this fact, in May 2012, President Dilma Rousseff established an Africa Working Group to help strengthen ties. The announcement in late May 2013 that Brazil was to cancel/restructure $900 million of debt from twelve African countries may be seen as a sign that Rousseff intends to continue the broad Africa policies inherited from Lula. Attending the AU 50th anniversary celebrations in 2013, Rousseff completed her third trip to Africa in three months (*Agence France-Presse*, 27 May 2013).

Brazil's policies towards Africa are hinged on its global ambitions, something which the BRICS designation implicitly prepares the ground for. The asymmetrical nature of the global system makes the Global South and Africa especially appealing to Brazil in terms of what the country has to gain by engagement. A mixture of both self-interest and solidarity characterises diplomacy and perhaps this is an indication that Brazil itself has not formed a coherent foreign policy towards Africa. While it seeks favourable terms of trade to ensure future economic growth, it also hopes for the backing of African nations in order to pursue its political agenda at the global level. Often, explanations of a 'debt' towards Africa are articulated; however this is simply rhetoric to legitimise Brazilian policies. While Brazil is increasing its role, it remains to be seen how much it is to Africa's benefit. There are certainly many beneficial development projects and Brazil provides investment and infrastructure opportunities, but it is also perpetuating a divide of inequality between Brazil and the developing world. Whilst claiming to encourage a 'South of equals', Brazil is in fact hoping to act as one of its leaders and engages in similarly unfavourable terms of trade towards Africa as the North does:

> The tactic most frequently used by Brazil is to position itself as a North–South balancer by trumpeting its 'Southernness': either as representative of the global South, a position that is far from universally accepted, or by working to organize coalitions in the South around particular policy positions. Equally significant is the near-naked pursuit of Brazilian self-interest through the articulation of a South–South agenda that clearly creates opportunities for its internationalizing businesses. (Burges, 2013: 579)

In this sense, Brazil might be seen as a classic emerging power, advancing *some* revisionist positions, but keen to maintain order in the system that facilitates its own growth. This is expressed through a predilection for multilateralism as the basis for international relations. Thus strong support for the UN and other governance bodies is central to Brazilian foreign policy, though this is coupled with a desire to diminish outright Western dominance in these organisations. It is important in this respect however to point out that Brazil does not challenge the substance of extant norms. Brazil is only uncomfortable with the institutionalisation of Western supremacy.

Some commentators have applauded Brazil's 'middle-ground approach' between the heavily state-backed and highly political Chinese involvement and the Indian focus on entrepreneurialism and private enterprise (White, 2010: 229). Labels such as the 'quintessential soft power' (Sotero and Armijo, 2007: 51) and Brazilian 'soft imperialism' (Visentini, 2010: 1) have been used to describe Brazilian diplomacy. In fact, Brazil uses cultural ties to create an 'imagined community', but this brings as much benefit to Brazil as it does to Africa (Vieira et al., 2010: 184). Brazilian policymakers understand that they are unable to compete with the present and future dominance of the United States and Europe in Africa and cannot effectively challenge either China or

India there. One advantage these countries do not possess though are the historic and cultural ties to the continent and this is why such an emphasis (call it soft power or not) is present in Brazil's Africa policies. Brazil's former foreign minister, Celso Amorim, explained this as 'the use of culture and civilisation, not threats. It is a belief in dialogue ... [leading to] Brazil's emergence as a leading exponent of soft power' (quoted by Lustig, 2010).

Yet there remains a problem that will need addressing with regard to Brazil–Africa relations. This is the reality that the Brazilian economy is unlikely to have the strength to sustain a foreign policy based on trade and investment. Currently, Brazil's economy depends heavily upon commodity trade and the national goal is to move away from this profile (Barbosa et al., 2009: 70). Brazil's trade relations with Africa will likely continue to grow in the short to medium-term, but unless something dramatic happens, Brazil's economic relations with the continent are vulnerable as Brazil steadily relies on its own sources of energy. A relationship based on exporting biofuel technology and investing in some extractive interests whilst pressing for Africa to get behind Brasília in pushing Brazilian interests at the global level appears limited in its durability – or indeed attractiveness for African elites. Many African elites like the talk of 'restructuring' the global order and are excited by the idea that the BRICS are supposedly poised to topple the North-dominated world order. Yet:

> While at times this means that there might appear to be a language of rebellion and substantive revision in Brazil's foreign policy statements, even ostensibly isolationist ideas such as Lula's new international economic geography [were] fundamentally predicated on maintenance of the existing global governance structures. The Brazilian aim is not to overturn these decision-making tables, but rather to gain an important seat with decision-influencing power that will allow the advancement of its own interests. (Burges, 2013: 578)

As this rather narrow set of interests are advanced and becomes clearer, it will likely disappoint African leaders. How Brazil navigates this situation will be of intense interest.

3
Russia in Africa

Along with the other BRICS countries, Russia has a renewed interest in Africa, yet compared to the others Russia is only starting to (re)develop economic and political relations with the continent. This follows a long hiatus when Africa was pushed far down the list of priorities for Moscow after the Soviet Union collapsed. Russia is 'the BRICS' most atypical actor. It is not an emerging power, strictly speaking, but rather a former superpower eager to regain a part of the political status it lost in the aftermath of the Cold War' (Laïdi, 2012: 619). Consequently, there have been various questions placed against Russia's very status (see MacFarlane, 2006; Bremmer, 2006).

With regard to Africa, domestic economic retreat and a focus on developing and improving relations with the capitalist heartlands resulted in Moscow drastically reducing its presence in the 1990s. As a consequence, of the BRICS states, Russia is the country which is having to play catch-up to the rest and as a result, is lagging behind the others, with the least presence. Then Russian President Dmitry Medvedev summed up the situation during a visit to Africa in 2009 stating that Russia was 'almost too late in engaging with Africa'. 'Work with our African partners should have been started earlier' (*Russia Today*, 2009). However, recognising the potential the continent has for Russian capital, Moscow and its corporations (many state-owned) are beginning to seek to reverse this situation and this has been especially evident over the last decade.

Under both Presidents Vladimir Putin (2000–2008, 2012–) and Dmitry Medvedev (2008–2012), Moscow sought to undertake significant new initiatives in Africa. As a major producer and exporter of oil and natural gas, Russia does not (unlike China and India) need to access energy from Africa. Rather, Moscow seeks to increase its influence over global energy sources to consolidate its own economic and political position (Treisman, 2011). As such, Russia is for the most part interested in oil and natural gas supplies from Africa to Europe: 'Africa's rich untapped oil and natural gas reserves provide an opportunity for Russia's outbound exploration drive and strategic goal of remaining the world's largest exporter of oil (second to Saudi Arabia) and natural gas, and maintaining Europe's dependence on its export of natural gas' (African Development Bank, 2011b: 3). Such dynamics are entirely predictable given that '[i]n Russian foreign policy circles, realist thinking, which focuses on geopolitics and balance-of-power calculations, predominates' (Jordan, 2010: 83). Indeed, Moscow pursues 'a foreign policy attitude that relies on the control of economic and energy resources. Engaging in cooperation with African countries in the oil, gas, platinum-group metal and diamond markets, Russia is attempting to be the world leader in production and market development' (Fidan and Aras, 2010: 59). Consequently, 'Russia's outward investment is dominated by large resource-based corporations that seek to gain greater access to the African market of fuel, energy and metallurgy, and expand Russian investment flows to Africa (African Development Bank, 2011b: 3). Yet despite this upsurge in interest in trade with Africa, it might be said that still, Russia has no concrete foreign policy toward the continent and is outpaced by the other BRICS states. Russian interests primarily spring from two main sources: trade and expanding Russia's global role and prestige.

Historical ties

Russia's interaction with Africa is obviously not new, and the shape these relationships have taken in the past influences Russia's contemporary ties, albeit at times in a negative fashion. Whilst it is true that relations between the Soviet Union and Africa were widespread, these should not be exaggerated for, as Desfosses (1987: 3) noted at the time, these were in the wider scheme of things, persistently a 'low priority' for Moscow. Initially, under Joseph Stalin the emergent African elites were dismissed as bourgeois imperialist lackeys, uninterested in revolution or any significant reassessment of Africa's place in the world other than tokenistic national independence. However, under Nikita Khrushchev, Moscow saw the nationalist leaders as actors who could be 'used in a concerted effort to undermine the West's influence' (Ogunbadejo, 1980: 297). For the Soviets then, the African continent became largely a geopolitical region where strategic and ideological posturing against the capitalist West (and to a lesser extent, China) could be exercised.

Moscow played an ever more important role in Africa from the late 1960s onwards and various countries, particularly those who expressed an interest in or identity as socialist, received substantial technical and economic assistance, as well as a steady supply of Soviet weaponry. During this period, the Soviet Union appeared to be determined to exert influence in Africa, and its ability to do so was assisted by developments within the continent, not least the late collapse of the Portuguese empire and the simultaneous demise of Haile Selassie's regime in Ethiopia. The decline in interest in Africa by Beijing at the same time facilitated this progression. The Sino-Soviet split and the way this played out in Africa had been a very significant dynamism that affected the continent's international relations in a variety of ways, not least in splitting the various anti-colonial movements into contending pro-Moscow and pro-Beijing wings (see Taylor, 2006a).

For Africa, having ideological and geopolitical struggles played out on its soil had largely negative consequences. As the 1960s developed, Moscow's Africa policies hinged on relations with individual countries, based on 'the strategic importance of the country concerned, its economic importance as a market for Soviet exports or a provider of raw materials, and the importance of the Western powers' influence in the region' (Ogunbadejo, 1980: 299). As Desfosses (1987: 3) notes, Moscow at all times acted in its own particular economic interests. Eager to win allies, both sides in the Cold War ignored concerns over governance, sustainable development and elite manipulation of the rivalry. Yet having never herself possessed African colonies and in fact being active in the dismantling of the colonial system, as well as expressing a strong sense of solidarity towards the developing world, Moscow enjoyed a certain comparative advantage, at least in particular quarters (Shubin, 2008). This still has (limited) capital for Russia today. For instance, speaking in Moscow in 2010, South African President Jacob Zuma remarked that 'We [South Africa] have fond memories of that solidarity and friendship, which existed when friends of the oppressed in South Africa and Africa were very few' (Zuma, 2010). Equally however, the sudden severing of many of Moscow's ties with Africa in the aftermath of the restoration of capitalism left a bitter legacy in other quarters.

Problematically, with the context of the Cold War ever-present, parts of Africa were reduced to ideological battlegrounds and the phenomena of proxy wars in Africa often characterised any upsurge of interest in a particular country by either Moscow or Washington. Regimes in Angola, Ethiopia, Guinea-Bissau and Mozambique enjoyed Soviet largesse, but the cost was often unbridled hostility by the West (Patman, 1995: 284). As a consequence of this, Moscow was compelled to deliver billions of dollars' worth of weapons to help defend the socialist regimes in Africa (Albright, 1980). The end result was that much of Africa's military capacity depended on Soviet-built arms and training. Indeed, in Algeria, Angola and Ethiopia, as much as 90 per cent of military equipment was Soviet-made (Shubin, 2004: 108). But weaponry was not the only focus of the Soviet Union and, by the 1980s, Moscow had made hundreds of trade agreements with African countries. Relations were further strengthened by the more than 50,000 African students who studied at Soviet universities, many at the Patrice Lumumba University in Moscow, as well as the thousands of African military and political leaders who trained there (Quist-Adade, 2007).

However, as the 1980s progressed – and particularly after the advent of Mikhael Gorbachev's tenure – the Soviet Union's interest in Africa declined precipitously (see Webber, 1992). Despite all of the political and military efforts, no more than a dozen African nations were ever even vaguely socialist-oriented. Heavily supported by Soviet largesse during the Cold War, these states and their dependent relationship with Moscow became a political issue as economic woes began to embroil Moscow. It was during this time that 'Africa became somewhat of a scapegoat for Russian ills' (Shubin, 2004: 103). It *was* true that by 1989, Sub-Saharan states owed the Soviet Union $14 billion, 16 per cent of all debt owed to Moscow, and a variety of politicians, including Boris Yeltsin, began to assert that assistance to developing countries was in fact a major cause of Russia's economic collapse. This was then extended to the assertion that all links with places such as Africa were costly and practically worthless: 'in reality, the USSR's economic co-operation with African countries was, by and large, mutually advantageous. Nonetheless, these false claims proved damaging and especially dangerous because they encouraged xenophobia and racism in "post-Soviet" Russia' (Shubin, 2010: 5).

Typically, Yeltsin suddenly announced that African countries had to swiftly repay to Moscow their debts, something which alienated many African leaders. Aid to Africa was slashed from 12.5 billion roubles in 1989 to only 400 million roubles in 1990 (Donaldson and Nogee, 2005: 345). The desire to evacuate from Africa led to decisions that damaged Moscow's reputation on the continent further, such as the termination of a multi-million dollar steel plant in Nigeria that was 98 per cent completed when construction stopped (Shubin, 2004: 103). Russo–African trade collapsed: on the eve of the Soviet Union's demise, Moscow–Africa trade was valued at about $1.3 billion per annum; by 1994 this had shrunk to just $740 million (Fidan and Aras, 2010: 49). It was unsurprising that the African press of the 1990s began to refer to Russia as 'the land that turned its back on the continent' (Chhiba, 2011).

With the eventual collapse of the Soviet Union and creation of the Russian Federation, Africa was pushed even further down any foreign policy agenda as Russia worked to rebuild its economic and political structures along capitalist lines (see Hughes, 1992). During this period, 'Africa and the South in general were sacrificed as an important vector of Russian foreign policy in favour of the West in a vain hope for technology transfer and soft credits. The West applauded such changes' (Shubin, 2004: 103). Reforms demanded by the international financial institutions helped force Moscow to withdraw Russian interest from most of the world, Africa included. By 1992, nine Russian embassies and four Russian consulates in Africa had been closed and Russian diplomatic staff at the remaining offices drastically reduced (Arkhangelskaya, 2013: 11). Russian cultural centres were closed and, reflecting the lack of interest in the continent, trade attaché numbers were slashed. In turn, African countries reciprocated by cutting the numbers of their diplomats in Moscow. It was coincidentally during this period that China accomplished great progress on the continent: since then Moscow has sought to claw back lost prestige.

Russia's deteriorating status as a global power became very obvious. The lack of Moscow's involvement in the Horn of Africa when that region was undergoing monumental change was emblematic, wherein the lack of a coherent Russian response to events in Ethiopia and Somalia was interpreted as an 'example of the limitations of Russian diplomacy in Africa after the Cold War' (Patman, 1995: 294). Although Russia had co-authored the 1992 Security Council resolution endorsing international intervention in Somalia, besides a conditional offer of medical aid, Russia was utterly uninvolved. Meanwhile, Ethiopia ignored Moscow during its own transition and turned rather to the United States.

Decline in trade relations

As noted, trade with Africa was badly damaged during the reassertion of capitalism in Russia. The Russian Federation had inherited a large number of bilateral trade agreements with Africa from the Soviet Union, but there was little substance in many of these and by 1992 Africa made up only 2 per cent of Russia's total trade (Donaldson and Nogee, 2005: 345). This loss of trade was largely a result of the end of state management of foreign economic activity and then a subsequent lack of support for outward foreign investment (Shubin, 2004: 107). Indeed, 'the major problem Russian companies face[d] in their investments abroad [was] the absence of a system for obtaining financing from the government and commercial institutions' (Klomegah, 2012: 6).

Typically (although still a positive), the arms trade with Africa was reduced considerably. Sales fell from $12 billion a year in the early 1980s to $7.8 billion in 1991 and $2.5 billion by 1993 (Truscott, 1997: 55). In 1990 alone, African arms imports from *all* sources fell by 80 per cent and much of this decline was brought about by the fall in Russian exports (Patman, 1995: 295). Both Western suppliers as well as those based in the Ukraine and Belarus who had inherited large Soviet stockpiles of weapons took much of Russia's market share. This situation was not helped by the fact that as the economic situation in Moscow worsened, credit was abandoned and cash payments were demanded in advance. As most African countries already had huge military debts and were unable to pay cash, Russian weaponry became decidedly unattractive. Emblematic of this period in Russian history, in 1992 then Foreign Minister Andrey Kozyrev visited Luanda and broached the multi-billion dollar debt owed to Moscow by Angola (much of it arms-related). Luanda flatly refused to pay off the debt, arguing that it was owed to the Soviet Union and not the Russian Federation (Donaldson and Nogee, 2005: 345). A weakened Russia was unable to do anything.

Although Vladimir Putin is often seen as the key figure in turning Moscow's foreign policy around, it should be noted that a new phase in

Russian foreign policy 'began even before Yeltsin's resignation, following the dismissal in 1996 of Yeltsin's first foreign minister, Andrey Kozyrev, who was notorious for his acquiescence to the West, and the appointment of Yevgeny Primakov. Primakov was an outstanding expert on the Third World' (Arkhangelskaya and Shubin, 2013a: 7). However, it was only after Yeltsin's resignation in 1999 that there was a serious overhaul of Russia's foreign policies, outlined in the *Concept of the Foreign Policy of the Russian Federation*, signed by Putin in June 2000. On Africa, the *Concept* stated:

> Russia will expand interaction with African states and assist an earliest possible settlement of regional military conflicts in Africa. It is also necessary to develop a political dialogue with the Organisation of African Unity (OAU) and with sub-regional organisations and to use their capabilities for enabling Russia to join multilateral economic projects in the continent. (Quoted in Jordan, 2010: 88)

Though the policy paper made it clear that Africa was not a top priority for Russia, the development of interest in the continent was hinted at, as a newly assertive Russia began to rebuild. This was related to the contours of capitalism post-Yeltsin, something which continues today. 'Under Putin's economic record during his first term can be characterised as largely liberal [but] the dominant stance of Putin's policy towards business during his second term was *étatisation*. In particular, the state increased its stake in strategic economic sectors via nationalisation and created vertically integrated state corporations' (Vasileva, 2014: 110). This explains why Moscow's activity in Africa is dominated by Russian mega-corporations.

From 2000 onwards then, Moscow sought to slowly pick up the pieces of its shattered African policies, in part building on relations that had continued during the post-Soviet chaos. During the transition, Africa did continue to export certain key resources to Russia, and a very small number of Russian companies traded with the continent, though the focus was mainly on North Africa. South Africa was the one exception to this; trade between Russia and Pretoria actually grew during the chaos. This was somewhat unexpected, as there had been no official ties between the two countries since 1956. Indicative of this was that South Africa owed only a small debt to Russia of $50 million, which had obviously remained unpaid for decades (Donaldson and Nogee, 2005: 346). However, Moscow *was* a strong supporter of both the African National Congress and the South African Communist Party (see Shubin, 1999). This helped facilitate access as apartheid came to an end, as did the pragmatism/opportunism arising from the end of the Cold War. According to Shubin (ibid.: 34), during this period policy was 'largely determined by personalities or clans, acting either in their own narrow interests or blinkered by "re-ideologization", and certainly not in Russia's national interests'. These developments included the premature switching of support from the ANC to the White minority government. Indeed, even before official ties were established, Moscow entered into a secret $5 billion marketing deal with the De Beers diamond company in 1990, granting De Beers exclusive rights to the sale of 95 per cent of diamonds exported by Moscow for 30 years (Patman, 1995: 293). By 1991, the transition in South Africa led Russia to resume official relations and Russia and South Africa were cast as 'natural partners, because of symmetries between the two economies: together they produce 80 per cent of the world's gold, platinum, and other precious metals' (ibid.).

Contemporary relations

As with the other BRICS countries, the 2000s have been a period of economic and political upsurge. The Russian economy, not least, has made a strong comeback since 2000, with Russia's GDP rising from a low of $195 billion in 1999 to $1.61 trillion on the eve of the financial crisis in 2008 (World Bank, 2011). Between 2000 and 2011, Russian average annual GDP growth was 6.9 per cent. Russia is the world's second largest producer and exporter of oil as well as the world's largest producer, exporter and proven reserves-holder of natural gas. Overall, Russia's economic structure makes it a net exporter, with $542.5 billion exported in 2012, compared to $358.1 billion of imports. Oil and gas exports account for over 65 per cent of total Russian exports and contribute 30 per cent of Russia's total GDP as well as up to 40 per cent of Moscow's revenues (African Development Bank, 2011b: 1). Along with the expansion of the Russian economy has come the re-emergence of Russo–African trade, rising from $740 million in 1994 to circa $10 billion in 2012, although this figure still represents less than 2 per cent of global Russian trade (Arkhangelskaya and Shubin, 2013b: 24).

Over the last ten years there has been a reversal of the situation observed in the 1990s and, with his ascendancy to the presidency in 2000, Vladimir Putin acted to recover from Yeltsin's 'lost decade' under a new, stronger and more globally grounded foreign policy (Stent, 2008). This was grounded in an acceptance of the capitalist paradigm, albeit with Russian characteristics, to coin a phrase (Treisman, 2011). 'Putin clearly understood that Russia's future as a leading power required its integration into the global economy and the preservation of the core market institutions that had been introduced – at great social cost – in the 1990s' (Rutland, 2012: 21). Like the other BRICS states, this is practised through a middle power-type role:

> Russia's pursuit of multilateral approach has dual characteristics. As a medium-sized great power in world politics, Russia tends to perform rhetorically as a proponent of the kind of multilateralism embodied in the United Nations. On the other hand, Russia has revealed stronger

ambitions to assert itself as a regional power in its immediate neighbourhood. Here, it tends to act either unilaterally or as an 'instrumental multilateralist', predominantly making use of regional institutions to legitimise its actions. In this context, Russia can be seen as both an instrumental and a principled multilateralist, in other words, multilateralism in Russian foreign policy is both a tool and a value. (Lee, 2010)

The BRICS might be said to serve a useful purpose for Moscow in balancing its links with the core in groupings such as the G-8 (and soon perhaps the Organisation for Economic Co-operation and Development – OECD) and with 'the rest':

> This duality allows Russia many useful advantages. On the one hand, G-8 and OECD connections provide the lustre of equality with wealthy and powerful nations in the West, a valuable badge especially on the domestic front. On the other hand, [Moscow] can also remain aloof from that group by using its BRICS and G-20 relationships as a platform from which to contest Western hegemony and avoid the blame for the economic debacle associated with neoliberal economic policies. (Rowlands, 2012: 635)

This is important for Putin as it plays to different audiences at different levels: 'Putin want[s] Russia to be accepted as part of the global community through entry to organisations such as the Group of Eight (G-8) or the WTO, but, at the same time, he portray[s] himself to domestic audiences as a strong leader standing up to the West and insisting on Russia's uniqueness' (Rutland, 2012: 24). Thus, Russia's membership of BRICS has been characterised as 'a stroke of diplomatic ju-jitsu aimed at the West'. Moscow 'transformed a successful investment strategy into Russia's own novel international agenda' (Roberts, 2010: 39). In other words, an instrumental – if not opportunistic – policy aimed at external projection and the soothing of some domestic constituencies.

Certainly, BRICS allows Russia the possibilities of diplomatic support when dealing with the West. 'The BRICS form a coalition that allows Russia to exist in a broader group when interacting with the West. It is no coincidence that Moscow was most willing to politicise the BRICS at a time when relations with Washington were deteriorating' (Laïdi, 2012: 619). As Roberts (2010: 41) avers, 'Russia has been the leading proponent of transforming the BRICs from just another investment strategy into a recognised international coalition bearing significant implications for international relations'. Yet:

> Russia's political move is not intended as a vehicle to balance American power. Nor is Moscow's BRICs agenda a revolutionary gamble to overthrow the Western order, notwithstanding the Kremlin's frequent bellicose rhetoric, a teapot war against Georgia, and concerted if unsuccessful efforts to build an autonomous regional sphere of influence. As theorists of unipolarity would predict, Russia has adjusted, however

fitfully, to the constraints of America's overwhelming power for almost twenty years. Indeed, Russia has been preoccupied during this period with integrating itself into the Western order. (ibid.)

Certainly, whilst 'Russia sees itself as neither East nor West' and thus multilateralism is a useful policy tool, there are residual 'lingering hopes among a certain part of the Russian ruling elite that a full-scale alliance with the United States is still a possibility, with Russia becoming part of the collective West (and then, goodbye, unloved BRICS!)' (Martynov, 2011: 77). This reality is a good illustration of the incongruity between Moscow's diplomatic ambitions and its economic capabilities (Shevtsova, 2007). Nevertheless, underpinned by the growth in the Russian economy, a more assertive foreign policy under Putin, and the increase in interest in African markets and the economic opportunities found on the continent, has brought Russia and Africa back together. This could be observed early on by the number of visits: 'From 2001 to 2005, Russian interest in Africa began growing, and Russia–Africa relations gained positive dynamism. In 2001, the Presidents of Algeria, Gabon, Guinea, Egypt, Nigeria, and Prime Minister of Ethiopia visited Moscow' (Fidan and Aras, 2010: 51).

This development was further driven by Putin's progressive moving away from the Atlanticist tendencies of the Yeltsin era (Tsygankov, 2012a). Instead, Putin has sought to reassert Russia's position as a global power not beholden to anyone and often in response to an overweening United States (Larson and Shevchenko, 2010). Various Western initiatives that are seen to undermine Moscow have helped drive this process forward (see Kanet, 2011). These would include *inter alia* the expansion of NATO eastward up to Russia's borders; the Balkans Crisis and the aggressive response of the West towards Serbia (leading to Kosovo's 'independence'); harsh criticism directed against Russia regarding the conflict in Chechnya and over human rights more broadly; the unilateralism of the United States, as exemplified by the invasion and regime change in Iraq; hostility towards Russia for its relations with Iran and Syria; and policies by the West during Russia's confrontation with Georgia (see Lucas, 2008).

Africa can play a role here as a support constituency and this influences how Moscow approaches the continent diplomatically. For instance, in 2008 Russia voted *against* imposing sanctions and arms embargos on Robert Mugabe's Zimbabwe, with Russia's ambassador to the UN stating that Moscow saw no threat to international peace and security and that the situation in Zimbabwe had not taken on trans-border dimensions (*The Guardian*, 11 July 2008). Of course, at the same time anti-Zimbabwean moves by the West were not particularly popular in Africa and, equally, sanctions would have frozen Russian arms sales to Harare. Attracting African support for Russian policy positions is also pursued, as in August 2012 when Russian Deputy Foreign Minister Mikhail Bogdanov and Special Presidential Envoy to the Middle East and Africa, Mikhail

Margelov, visited Ethiopia, Liberia, Madagascar, Uganda and Zimbabwe to drum up support for Moscow's position on Syria.

It may be averred that 'a new attitude in Russian foreign policy both towards the West and towards the developing world has emerged' (Shubin, 2004: 104). In this regard, Russia's attitude towards Africa is similar to the other BRICS: Africa is a useful support constituency at the global level. 'From Russia's perspective, there are important geo-political implications for working with Africa. The continent's 54 states represent a key voting bloc within the structures of global governance' (Klomegah, 2012: 6). In the context of an aggressive dominant power:

> Russian–African relations can play an important role in opposing the tendency of one country or a limited group of countries to impose their will on the rest of the world and, from the Russian perspective, in particular to prevent Russia from being isolated. Most African countries and Russia are committed to the idea of a multi-polar world, and consider that the UN should play the central role in this multi-polar world. The states of the African continent constitute about a quarter of the members of the UN, while Russia is a permanent member of the UN Security Council, and the UN is an arena in which Russia and Africa collaborate fruitfully. (Shubin, 2010: 6)

Indeed, collaboration is in the interests of both Russia and Africa 'because 60% of all of world resources, including biogenetical resources, fresh water and minerals, are located in either Russia or Africa. Therefore, both sides stand to benefit from joining forces to safeguard their sovereign right to control this wealth, especially in the face of attempts to declare these resources "an international asset", under a false pretext of "reestablishing justice"' (ibid.).

Having said that, we should not exaggerate Russian hostility to a Western-led global economic order. 'Moscow does accept Western leadership in the normative field ... There is a passage in the 2008 Foreign Policy Doctrine that ... while it criticises "the historic West" for clinging to its "monopoly in global processes", it nevertheless insists that the future inter-civilisational "competition between different value systems and development models" is going to take place "within the framework of universal democratic and market economy principles"' (Makarychev and Morozov, 2011: 357). Indeed, 'while the BRIC (Brazil, Russia, India, and China) countries are rapidly expanding their economic and political influence across the globe, there are no signs as yet of an anti-American alliance forming between them. On the contrary ... Russia's re-emergence on the global stage has coincided with a new emphasis on the part of the Kremlin to underline Russia's European credentials, and thus (in some ways) to be part of the "western club" of states' (Jurado, 2008: 6). 'Putin's continued pursuit of market reforms [is] based on his own calculation of what [is] in Russia's strategic interests – and what ... serve[s] the more venal interests of his own political coterie' (Rutland, 2012: 24). What connections that exist between China and Russia are largely expedient and pragmatic, the BRICS included. Indeed any putative Russo–China nexus is purely an 'axis of convenience' (Lo, 2008). It would be an error to mistake the BRICS as indicating any particular warmth between China and Russia.

The presidentialist style of rule in Russia has facilitated quick decision-making by the elites, which has also lubricated Russo–African ties (Roxburgh, 2011). The constitution of 1993 established a presidential republic with a strong head of state, granting the president a dominant say in foreign policy matters, with powers ranging from the right to declare and end wars to the appointment of ambassadors (Galeotti, 1995: 88). Both Putin and Medvedev have been proactive in shaping foreign policy (Stuermer, 2009). Constitutionally, the Duma and the Prime Minister have very little role in international relations (although that never stopped Putin when he held that position) and the Ministry of Foreign Affairs is directly subordinate to the president. It is in effect an arm of the executive, as opposed to an active decision-making entity (Lynch, 2001).

With a foreign policy that is largely formed by the president, looking at how the president goes about relations with Africa is a good way to measure policies. The foreign policy objectives of resource control and projection of influence are most clearly demonstrated by Putin's state visit to South Africa in 2006 and Medvedev's visits to Egypt, Nigeria, Angola and Namibia in 2009. The countries that they chose to visit, and the topics raised on these visits made it very clear where Russian interests lay. On the 2009 tour, one of the deals announced was a $2.5 billion partnership between Gazprom (Russia's largest oil company) and the state-run Nigerian National Petroleum Corporation (NNPC), to be known as Nigaz (*Russia Today*, 2009). At the time, this was the single largest gas contract Nigeria had ever signed. In concrete terms the deal signalled a major monopolistic move by Russia. In the same year that Nigaz was announced, Gazprom, already controller of over a quarter of all gas supplies to Europe, signed a deal with the Algerian firm Sonotrach (Europe's third largest gas supplier) to seek out and commercialise gas supplies together (*New York Times*, 3 September 2009). These moves were observed with concern by a gas-dependent Europe.

Russian engagement with Africa is, as these and similar examples demonstrate, overwhelmingly economic in nature. The *Foreign Economic Strategy of the Russian Federation to 2020*, released by the Ministry of Economic Development of the Russian Federation in 2008, provides an interesting insight into Russian aims in Africa:

> Africa, being a swiftly growing region, represents a strategic interest to the Russian economy, including as a source of natural resources, a market for investment projects and a market for exports of machinery and technical products exports ... The priorities of the foreign economic strategy in the region are:

- prospecting, mining, oil, construction and mining, purchasing gas, oil, uranium, and bauxite assets (Angola, Nigeria, Sudan, South Africa, Namibia, etc.);
- construction of power facilities – hydroelectric power plants on the River Congo (Angola, Zambia, Namibia, and Equatorial Guinea) and nuclear power plants (South Africa and Nigeria);
- creating a floating nuclear power plant, and South African participation in the international project to build a nuclear enrichment center in Russia;
- railway Construction (Nigeria, Guinea, and Angola);
- creation of Russian trade houses for the promotion and maintenance of Russian engineering products (Nigeria and South Africa).

As with the regions of the Middle East, an urgent task for Africa is the participation of Russian companies in the privatization of industrial assets, including those created with technical assistance from the former Soviet Union (Iran, Turkey, Morocco, Nigeria, Guinea, and Angola) (Ministry of Economic Development of the Russian Federation, 2008).

Relations are indeed centred on just a few large Russian resource-based corporations which are close to the presidency, creating what some have called Russia's 'Petrostate' (Goldman, 2008). In the run up to the 2008 financial crisis, the bulk of Russian commercial activity in Africa was undertaken by just seventeen corporations, operating 44 planned or existing projects in 13 African states. Of these corporations, the most active were Gazprom and Lukoil, Moscow's biggest oil and gas firms, with Alrosa, a diamond company, followed by Rusal, an aluminium firm (Shubin, 2010: 6). Russia's interests in Africa are understandably rooted in the acquisition and exploitation of primary resources: 'The common interests lie in the field of resources [and] infrastructural development, particularly in the sphere of energy resources and nuclear power' (Arkhangelskaya, 2013: 11). If this is not aimed at seeking to monopolise gas, then Russian companies seem to be seeking natural resources vital to Moscow. As observed in one analysis: 'With the dissolution of the Soviet Union, Russia found itself partly deprived of vital minerals for its economy. Imports cover its deficit of certain minerals: manganese (almost 100 percent), chrome (80 percent) and bauxites (60 percent). It also has undeveloped deposits situated mostly in the remote areas of Siberia and far east' (Arkhangelskaya and Shubin, 2013b: 24). What is clear is that so far only the largest Russian corporations, active in the largest and most lucrative sectors of the Russian economy and often 'national champions' in terms of their economic clout, have managed to find a niche in Africa.

Russian policy towards Africa

The Russian leadership has been eager since 2000 to emphasise their 'return' to Africa, and to the global political scene in general. It should be noted that Medvedev seemed more focused on Moscow's ties with Africa than Putin (Putin only visited Morocco and South Africa during his first presidential term of 2000–2008) and the nature of Russian foreign policymaking will likely play a role in the future course of events. Notably, Medvedev on his 2009 Africa trip insisted that 'Africa is waiting for our support' and that renewed 'work with our African partners should have been started earlier' (*Russia Today*, 2009), an implicit criticism of Putin's policies. Yet the fact that Putin is clearly wed to the idea of Russia once again being a strong actor in global affairs, it is possible that Africa's sheer political presence at forums such as the UN may concentrate Putin's mind *vis-à-vis* the continent.

However, while the Kremlin and sympathetic Russian media outlets are eager to promote 21st Century Russia as a strong and versatile actor, all is not so straightforward. Indeed, complexities may be identified in two distinct directions. Firstly, it seems that Moscow's interests in and policies towards Africa, despite the rhetoric of equality that often pervades Russian diplomatic discourse about Africa, are actually rooted in a decidedly European foreign policy interest (see below). The second issue relates again to reality versus rhetoric: upon further examination it is clear that Russia's activities in Africa are minor in the overall grand scheme of things.

Russia has heavily employed the notion of pragmatism in explaining its foreign policy. In its 2000 *Foreign Policy Concept*, it was asserted that the state must always maintain a balance between 'objectives and possibilities for obtaining these objectives', before going on to clearly stipulate that the primary aims of the Russian state are to integrate into the world economy in order to ensure favourable market conditions for Russian-based business and 'maximise economic returns' to the state (Ministry of Foreign Affairs of the Russian Federation, 2000). 'In the economic arena, Russia's main focus remains greater integration with the EU's economy and the WTO. In late 2011, Russia finally completed its negotiations over its membership in the WTO' (Tsygankov, 2012b: 4).

According to Kuchins and Zevelev (2012: 190), Moscow places its main focus in foreign policy on binding the three "wings" of European-derived civilisations together (Russia, the EU and North America). Within this policy 'is the stated import of deeper integration among the three wings of European civilisation to maintain their competiveness globally, and the implication that the three should not compete against each other but rather cooperate to better compete against others'. Such an unwritten policy clashes with the very idea of the BRICS – as Kuchins and Zevelev

note, 'Suffice to say that the foreign minister and other Russian political figures do not speak in this manner in Beijing and most other places
outside the famed belt from Vancouver to Vladivostok' (ibid.). This basic
contradiction is of great interest when evaluating the staying power of
the BRICS.

Returning to the continent, the specific role of Africa in Russia's
foreign policy outlook is particularly surprising when viewed against
the political vocalising mentioned above. The Kremlin has published
three official *Concepts* regarding foreign policy to date (in 1993, 2000
and 2008). In this, regional priorities are ranked. In stark contrast to official claims about the importance of Africa to Russia, in all three of these
documents Africa appears in the ninth place (followed only by Latin
America) (Ministry of Foreign Affairs of the Russian Federation, 2008). In
the 1993 *Concept* document no particular attention was given to Africa,
mentioned only in passing, in keeping with Yeltsin's orientation at the
time. The 2000 document was certainly more assertive than its predecessor, again in keeping with the rapidly rising wealth and confidence of
the era, and moved Europe up from fifth place to second, while retaining
a minor place for Africa. The most recent publication in 2008 was the first
to devote any significant attention to Africa, asserting in Section IV the
rather bland and formulaic:

> Russia will enhance its multi–pronged interaction with African States
> at the multilateral and bilateral levels, including through the dialogue
> and cooperation within the G-8, and contribute to a prompt resolution
> of regional conflicts and crisis situations in Africa. We will develop
> political dialogue with the African Union and sub-regional organ-
> isations taking advantage of their capabilities to involve Russia in
> economic projects implemented on the continent. (ibid.)

This generic approach to regional issues was accompanied by no change
in Africa's official priority to Moscow and the continent remained near
the bottom of the list. Though there is a strong concern about identity,
spheres of influence and the use of resources as a gambling chip, the
situation regarding Africa *does* fit with Moscow's current overall foreign
policy whereby a lack of coherency dominates. To date, despite Moscow's
apparent resurgence, there does not appear to be any grand strategic
vision on any front (Legvold, 2001: 62).

With regards to aid, until recently Russian developmental assistance
has been somewhat limited (it should be noted that it was not until 2010
that Britain stopped its aid programme to Russia). Russian aid is limited
to a few countries in Africa, namely Ethiopia, Somalia, Guinea, Kenya and
Djibouti (*Russia Today*, 2012). Indeed, as one Kremlin official asserted,
'the most important aspect of economic cooperation in our foreign policy
is to encourage African countries to trade with us and to not only depend
on development aid' (Klomegah, 2009b). Although Russia remains one
of the largest economies in the world, it is not a member of the OECD,

and there was no Russian contribution to the Gleneagles commitment to increase development assistance to Sub-Saharan Africa to $25 billion a year by 2010. In 2010, Moscow only spent $472 million on foreign assistance, a drop from $785 million in 2009 and a year-on-year decrease of 40 per cent. Given that in 2007 Russia committed itself to the spending target of 0.7 per cent of gross national income (GNI), this figure is somewhat farcical: if it had met the 0.7 per cent target in 2009, Russia would have budgeted $9.27 billion.

The overwhelming bulk of Moscow's aid goes to neighbouring former Soviet republics, whilst outside the region Russian aid goes through multilateral agencies such as the United Nations. Given that 'Russia has said the role of its foreign aid is to "strengthen the credibility of Russia and promote an unbiased attitude to the Russian Federation in the international community"', this is problematic (*The Guardian*, 25 May 2011). To somewhat address this, a direct state-to-state international aid agency was announced in mid-2012. However, the fact that the planned agency was to be staffed by only 50 people spoke volumes about Russia's aspirations to be a major aid provider.

Having said that, in 2012 Russia did move to write off the debt of over $20 billion owed to the Soviet Union (and inherited by the Russian Federation) by several African countries: Ethiopia ($4.8 billion), Libya ($4.5 billion), Algeria ($4.3 billion) and Angola ($3.5 billion) (Vasilenko, 2012). This followed the 2008 write-off of $16 billion of debt owed by African countries. At the same time, Russia transferred $50 million to the World Bank's foundation for poor countries, mainly directed to Sub-Saharan Africa and allocated $43 million to the World Bank programme to improve education in developing countries, especially African countries. At that time, more than 8,000 students from Africa were studying at Russian higher education institutions, with more than a half of them doing so for free (ibid.). Due to Soviet involvement in the continent, at the turn of the century, 'of all the debts of African countries to be written off, 20 per cent [fell] on the Russian Federation. It [was] 26 billion dollars' (Shubin, 2004: 114).

Contemporary economic ties: the European prism

In stark contrast to the political rhetoric, real economic interaction between Russia and Africa is 'well short of the full potential' (Shubin, 2010: 6). One example of this can be found in the surprising absence of a Russia–Africa forum. In contrast, the United States, France, China, India, Japan, South Korea and most other major economic actors in Africa now have such forums. The best that Moscow has at present is the 'Russia–Africa Business Council', initiated in 2002 by 60 Russian businessmen active in the oil, gas, finance and tourism sectors. It is true that Medvedev appointed a new special envoy on African affairs (the aforementioned Mikhail Margelov) but this was all rather ad hoc and reactive, probably as a result of the fact that in comparison to other developed and emerging markets, such as the EU, China or India, Russian trade with Africa is of 'quite minimal' importance to the continent (African Development Bank, 2011b: 1). A business forum was organised in Addis Ababa in 2011, attended by 250 African businessmen, as well as governmental representatives from Ethiopia, Zimbabwe, Sudan, Niger and Mali and representatives from Gazprombank, Lukoil and the Russian Railroad Company. Compared to the Forum on China-Africa Cooperation (FOCAC) or the India–Africa Forum Summit, Moscow's efforts in this regard are, to say the least, risible.

While arguing that BRICS investment in Africa goes deeper than simple self-interested commercialism, analysts have generally failed to demonstrate real evidence of this in the case of Russia specifically. This is a problem if one wishes to make the argument that the BRICS are all going into Africa in an equally vigorous manner (see Schoeman, 2011). In fact, if one examines BRICS–Africa trade links as a totality, Russia is *way* behind the others. The BRICS–Africa relationship is in fact predicated on Chinese, Indian and Brazilian ties, with Russian linkages significantly less important. For instance, Africa's merchandise exports to the BRICS countries in 2011 totalled about $117.6 billion, of which only 1 per cent went to Russia. In contrast, exports to Brazil, India and China made up 13, 25 and 50 per cent respectively (UNECA, 2013a: 10).

Of the BRICS nations it is true that Russia's trade with Africa has grown at a greater rate than, say, Brazil's, but 'the importance of Russia as a trading partner to African countries is quite minimal when compared to other developed countries and emerging markets such as the European Union, the United States, China, India, and Brazil' (African Development Bank, 2011a: 1). Partly, this is because 'Russian private business is still relatively young and inexperienced. It has limited knowledge of Africa and does not always take into account the specific character of this market. Most Russian companies lack the marketing skills necessary to enter the highly competitive markets in Africa' (Deych, 2012: 12).

However, a number of Russian economic investments are worthy of note. Not least is the proposed trans-Saharan gas pipeline from Nigeria to Algeria for exporting Nigeria natural gas into southern Europe. Such a pipeline would present the first major competition for Russian gas suppliers in the European market. In response, Gazprom obtained concessions from the Nigerian government in September 2008, and signed a $2.5 billion deal with Nigeria's state oil-company to invest in the aforementioned Nigaz joint venture (*The Guardian*, 30 June 2009). In doing so, Gazprom beat Chinese and American competitors to the deal by promising development aid such as electricity generation and offering to develop a civilian nuclear infrastructure, as well as agreeing to help fund the 2,700-mile trans-Saharan pipeline (*BBC News*, 23 June 2009). By engaging directly with the Nigerian government and ensuring that

Gazprom has a stake in the project, Moscow is seeking to ensure that the new supply chain, when it comes on line, will not undercut Russia's gas monopoly to Europe. With ongoing developments in Ukraine at the time of writing, such concerns can only be exacerbated.

In addition, Gazprom Neft, the oil arm of Gazprom, has been involved in the Elephant oil project in Libya. Until the fall of Gaddafi, Gazprom Neft had been set to acquire half of Italian group Eni's 33.3 per cent stake in the Elephant project, valued at $170 million. The project aims to pipe natural gas from Libya across the Mediterranean to Europe. At the time of writing Gazprom Neft and Eni had reached an agreement to prolong Gazprom's option for buying the shares in the Elephant project. If the deal goes through, it would strengthen Gazprom's goals *vis-à-vis* supply routes to southern Europe. Libya has the fourth largest natural gas reserve in Africa after Algeria, Nigeria and Egypt.

Besides Libya and Nigeria, Gazprom is also active in Algeria seeking production contracts. Algeria, which already supplies 13 per cent of Europe's total gas requirements, is of immense strategic importance in this regard and Gazprom is clearly interested in extending its reach there. 'By promoting the formation of a natural gas cartel, Russia would potentially control most gas pipelines into Europe, fostering the possibility of a Russian monopoly over significant parts of Europe's energy sector' (Boussena and Locatelli, 2013). Because of Gazprom's holdings in Central Asia, Russia already controls natural gas supplies from the east, so control of the African supply would leave Europe with little manoeuvrability to find alternative energy supplies.

Despite its own strong resource reserves, as mentioned previously Moscow's interests in overseas commodities, particularly the under-exploited raw materials of Africa, makes sense. This relates to the domestic situation, whereby:

> Although Russia possesses extremely rich supplies of natural resources, domestic capabilities for fully meeting industry's needs for high-quality raw material and at competitive prices are shrinking. Many profitably exploitable deposits have been exhausted or are on the brink of exhaustion ... Russia has been experiencing a significant shortage of several of the most important minerals, including almost 100% of manganese, 80% of chromium, 60% of bauxite, and so on. New Russian deposits of many important minerals are largely found in the northern latitudes and their development is associated with large investments and long introduction into service. (Abramova and Fituni, 2011: 10)

Other than Brazil's ethanol industry, no other BRICS is a significant energy exporter apart from Russia. Interest from Moscow in raw energy materials beyond Russian borders is thus distinct within the grouping. China and India, for example, seek African oil as necessary inputs into their growing economies. Russia, on the other hand, seeks African oil and gas in order to monopolise as much of the market as possible and hence maintain Moscow's strong position in the global energy sector: 'Russia is striving to become the most influential player in the world oil and gas market. However, it will be very difficult for the country to materialise these plans by means of its own resources alone' (Abramova and Fituni, 2011: 10). As one commentator has asserted, Russia's interest in African oil then 'should be seen as a move to create a bloc of countries rich in energy resources. The existence of such a bloc, in Russia's thinking, would increase the political weight of its participants and thus change the balance of power and influence in the world' (*The Guardian*, 26 June 2009).

Russia's deeper economic aims in Africa lie in the control of 'access to the gas that heats western and central Europe' (Klomegah, 2010). The continued exploitation of the lucrative European gas market is very much in Russia's interests and it stands to reason that foreign policy aims revolve around this. Russian policy consequently views Africa through a European lens. Moscow's economic interests are firmly rooted in the control of oil and gas sales, and Europe is a strong export market that Russia already dominates; Africa is ripe for the further entrenchment of this control. Whilst Russian corporations have demonstrated increased interest in Africa and the Kremlin has stepped up its rhetorical commitments, as previously mentioned there has been no real rise in Africa's official importance to Moscow. However, there *has* been a strong rise in the real importance of Europe and a significant increase in the control of African supplies by Russian firms. There are many reasons for Russia to find its relations with Europe deeply important and equally strong reasons for Russia to find Africa useful within the wider Russo-European relationship, as well as for Moscow's wider global ambitions.

However, future developments in the global energy industries may not augur well for Russia, may lessen European dependence on energy imports and, in the long-term, impact upon Russo–African relations. The energy landscape is going through an ongoing and incomplete change as unconventional gas, tight oil and new technologies of coal generation are 'rewriting the rule book in what had been regulated and stagnant energy markets, uncomfortably dependent on Russian pipeline gas' (Sherr, 2013: 66). It is too early to state equivocally how this will play out and then possibly affect Moscow and its corporations' stance towards Africa. However, what is sure is that 'the assumption of growing European dependence on Russian energy now looks vulnerable' (ibid.).

Weapons to Africa

The Russia arms industry is actively seeking new buyers, and has found a market in Africa, with a total 1.1 billion dollars' worth of arms sold by Russia to Africa between 2000 and 2007 (Klomegah, 2009a). This has led to criticism by the West of Russian involvement in certain African situations, Sudan being the prime example. Russia exported $21 million worth of aircraft and equipment and $13.7 worth of helicopters to Sudan in 2005 during the Darfur conflict, provoking Amnesty International to accuse Russia, along with China, of violating a United Nations arms embargo. Military helicopters, particularly the Russian Mi-24 gunships sold to the Sudanese air force, were allegedly used to launch attacks in which civilians were subjected to indiscriminate fire.

Russia has also been accused of selling arms outside of official channels, in smuggling and contraband rings, further contributing to violence in Africa. 'The illegal trade in Russian arms is by definition impossible to fully capture, but should be in the region of at least 20 per cent of the official figure, judging by the rate of conflict proliferation in central Africa' (*Inter Press Service*, 29 January 2009). Russia has refused to support negotiations on a global treaty to regulate the weapons trade and in fact Putin has asserted: 'We must focus on expanding Russia's presence on the global arms market'. 'This applies to the geography of our deliveries and to the list of products and services' (*The Guardian*, 3 July 2012). Yet as a permanent member of the UN Security Council, Russia has been actively involved in conflict prevention and peacekeeping in Africa, mostly in observer-type missions, in countries such as the DR Congo and Western Sahara. Russia *did* dispatch a military contingent of 115 persons with four Mi-24 attack helicopters to Sierra Leone, the only permanent member of the Security Council to deploy troops as party of the United Nations Mission in Sierra Leone (UNAMSIL). In general, however, Russia seems as reluctant as the other permanent members to get entangled in African conflicts – and has even fewer ties with the continent to motivate it to do so.

Conclusion

Unlike Brasília, Delhi or Beijing, Russia does not ostentatiously self-identify with the Global South, although it sees it as a useful forum to help Russia assimilate into the liberal world economy and occasionally will advance the claim that Russian was not an imperial power in Africa. According to a report in early 2013, 'Participation in the BRICS was the most promising route for Russia's integration into the global economy ... "The positive prospects of the BRICS are obvious"', Prime Minister Dmitry Medvedev was quoted as saying (*Xinhua* Moscow, 16 January 2013). In fact, 'Moscow's focus on economic modernisation and globalisation to overcome economic backwardness predates the BRICs and helps explain why a Goldman Sachs marketing strategy captured the imagination of the Kremlin and developed into BRICs mania' (Roberts, 2010: 43). But in this grand scheme of things and with global pretensions driving the BRICS grouping, in the case of Russia, Africa appears to be a side-issue, perhaps contrasting with its importance for the other BRICS.

What this means for Moscow's position *vis-à-vis* African development and any structural reordering of the global system that might benefit the continent is clear: 'As a rentier state, its vision of the international economic system is warped by the very nature of its economy, which is based on the value of hydrocarbons. Therefore, Russia does not have, unlike the other BRICS, a real strategy of growth and development. Therefore, Moscow only joins the BRICS on sovereignty-related issues, and even then, only if the BRICS agree on what they mean by sovereignty' (Laïdi, 2012: 620). In short, Russian interest in both Africa and the rising powers group hinges mainly on gaining geostrategic leverage.

As has been noted, unlike the rest of the BRICS, Russia is a net energy *exporter*. However, the structural nature of Russo–African trade remains concentrated in primary commodities, something which places Russia within the 'typical' mode of emerging economies' trade with the continent. Of interest, Russia and China target very different niches on the continent, which makes talk of any Sino–Russian competition in Africa overblown. Russia cannot compete with low Chinese textile prices, and does not compete with Chinese infrastructure works, but equally China is not in a position to compete with the highly technical projects Russia pursues in Africa, such as the Angolan satellite project (AngoSat) or the building of nuclear power stations. Indeed, when NigComSat-1, a Nigerian communication satellite, was launched in 2007 aboard a Chinese rocket, it ended in ignominy less than a year later when the satellite ran out of power and failed in orbit, resulting in 'an embarrassing failure' (*This Day*, Abuja, 31 January 2013). Worryingly, though 'Chinese nuclear technology can be regarded as approaching global levels, with similar design, safety and operational standards ... to reduce costs, Chinese designs often cut back on safety' (He Zuoxiu, 2013). African countries might be advised to steer clear of bargain-basement Chinese nuclear reactors. Having said that, Moscow does not seem to have taken the lead in any comparative advantage in such industries and, overall, Russian actions on the continent suffer from a lack of a coherency.

To underline, Russia's relations with Africa are firmly rooted in the activities of a few large resource-based corporations, with obvious implications for the continent. Russian rhetoric speaks of the desire to promote commercial, political and related interactions with Africa but the reality of Africa's importance to Russia is less profound and Africa lies near the bottom of the Kremlin's strategic interests. Trade statistics are indicative of this relationship's reality and, while hugely increased, are miniscule on a general Russian scale and lag behind other actors trading with Africa, be they traditional or emerging partners.

Something which also hinders Russian expansion in Africa is the issue of reputation (see Bondarenko, 2012). 'Today, there are in Africa two basic views on Russia that have developed – Russia as the successor to the Soviet Union and Russia – as a country that has made a step back' (Arkhangelskaya, 2012: 6). As one analysis frames it:

> Russia also has an image problem in Africa. The new post-Cold War generation in Africa (those who grew up and were socialised in the aftermath of the Soviet Union) do not know much about Africa's formerly close relations with the Soviets. While other countries have filled African markets with investment and consumer goods, thus promoting positive images of themselves, Russia has not. Furthermore, racially motivated attacks by Russian ultra-nationalist groups against African students and workers have damaged the image of Russia in Africa. (Fidan and Aras, 2010: 55–6)

Russia's growing involvement in Africa obviously raises two questions: will involvement continue to deepen, and what are the consequences for Africa? Russian firms are clearly dedicated to continued investment in Africa, but they face competition. Russian actors seem to be seizing opportunities to exploit Africa's resources with little compulsion, and Russian firms continue to take advantage of the uneven global system and Africa's unequal inclusion. There seems to be little attempt to address or compensate for such a milieu and Moscow seems to be more interested in Africa's natural resources without any comprehensive preferential trade deal with the continent. As the African Development Bank (2011b: 6) warns, 'Increasing Russian investments in Africa ... might represent significant economic opportunities for resource-rich African countries, [but] there is a risk that, coupled with limited domestic policies, they might generate negative social and environmental outcomes for Africa'. Whilst they may generate revenues for the national economies of oil- and resource-rich countries in Africa, dependency deepens.

A foreign policy based largely on the person of the president, a disinterested public and an indifferent – if not at times hostile – media all act as obstacles to the formation of a more positive foreign policy towards Africa. While the Soviet Union was deeply involved in Africa, this involvement faded after the Cold War, as the Russian Federation tried to restructure its political and economic systems. Russian (re-)involvement in Africa is only just now beginning to develop. The renewed interest is driven by Africa's natural resources and a desire to be an influential global actor. Indeed, 'African countries can be regarded as Russia's foreign policy reserve. African countries are the first to support Russia in cases when Russia insists on its own stance in the international arena or resists pressure from the West' (Fidan and Aras, 2010: 57). Consequently, 'while Africa may not be an immediate policy priority, at a longer-term strategic level, the desire remains for Moscow to establish and maintain a more clear and defined presence in the region. Russia's dependency on natural resources to maintain its state budget and ensure future reserves for its export-based economy will ensure Moscow's continued interest in

Sub-Saharan Africa' (Giles, 2013: 41).Yet the implications that this and other manifestations of Russia's ties with Africa have for the continent suggests a reification of Africa's dependent relationships. Ironically, this may be increased by other factors hinged around dependency: 'Africa's dependence on China could … wind up being Russia's advantage. Many of the continent's countries are already talking about Chinese "colonialism," and are looking for partners from other countries to decrease their dependence on Beijing' (Kommersant, 2011). If this is the case, the diversification of dependency through engagement with Russian interests is no solution to Africa's problems. Ongoing developments can only intensify the extant character of Russo-African economic relations.

4

India
in Africa

The holding of the second Africa–India Forum summit in Addis Ababa in May 2011 exemplified the burgeoning ties between New Delhi and the continent. Such connections represent a further diversification of Africa's international relations away from 'traditional' North–South linkages. However, this diversification also poses potential problems given the nature of many of the linkages that the emerging economies bring in their relationships with various African countries. In this light, this chapter seeks to analyse some of the main implications of the growing Indian relationship with Africa. What is important to note is that the upsurge in Indian interest in Africa has taken place within the wider context of the adoption, in 1991, of a neoliberal economic policy framework. '[T]his shift was a momentous development and a leading World Bank economist reportedly celebrated it as among the "three most important events of the twentieth century", alongside the collapse of the Soviet Union and China's transition to "market reforms" (Jha, 2005: 3677). For others, it is 'probably the most significant [discontinuity] since the country's independence from colonial rule in 1947' (Mazumdar, 2014: 79). The immediate stimulus for this abrupt change was a balance of payments crisis instigated by the effects of the first Iraq war which hugely increased India's oil import bill whilst exports slumped, credit dried up and capital flight from non-resident Indians' deposits from Indian banks increased exponentially (Ghosh, 2006). This crisis was seized on by important elements in leading classes to push for a dismantling of the Nehruvian *dirigiste* state, enthusiastically supported by those within India with aspirations for accumulation under the new dispensation.

This moment had long been percolating, with reformers increasingly pushing for change (Desai, 2012). The crisis of 1991 opened the opportunity for this *volte face*. 'Policy reform was favoured by state elites under the influence of new ideas, eliciting a change in the ideological orientation from those that shaped earlier policies. These elites included political leaders and bureaucrats … Together they formed an "epistemic community" with new goals, and sought the reconstruction or modification of previous policies' (Shastri, 1997: 28). Now, '[Indians] are told by the ruling political establishment, and reported prominently in the media, that [the] growing international stature of India has been possible due to the process of globalisation. Despite its many shortcomings, we are told further, if less directly, that we need to play the game according to the global rules set by the United States' (Bhaduri, 2010: 40).

Whilst it was the Congress Party and Manmohan Singh as Finance Minister that initiated the neoliberal reforms, when Congress lost power in 1996 and then in 1998, it was the new government led by the Hindu chauvinist party, the Bharatiya Janata Party (BJP), consolidating power in 1998, that carried forward the reforms with enthusiasm, which has continued to this day under successive governments. '[I]t would be a fair assessment that the IMF-World Bank perspective has been very well entrenched in shaping the policies of the central as well as a number of state governments. For instance, in the case of central government, the key economic ministries have been headed, almost uninterruptedly since the early 1990s, by the same people although political parties heading the government have been tossed around quite a bit by the electorate, by some of the staunchest advocates of neoliberalism' (Jha, 2005: 3677–8). This has been supported by dominant fractions of the Indian bourgeoisie who have increasingly become outward-oriented – and supportive of the existing global order:

> A large part of the Indian bourgeoisie is now prepared to settle for rentier status, and to collaborate with foreign capital. Politically, there is a growing sense among the Indian bourgeoisie that American political and strategic dominance can't be challenged, and although they would like to see it tamed, it is out of their hands. So they are willing to settle for the best they can get, by trying to become more important regionally and internationally through greater collaboration with the US. (Lal and Vanaik, 2004)

Since 2004, a Congress-led United Progressive Alliance (UPA) coalition has been in power, with Manmohan Singh as Prime Minister. He has had to face domestic constituencies threatened by liberalisation (particularly, but not exclusively, in the retail sector) who remain resistant to the reform process. As a result, 'Singh's United Progressive Alliance (UPA) government is trying to have it both ways; embracing globalisation and protecting domestic popular interests' (Ollapally and Rajagopalan, 2012: 88). Of interest, China's path to development is extolled within certain circles in India as the way to go, the way to promote and 'modernise' India. This is an interesting development given that, traditionally, Indian policymakers have been wary of Beijing, often with strong memories of the 1962 Sino-Indian War: 'Our one-time China-haters have become its greatest economic admirers ... "China's path is our path"' (Bhaduri, 2010: 44). Equally, as Thussu (2012: 441) notes, 'a particular version of India is being promoted, with grandeurs of an emerging superpower, following in the footsteps of Uncle Sam. This reinforces a reconfigured hegemony that legitimises the neoliberal agenda, predicated on free-market fundamentalism.'

Under such impulses, Indian foreign policy is moving away from its non-aligned position to one of multi-alignment. India's foreign policy debates are centred on three key positions. The first revolves around the hawks on Pakistan, which need not be discussed further here. The second centres on those who argue that India's future lies with a close alignment with the United States. This position is held at the highest level: 'in 2003, then prime minister Atal Bihari Vajpayee reportedly confessed that strategic partnership with the United States was essential to his twenty-year program to attain great-power status; "otherwise India's ability to project power and influence abroad anywhere would be greatly compromised"' (Research Unit for Political Economy, 2005: 16). Often, such arguments are also hawkish *vis-à-vis* Beijing. The third position argues that India's best option is to try and manage both China and the United States equitably, extracting maximum benefits from the relationships. This position, which might be cast as strategic ambivalence or strategic autonomy, is what seems to be ascendant in India's membership of the BRICS and also in any debates regarding India's Africa policies, where New Delhi is conscious that it is playing catch-up on the continent to most other actors, particularly China. Here, India's business community and its organic intellectuals are most influential in framing the terms of the debate. India's efforts to develop ties with Africa may be seen within this context, as can New Delhi's membership of the BRICS. Yet the fundamental aim of pursuing neoliberal policies and marinating strong relations with Washington remains central.

Within India itself there are on-going debates and tensions over the direction of foreign policy (Taylor, 2012). The pendulum at present seems moving towards a greater warmth towards the West, specifically the United States. As Prashad (2011, quoting cables from the U.S. Embassy, Delhi, exposed by Wikileaks) has detailed, this has led to the undermining and replacement of actors seen hostile to the rapprochement:

> Remarkably, at a lunch meeting between [then-Indian Permanent Representative to the United Nations, Nirupam] Sen's Deputy, Ajai Malhotra, and [John] Bolton's Deputy, Alejandro Wolff, the Indian said that he 'had been sent to New York with instructions from Indian Foreign Secretary Shyam Saran to cooperate with the USG [U.S. government] on the broad range of issues,' and, as Wolff put it, 'to check his boss's antiquated instincts.' Malhotra criticised Sen's 'confrontational attitude to the USG'.

In May 2009, the Indian government ended Sen's tenure, and sent as his replacement Hardeep Singh Puri, whose appointment pleased the US government. In a meeting on May 1 with Political Counsellor Ted Osius in New Delhi, Malhotra indicated that he wanted to increase

U.S.–India engagement 'to a higher degree of convergence'. Head of the India–U.S. Forum of Parliamentarians, Ramesh Chandran put it plainly, 'Noting Puri's Moscow-educated, UN predecessor Nirupam Sen's proclivity to cling to a leftist non-aligned mentality, Chandran favorably compared Puri whom he contended has a much more modern and twenty-first century way of thinking' – in other words, one subservient to the U.S. narrative of world affairs. (ibid.)

Indeed, 'The BRICS grouping is yet another effort in India's bid to create a "swing space" in the evolving international architecture by embracing new relationships, not avoiding them. The audacity of the BRICS grouping is that it goes beyond the global, regional and bilateral links among states that have come to define the new architecture. BRICS is multilateral but not geographically tied and not an encompassing global grouping' (Legro, 2012: 643). This reflects a paradox in Indian foreign policy: 'Indian policymakers are reluctant to abandon the current "nonaligned" status. And they are genuinely interested in working with the United States instead of challenging the American dominance' (Sinha and Dorschner, 2010: 88). In spite of New Delhi's involvement in the BRICS, wariness characterises Indian attitudes towards some of their ostensible partners. In particular, 'there remains considerable suspicion of China and guarded and lukewarm fondness for Russia' (ibid.: 97). In fact:

> For the Indians, nonaligned means: dependent on nobody. At the same time, the Indians clearly see that their most important political relationships are those with Washington and Beijing. The BRICS' role is accordingly diminished. At best it is one of several instruments for India to use in managing its relationship with China. There is little doubt that if China was not a part of this group India would not invest much in it. India's political involvement in the BRICS can be seen as the by-product of a global strategy whose overriding concern is to contain China's rise. (Laïdi, 2012: 624)

Whilst many current analyses of Indian foreign policy stem from an emerging (and arguably premature) Indian triumphalism (see, e.g., Mathew, Ganesh and Dayasindhu, 2008; Nanda, 2008; Sanyal, 2008), the modalities of Indo–African relations are taking place within the milieu of a burgeoning – and increasingly confident – India (see Goldstein et al., 2005). Having moved from the slow 'Hindu rate of growth', India's recent economic trajectory has propelled Indo–African ties. It is within this broader milieu that Indian policies towards the BRICS and Africa should be contextualised, where New Delhi's elites actively seek to embrace an objectified 'globalisation' as a means to benefit powerful externally-oriented factions: 'the Indian government has taken a much more positive attitude towards [the] internationalised trend and liberalised foreign exchange policies, foreign ownership ceilings, access to international capital markets, and other rules and regulations, all with the aim of promoting outward investments' (Hattari and Rajan, 2010: 512).

Foundations

Indo–African relations can be traced to ancient times (Beri, 2003) and Africa is host to a long-established Indian diaspora (a smaller long-established African diaspora also exists in India – see Karmwar, 2010). In the contemporary period a new set of dynamics with rapidly expanding relations are emerging, 2005–06 being dubbed 'Our Years of Africa' (Suri, 2008: 2). India's trade with Africa has doubled in recent years, from $24.98 billion in 2006–07 to $52.81 billion in 2010–11 (*Business Day*, 28 January 2013). There are diverse motives for the variety of Indian actors currently establishing themselves in Africa. From the Indian state's perspective, energy security has been seen as paramount (Bava, 2007: 3), as has the ambition to be taken seriously as an important global player (Sahni, 2007: 21–3). This stems from the celebratory rhetoric around India's supposed emergence as a, if not *the*, next superpower (see Nayar and Paul, 2003; for alternate views, see Mundkur, 2011; Drèze and Sen, 2013).

There is no doubt that New Delhi's politicians harbour ambitions to take up a permanent seat on the UN Security Council (Jobelius, 2007: 4). Equally, as India's economy continues to grow, Indian business interests have ambitions of themselves to expand their commercial empires. With Africa being described by Manmohan Singh as 'a major growth pole of the world' (*Times of India*, 24 May 2011), the continent is seen as providing political support to India as well as important opportunities for new investment sites and new export markets (Agrawal, 2007: 7). Consequently, 'economic activity between Africa and Asia is booming like never before' (Broadman, 2008: 97).

Until recently, India's economy was one of the fastest growing in the world, leading some analysts to predict a potential growth rate of circa 8.4 per cent per year until 2020 (Poddar and Yi, 2007: 9). This was then extrapolated to suggest that by 2042, India would overtake the United States to become the world's second largest economy, behind China (Ganguly and Pardesi, 2007: 10). However, of late India's economy has experienced problems, weighed down by high inflation, a weak currency and a drop in foreign investment. Key sectors such as mining and manufacturing have been hit, whilst slowing growth – coupled with a recovery in the North post-2008 – has made India (and other emerging economies) a less attractive option for foreign investors.

As mentioned, contact between India and Africa is long established and Indian trade with the eastern African seaboard is ancient (Prasad, 2003). Colonisation led to the incorporation of the Indian subcontinent and large swathes of Africa into the British Empire, which then facilitated the establishment of a substantial Indian diaspora in Africa, which constitutes a radical difference between India and most other international actors involved in Africa. There is at present a great interest within India in what are termed People of Indian Origin (PIOs) in Africa. Around 10 per cent of the global Indian diaspora is located in Africa (Dubey, 2010) and these are relatively assimilated. According to one study, 'in a 2006 survey of 450 business owners in Africa, almost half the respondents who were ethnically Indian had taken on African nationalities (with most of the other half retaining their Indian nationality), compared with only four percent of firm owners who were ethnically Chinese (the other 96 percent had retained their Chinese nationality)' (Broadman, 2008: 99). PIOs are currently seen by New Delhi as having the potential ability to facilitate cooperation and communication between Africa and India, as well as serve as economic agents for Indian commercial interests. This last point needs to be carefully managed by New Delhi as historic resentment against economically powerful ethnic Indians has long been a feature of a number of African countries – and is something which will not be helped by any notion that such actors are somehow advancing India's agenda in any form.

Crucially, in light of much current Indian rhetoric about its relations with Africa, the struggle for Indian independence inspired African nationalism and is a powerful legacy that continues to have redolence today – even if only at the state level. However, whilst Gandhi may have set down the moralistic underpinnings for Indo–African relations, it was Jawaharlal Nehru who provided a political framework, with a strong element of South–South solidarity infusing India's early post-colonial foreign policies. Central to Nehru's ambitions in this regard was the 'gradual creation of friendly, cooperative, and mutually constructive relationships between India and the various countries of Africa' (Park, 1965: 350). Nehru in fact referred to Africa as a 'sister continent' (Sharma, 2007: 20) and Africa became important in Nehru's vision for a fairer and more equal global system (Naidu, 2008: 116). The epochal Bandung Conference of 1955 was in fact organised by India and other Asian countries to promote economic and cultural cooperation between Asia and Africa and oppose colonialism and neo-imperialism. The subsequent Non-Aligned Movement, with which Nehru became heavily associated, reinforced his position as 'the post-colonialist leading voice against imperialism, colonialism, domination, interference or hegemony' (Bhattacharya, 2010: 65). However, because of the constraints of the Cold War and superpower chicanery (and, equally, India's relative material poverty), such aspirations were largely confined to the realm of rhetoric. Indeed, it has not been until the post-Cold War period and India's exponential economic growth that Indo–African relations have moved substantially forward, accompanied by a greater 'pragmatism and a sober realisation of new challenges facing both India and Africa as they get ready to take their place under the global sun' (Singh, 2006).

Political ties

Officially, Indian foreign policy roots itself in Nehruvian inclinations for multilateralism and South–South solidarity (Agrawal, 2007: 7). According to some commentators, this has stimulated India's long-held interest in UN peacekeeping (Chiriyankandath, 2004: 200) and Indian peacekeepers have now been occupied with over 40 UN peacekeeping missions (Jobelius, 2007: 8), many of these in Africa. New Delhi is enthusiastic in its support of the UN system which often stands in contrast to much Western practice (Bava, 2007). Using its leverage, New Delhi has at times sought to open up a certain amount of political space within multilateral institutions where developing countries might cooperate (ibid.) and as part of this strategy, has underwritten the financial costs necessary for such cooperation (Hurrell and Narlikar, 2006: 7). Motives for such efforts come from the fact that:

> [T]he Indian economy is becoming highly reliant on foreign markets for its survival and growth ... India's growth in its exports of goods, services, and people create a big stake for India in sustaining open markets globally. Multilateralism is being seen as an important means for India's economic management, especially in dealing with major powers. (Ollapally and Rajagopalan, 2012: 98)

To reflect its growing status, India seeks a number of goals, for example, a permanent seat on the UN Security Council (UNSC). As 'an observable manifestation of friendship is the pattern of UN votes' (Alesina and Dollar, 2000: 46), it is likely that some political interest by India is aimed at strengthening bonds with countries in the expectation that benefits will accrue. This tactic paid off in 2006 when the chair of the Council of Ministers of ECOWAS (the Economic Community of West African States) threw the weight of the fifteen-member sub-regional group behind India's bid to be a Permanent Member of the UNSC. Pranab Mukherjee, India's External Affairs Minister, later declared at the India–Africa Summit in 2008 that 'the support of Africa for reform and expansion of the UN Security Council, in both permanent and non-permanent categories, is critical' (Mukherjee, 2008: 59).

As part of its general commitment to multilateralism, India has long emphasised both a cooperative new world order and the mutuality of Southern interests in combating global inequality. This rhetoric plays out well across Africa and has at times enabled New Delhi to project itself as the spokesperson of the Global South (Narayan, 2005: 2), a role that India often (even if only implicitly) competes for with China (Ford, 2006). In emphasising the claimed mutual interests behind Indo–African ties, the Indian government has in fact asserted that 'India's contemporary Africa policy is aligned to a confluence of interests around justice in the global order levelled at increasing the leverage and influence of their [its] respective global positions and promoting a new international order' (quoted in Naidu, 2007: 2). This resonates in many quarters in Africa, confirmed by Jean Ping, former Chairman of the African Union Commission, who stated that 'Africa is paying special attention to developing relations with emerging powers of the South. Our common aim is to promote multilateralism as a paradigm in international relations' (*Times of India*, 25 May 2011).

The mutual desire by both India and the AU to reform the UN Security Council and secure permanent seats has been a consistent theme in recent Indo–African relations. This is not only linked to the demand to secure their 'rightful places' in world affairs, but also in the case of India, would alleviate the inconvenience and inferiority that India feels *vis-à-vis* China. India's diplomatic strategy cannot be said to be grounded in an idealism predicated purely on South–South solidarity, and contemporary India's foreign policy is more pragmatic than previous incarnations. Although New Delhi continues an interest in non-alignment and notions of South–South solidarity, the focus these days is very much on the importance of national interests, particularly economic in nature. This is linked to a wider move within India away from statist economic policies to those more in line with neoliberalism. 'In the dominant discourse – both in India and internationally – the latter policy shift [towards neoliberalism] is credited with having put India on a fast growth path for the first time in its history' (Desai, 2007: 785).

In this way, India might be said to be following in the economic (and hence political) footsteps of China. Indeed, 'since 1991...India has begun to liberalise its economy in a belated effort to achieve the growth and investment seen in China, as well as to stave off bankruptcy' (Alden and Viera, 2005: 1088). A surging economy within India requires new markets and new sites for Indian investment opportunities. 'India ha[s] a special significance for the BRICs thesis [of an exponential upward trajectory of emerging economies pursuing liberalisation]. Given its demographic bias, the thesis rested disproportionately on the Chinese and Indian cases. While India's contribution to the aggregates for the BRICs were more modest than China's, India's statistics were more reliable and India was closer to the sort of market economy assumed by the BRICs thesis' (Desai, 2007: 786). Competition with Chinese companies then stimulated recent Indian energies in parts of Africa. As Brahma Chellaney, of the Centre for Policy Research in New Delhi asserted, 'India is massively playing catch-up to China in Africa, and only in recent years is it trying to engage the continent in a serious way' (*Sydney Morning Herald*, 25 May 2011).

Of note, during the 1990s India was shutting diplomatic missions in Africa as an economic measure; today it has 33 embassies, high commissions and consulate-generals across the continent and the Indian Ministry of External Affairs is increasing its diplomatic initiatives by establishing three joint secretariats to manage three regional divisions that encompass the continent. India has also copied China's Forum on China-Africa Cooperation (FOCAC) (see Taylor, 2011b) in developing its own India–Africa summit. The first India–Africa summit in New Delhi occurred in April 2008 and 'marked the culmination of India's renewed focus on Africa' (Kragelund, 2011: 596). Fourteen African countries attended the summit, which gave rise to two documents: the *India–Africa Framework for Cooperation Forum* and the *Delhi Declaration*. Both stressed the usual ambitions of South–South cooperation, capacity building and mutual interests but of more interest were the proposals to develop a plan of action and various follow-up mechanisms to ensure implementation, a clear replication of FOCAC's own institutional framework. Subsequent to the summit, New Delhi declared a $5.4 billion credit line over the next five years (rising from $2.15 billion in the past five years), grants worth $500 million over the next five years and a unilateral opening of the Indian domestic economy to exports from all least developed countries (LDCs).

At the policy level, trade policy has been a crucial and important element of these meetings, which operates alongside New Delhi's commitment to both multilateralism and South–South solidarity. This is also reflected in India coordinating closely with leading African countries on the Doha Round of negotiations at the WTO and in Indian membership of the India, Brazil and South Africa Dialogue Forum (IBSA), formed in 2003 (see Taylor, 2009b), which 'created a new dynamic in international relations, drawing together the three most powerful economies of the southern hemisphere in a regional axis for the first time' (Lai, 2006: 4). Both IBSA and the Africa–India Forum were established with New Delhi's active involvement due to 'India's aim to change the world's perception of India – from being a recipient to being a donor – in order to boost its global political standing. Moreover, it was a realisation that political ties have lagged behind the growing economic ties between India and certain African countries' (Kragelund, 2011: 596).

The Indian economic presence in Africa

India–Africa trade has grown rapidly in the last few years, from $3.39 billion per year in 2000 (Majumdar, 2009) to over $70 billion in 2012–13 (*The Hindu*, 9 March 2014). As one Indian source put it: 'Trade between India and Africa has grown by more than 400 per cent in the past five years and is expected to grow at a rapid pace' (*Business Standard*, 19 May 2011). Currently, private sector investments by Indian firms into Africa are estimated to be $5 billion, excluding the $10.7 billion Bharti Airtel-Zain deal where Bharti Airtel, an Indian telecommunications company, bought Kuwaiti firm Zain's African assets. Around 245 Indian firms have investment linkages with Africa, whilst African investments in India are estimated to be $170 million cumulatively from 2000 to 2010 (*Finan-*

cial Times, 23 May 2011). Some of the top African investors in India are South Africa ($110 million), Morocco ($21 million), Kenya ($19 million), Seychelles ($17 million), Nigeria ($7 million), Tunisia ($4 million) and Ghana ($ 3million) (ibid.).

Mauritius is India's single largest offshore investor: between 2000 and 2009, $49 billion of foreign direct investment came from Mauritius to India, making up 42 per cent of India's total foreign direct investment (FDI) during this period (Vines and Oruitemeka, 2007). This special role of Mauritius is of interest:

> Mauritius is widely regarded as an offshore financial centre (OFC) that is used by most foreign investors as an intermediary to reach India, predominantly to capitalise on the tax rebates that the country offers so as to minimise their overall tax burden. Conversely, as Indian companies have become more globalised, many have chosen either to use their overseas locally incorporated subsidiaries to invest outside their home countries, or to establish holding companies and/or special purpose vehicles in OFCs, or other regional financial centres, such as Singapore or the Netherlands, to raise funds and invest in third countries. Apart from this so-called transshipping, a portion of these inflows, from Mauritius in particular and also other OFCs, could also be round-tripping back to India to escape capital gains or other taxes, or for other reasons, not unlike the investments dynamics between China and Hong Kong. (Hattari and Rajan, 2010: 502)

In fact, the Indian Finance Ministry has estimated that fake FDI from Mauritius costs India $600 million annually (*Mail & Guardian*, 15 March 2013). Mauritius is situated in the Indian Ocean and it is in this strategic space where New Delhi has become alarmed at the growing ability of their putative BRICS partner (China) to extend its naval power. In April 2013, a classified Indian document was leaked, entitled 'Indian Navy: Perceived Threats to Subsurface Deterrent Capability and Preparedness', prepared by the Integrated Defence Staff. The document asserted that China posed a grave danger to India's security interests in the Ocean through the 'String-of-Pearls' strategy, where Beijing has set up a network of ports and facilities in Bangladesh (Chittagong), Myanmar (Sittwe and Coco Island), Sri Lanka (Hambantota), Pakistan (Gwadar) and has also secured docking rights in Seychelles. This has been interpreted in some quarters as a deliberate attempt by China to gain strategic supremacy in the Indian Ocean (*Hindustan Times*, 7 April 2013). The news released in mid-2012 that Mauritius had offered India the use of North and South Agalega Islands as part of a trade and investment deal must be contextualised within this broader milieu (*Times of India*, 6 July 2012).

Some Indian commentators have sought to argue that India offers a more 'equal' trading partnership for Africa than the West (e.g. Sharma, 2007: 7). Initially, the balance of trade between India and Sub-Saharan Africa (SSA) was in India's favour and showed no sign of changing

(Chaturvedi and Mohanty, 2007: 55). However, the Department of Commerce's own *Export Import Data Bank* for 2009–10 showed that India imported 50 per cent more from Africa than it exported, primarily oil (Ministry of Commerce and Industry, 2011). As with the other BRICS, historical patterns are being reproduced, with 'evidence ... that Indian [outward foreign direct investment (OFDI)] is more market and resource-seeking than OFDI from most other countries in general' (Hattari and Rajan, 2010: 512). In 2010, primary commodities made up 91 per cent of Africa's exports to India, whilst manufactured goods dominated Africa's imports from India, accounting for 66.9 per cent of total imports (Standard Chartered, 2012: 5).

One aspect of Indian economic engagement with Africa that is of interest is the promotion by New Delhi of regional trade agreements. For instance, India has conducted a Joint Study Group on a Preferential Trade Agreement (PTA) with the Southern African Customs Union (SACU), incorporating Botswana, Lesotho, Namibia, South Africa and Swaziland. Such moves may reflect a wider process whereby the emergence of powerful Southern economies opens up new opportunities for Africa, as such regional agreements may allow African economies to interact with each other and with external actors in ways that bypass the conditionalities imposed upon the continent by the international financial institutions (Chaturvedi and Mohanty, 2007: 54). Such activity possibly also signifies the nascent formalisation of some resistance to the North's agenda setting (Hurrell and Narlikar, 2006: 1–3, 8). India's penchant for multilateral trade agreements may serve to profit some African economies by precluding economically predatory – if not destructive – behaviour that is arguably intrinsic to the WTO's unified methodology where Northern corporate interests seek advantage (Narayan, 2005: 7). Tellingly, the guest list at the April 2008 Indo–Africa Forum, consisted of the Chair of the AU, the heads of the initiating states involved in NEPAD (i.e. Algeria, Egypt, Nigeria, Senegal and South Africa) and the Chairs of the eight African regional groups (African Union, 2011), evidence confirming New Delhi's preference for regional rather than bilateral agreements (Vines and Sidiropoulos, 2008: 7).

In addition to state-led engagement with Africa, private Indian companies are leading the move into Africa and in fact dominate. 'Constrained in its ability to drive the economy's growth process through public investment, the state has to induce the private sector to play that role. Policy has therefore had to be oriented towards encouraging private investment and that ... in a context of global competition' (Mazumdar, 2014: 95). The mid-1990s saw the formation of a number of industry organisations such as the Associated Chambers of Commerce and Industry of India (ASSOCHAM), the Federation of Indian Export Organisations (FIEO) and the Federation of Indian Chambers of Commerce and Industry (FICCI). These have helped change the character of Indian economic interaction with Africa and such actors are increasingly important. Between 2005 and

2007 such companies invested nearly $400 million in Africa, with investment in infrastructure projects and enterprises increasing dramatically in recent years. New Delhi has actively 'urged African nations to encourage Indian industry to grow its footprint in the continent' (*Financial Express*, 21 March 2007). As with China, some Indian ventures in SSA add value to Africa's economies through investments in critical (yet under-funded) infrastructure projects. For instance, Rites and Ircon (state-owned engineering companies), are now active in Africa's rail and road development sector, where Rites has refurbished and leased locomotives in Sudan and Tanzania, supplied technical assistance to rail authorities in Kenya and Mozambique and consulted on the design and construction of roads in Uganda and Ethiopia. Meanwhile, Ircon has constructed 600 kilometres of rail in Mozambique, received a $31 million contract from the Ethiopian government to build 120 kilometres of roads and has been active in rail sectors in Angola, Nigeria, Sudan and Zambia (Naidu, 2007).

'Indian capitalism has always been characterised by the domination of the corporate sector by a relatively small number of business groups controlled by well-connected and powerful business families and individuals' (Mazumdar, 2014: 97). A prime example is the Tata Group, operating across SSA in a diverse array of economic sectors (Vines and Sidiropoulos, 2007). The Tata Group (with others) *has* helped to diversify African exports to a degree (Broadman, 2007: 12). For example, Tata has opened an instant coffee processing plant in Uganda and a vehicle assembly plant in Zambia (Naidu, 2007: 5). Both add value to raw materials and are obviously in the right direction when African diversification and industrialisation remain of such importance. Yet at the same time, the Tata Group asserts that it has 'aligned business opportunities with the objective of nation building' (Tata Group, 2008). Although private, the wider picture of aiding India's rise is seen as an intrinsic aspect of Tata's operations. Such rhetoric, tinged with mercantilist nationalism, contrasts strongly with the individualistic nature of most Western corporations, yet is emblematic of the fact that the liberalisation programme in India has led to 'an even closer relationship between the state and private capital' (Mazumdar, 2014: 94). Indeed, 'in a globalised context, private business enterprises have … become the standard bearers of "nationalism", "national interest" and "national achievement" so that national success tends to be seen as something that coincides with their success' (ibid.: 95).

African imports from India currently include machinery, transport equipment, paper and other wood products, textiles, plastics, and chemical and pharmaceutical products. Indian pharmaceutical manufacturers such as Cipla and Ranbaxy are progressively penetrating Africa's health markets, providing drugs at a fraction of the cost of Western drugs. Ranbaxy Laboratories, which has been involved in joint ventures in Nigeria since the late 1970s, are now taking advantage of WTO provisions that permit patents to be broken in the case of national emergencies. This is particularly important in the fight against HIV/AIDS, where the demand for low-cost anti-retrovirals is intense. Beyond India's major international companies, smaller Indian businesses are penetrating Africa's markets. In fact, between 2002 and 2005, Indian firms topped the list of FDI projects in Africa at 48, compared to 32 from China (Naidu, 2008: 125).

Some of India's companies have been criticised on the grounds that they conduct business in a dishonest manner, however. In 2006, Transparency International released its Bribe Payers Index which evaluates countries in the propensity of their businesses to pay bribes while operating abroad: India was deemed the worst (Sorbara, 2007). Despite the fact that this may not be an approved method of business, within the context of corrupt neopatrimonial African systems, it is to be expected. Yet there are also positive aspects of this trading relationship. Many Indian firms active in Africa are multinational corporations. Engaging in business with such corporations may help African companies expand their own engagement in network trade (Broadman, 2008). It is often argued that FDI has a general trend to draw trade flows from the host nation as new investors often have little knowledge of local contractors or local human, technical or financial capacity. Consequently, the sourcing of goods and services may take place outside of the host market. According to the Confederation of Indian Industry, Indian companies are more integrated into African economies and societies:

> There are some distinctive features of Indian operations in Africa. Indian companies investing in Africa vary in size and are typically either privately owned or under public-private ownership. Most Indian firms in Africa also acquire established businesses, or 'Brownfield investments'; are less vertically integrated; prefer to procure supplies locally or from international markets; engage in far more sales to private African entities; and encourage the local integration of their workers. (Confederation of Indian Industry, 2013: 18)

Most of Indian trade with the continent is with West and Southern Africa; West Africa primarily due to the on-going discoveries of oil reserves, and Southern Africa because of its developed markets (South Africa is in fact India's largest trading partner in SSA), with Indian imports from South Africa accounting for more than 50 per cent of India's total African imports, whilst Indian exports to South Africa make up about 25 per cent of Indian exports to SSA (ibid.).

It has been asserted that Indian companies see South Africa as 'the gateway into the rest of Africa' (ibid.). This perhaps explains why India has entered into negotiations for a preferential trade agreement with South Africa. The South African relationship actually demonstrates the two-way nature of Indo–African commerce. For instance, Airports Company South Africa (ACSA) won the bid in India for the modernisation of Mumbai airport, and in 2006 South African Breweries announced that they would invest $225 million in India over the next five years. The supermarket chain Shoprite Checkers has a presence in India with the first franchisee, Shoprite Hyper Mulund, open in Mumbai. The South African insurance giant Sanlam has entered into a joint venture with the Shriram Life Insurance Company for the provision of long-term insurance, and India's state-owned Power Grid Corporation appointed Eskom of South Africa to set up 800 kV sub-stations.

Energy

India currently ranks sixth in the world for energy demands. However, the International Energy Agency estimates that India will be required to increase its energy consumption by at least 3.6 per cent annually, leading the country's energy demand to double by 2025 (Haté, 2008: 1). Such an increase means that 'future projections are that by 2030 India is expected to become the world's third largest consumer of energy, bypassing Japan and Russia' (Naidu, 2007: 3). Energy, predominantly oil, coal and uranium are at the vanguard of New Delhi's foreign economic policy in Africa. The top six African exporters to India (Nigeria, South Africa, Angola, Egypt, Algeria and Morocco) account for 89 per cent of total African exports by value to India thanks mainly to exports of oil and gas, ores and gold. In 2011, the top six had a trade surplus of over US$ 24.5 billion (Confederation of Indian Industry, 2013: 16).

Currently, roughly 30 per cent of India's energy needs are met by oil (70 per cent of which is imported). It is projected that India will need to import 90 per cent of its gas and crude oil in a few years, possibly by 2025 (Beri, 2005: 372). As a result, Beri (ibid.: 320) has made the argument that 'energy security may be the biggest challenge to Indian policy-making in the coming decades'. In light of these energy needs, India is looking for new and diversified oil sources. Africa is an extremely attractive option: African oil is high quality and, with many new discoveries outside of conflict zones, it is open for foreign participation. Additionally, only Angola and Nigeria are SSA members of OPEC, which sets limits on member countries' output levels. According to one Indian analysis, 'the discovery of vast energy sources has raised the strategic importance of the continent' (ibid: 371). This then explains why in 2001 Southern Africa accounted for nearly 60 per cent of exports to India while oil-rich West Africa accounted for just above 16 per cent. By 2011, West Africa was the largest exporter to India with a share of 40 per cent, while the share of Southern Africa was 24 per cent (Confederation of Indian Industry, 2013: 16).

In response to India's strategic energy needs, New Delhi created the Energy Co-Ordination Committee in 2005. The objective of the committee (chaired by the Prime Minister) is to

Enable a systematic approach to policy formulation, promote co-ordination in interdepartmental action and function as a key mechanism for providing institutional support to decision-making in the area of energy planning and security. The other members of the committee included the ministers of finance, petroleum and natural gas, power, coal, nonconventional energy sources, as well as the National Security Advisor and senior officials from the ministries, including the Atomic Energy Commission. (Dadwal, 2011: 6)

In 2006, the committee published its final report, the Integrated Energy Report, which has subsequently become the de facto cornerstone of India's energy security policy (ibid.). One of the policy recommendations was the 'encouraging of Indian state-owned and private energy companies to acquire assets, through the purchase of equity in oil, gas and coal blocks or stakes in exploration and production (E&P) companies abroad' (ibid: 8).

It is in the oil sector where Indian investment perhaps poses the greatest risk for ordinary Africans. This is not specific to Indian corporations; the oil industry in general has often been accused of a disregard for governance in favour of rewarding contracts and Indian commentators have made this point alongside their international peers (see Sharma and Mahajan, 2007). An example of Indian indifference for ethical concerns might be the case where the overseas division of Oil and Natural Gas Corporation Limited (ONGC), namely, the ONGC Videsh Limited (OVL), an Indian public sector petroleum company invested $750 million to acquire two oil blocks in Sudan. Canadian company Talisman had previously sold the blocks due to pressure from human rights groups who had argued that the investment in these blocks fuelled conflict in Sudan (Beri, 2005: 378).

However, there are some ethical considerations in Indian corporations' presence in the African oil sector. In Nigeria, for instance, ONGC has 'not only carried out exploration and production successfully in very difficult terrains, but has also been responsive to the needs of local population in terms of development of healthcare facilities and education centres etc.' 'Corporate social responsibility projects undertaken by ONGC in and around its project sites ... have been immensely appreciated by the local community' (*This Day*, Lagos, 15 February 2009). OVL has invested $10 million in railway construction in Nigeria, a valuable investment in the country's dilapidated public infrastructure (Agrawal, 2007: 5). Of course, such investments are both tactical and no doubt with an eye on the bottom-line. They do nonetheless contribute to development and arguably contrast with the activities of some Western corporations.

Interestingly, Indian efforts to gain access to African oil shows less of the somewhat reckless attributes found in many of the Chinese efforts to do the same (see Taylor, 2006b). For instance, in January 2006 ONGC put in a winning $2 billion bid for an offshore Nigerian oil field, only to see the Indian Cabinet block the deal on the grounds that it was not commercially feasible. Consequently, the China National Offshore Oil Corporation bought a 45 per cent working interest in the field (*This Day*, Lagos, 21 April 2006). What was interesting here was that the Indian government deemed the deal as too risky, with potential political repercussions. Yet for the Chinese oil company, such concerns did not appear to be paramount – an interesting reflection on the comparative risks Beijing and New Delhi are willing to take to gain access to oil supplies, no doubt underpinned by the level of Chinese foreign exchange reserves.

Indian oil companies are expanding in Ghana; OVL and the Ghana National Petroleum Corporation (GNPC) agreed in October 2004 to begin joint oil exploration (Beri, 2005: 384). Indian rhetoric of the developmental spin-offs of such ventures is often underlined by official pronouncements: the Indian Minister of External Affairs has asserted that 'investment in this [oil] sector should directly assist in the building up of a trained and skilled workforce' (quoted in Sharma and Mahajan, 2007: 42).

OVL is also working in the Ivory Coast, Libya and Egypt whilst another Indian state-owned entity, the Indian Oil Corporation (IOC), has invested $1 billion in an Ivory Coast offshore block and possesses a Nigerian oil refinery worth $3.5 billion (Naidu, 2007). Other African countries where Indian oil companies are seeking contracts include Burkina Faso, Chad, Equatorial, Guinea, Guinea-Bissau, Niger, Democratic Republic of Congo and Senegal. India's energy footprint in Africa is becoming increasingly noticeable as Indian companies aggressively search for new sites of exploration and investment.

However, the activities of Indian corporations are probably no worse than other international actors whose companies are equally involved with less than salubrious regimes. In fact, the ability of the Indian state to influence (even curtail) deals done by the state-owned OVL perhaps arguably gives Indian activity an ethical edge over the strictly private (and profit-driven) activities of Western corporations. There are limits to this obviously – India was an enthusiastic investor in Sudan's oil industry (alongside the Chinese and Malaysians). That it was only the Chinese that received negative publicity for this suggests that the West gives a certain 'free pass' to its ostensible democratic partner.

Where there are possible factors that may undermine such trends is in the on-going competition with Chinese companies in Africa for energy contracts. Chinese companies already have a strong market presence in poorly governed states. The question is, will this reduce the likelihood of negative Indian involvement in such economies, or induce Indian companies to follow suit? Indian companies have already been subject to attempts by Chinese corporations to block access to certain African oilfields – the classic example being the ability of the Chinese to prevent the April 2004 agreement between Shell and OVL in Angola. Of note, the Indian government continued its economic aid programmes in Angola in spite of such developments. Explaining such a position, New Delhi has claimed that, unlike the US and China, India's energy security policy is based on 'an integrated set of policies to balance foreign policy, economic, environmental and social issues with the rising demand for energy' (Naidu, 2007: 2). This of course is for public consumption, but it does also reflect a desire by Indian policymakers not to be seen to be too nakedly mercenary in India's dealings with Africa, a stance that fits with overall Indian foreign policy towards Africa as noted above. Of course, how Indian capitalists behave is a different matter altogether.

Indian aid to Africa

India has emerged in recent years from being purely an aid recipient to an important aid donor. In 2003 the government announced it would no longer receive foreign aid except from a select few Western governments and it repaid $1.6 billion to 14 bilateral donors while increasing its own aid to other countries (Sinha, 2010: 77). As a result it has been termed an 'emerging' donor, but it may be more useful to use the appellation 'non-DAC' (Development Assistance Committee of the OECD) donor (Kragelund, 2011: 555), given that parts of Africa and other areas have now been receiving Indian aid for over half a century.

India's emergence as an aid donor is obviously linked to India's rapid economic growth: 'Development aid, or rather, a shift from mostly being an aid recipient to also being a donor [is] perceived ... as a means to acquire more international political leverage and ultimately obtain a seat in (an enlarged) UNSC' (ibid., 2011: 594–95). This has not occurred without some controversy, with critics arguing that New Delhi openly uses its foreign aid as an instrument to gain access to overseas markets for its goods and services, pave the way for Indian investment abroad, and secure access to natural resources (e.g. Agrawal, 2007; Kragelund, 2008). Meanwhile, within India itself, there is widespread criticism among Indian policy-makers of short-term projects that 'rapidly unravel following the ending of the three- or five-year funding cycle' (Price, 2011: 6).

As there is no central agency managing disbursals of Indian development assistance, it is difficult to ascertain exactly how much India gives. In 2006 it was suggested that New Delhi's development assistance programmes were at an annual level of over $350 million (Khanna and Mohan, 2006), whilst in 2009 'according to the various existing sources India's annual financial volume for development cooperation is currently estimated as being in between half a billion and one billion US$' (German Development Institute, 2009: 2). At the Africa–India Forum Summit in May 2011, it was announced that $5 billion aid for the next three years would be made available to Africa, with an additional $700 million for establishing new institutions and training programmes (*Times of India*, 24 May 2011).

According to one Indian source comparing China and India in Africa, 'India's strategy and strengths in Africa are quite different. China concentrates on resources-based investment, while India has focused on capacity building' (Ramachandran, 2007). Of note, India was the first Asian country (in 2005) to become a full-member of the Africa Capacity Building Foundation (ACBF) after guaranteeing $1 million to the ACBF to build capacity for sustainable development and poverty alleviation in Africa. A number of existing capacity building projects in Africa exemplify the focus on developing a string of higher education and vocational training institutions in Africa. The India–Africa Institute of Information Technology in Ghana will offer courses in computer software in consultation with Educational Consultants India, a state-run consulting firm. The India Africa Institute of Foreign Trade, based in Uganda, is to be set up over the next five years and will offer full-time and part-time Masters of Business Administration degrees. The India Africa Diamond Institute is to be based in Botswana and will, in collaboration with the Indian Diamond Institute, offer accredited diplomas and certificates in diamond processing, assortment and grading, gemmology, jewellery designing and manufacturing, computer application and management programmes. Finally, the India–Africa Institute of Education, Planning and Administration will provide academic and professional guidance to agencies and institutions engaged in educational planning and administration in Africa. It is to be based in Burundi (*New York Times*, 13 February 2011). In all, 19 training institutes will be set up across Africa by India, part of a commitment given at the first India–Africa Forum summit in 2008. This was then crystallised by an action plan that was launched in March 2010 and which outlined a detailed strategy for accelerating bilateral engagement across various sectors for the next four years. According to one report, 'The AU will determine the location of the institutes, the host country will provide the land and construct the buildings and India will run the centres for three years, after which they are intended to be self-sustaining' (Price, 2011: 4).

India has also cancelled the debts owed to New Delhi by countries under the Heavily Indebted Poor Countries (HIPC) initiative and also rationalised commercial debts. The total debt written off by New Delhi is however only about $37 million, so it is largely symbolic. But nations such as Ghana, Mozambique, Tanzania, Uganda and Zambia have benefited. India is also a major donor to the World Food Programme and has donated food to Namibia, Chad and Lesotho.

Indian emphasis *vis-à-vis* aid has gradually shifted from political aid (i.e. aid via the UN, the Organisation of African Unity and the Non-Aligned Movement to support African anti-colonial struggles) to development aid (McCormick, 2008). Partly, New Delhi has deployed developmental assistance as a means to attempt to counter Chinese activities, but also to help facilitate the opening up of new market opportunities and also to reinforce India's position within multilateral institutions as a means of enhancing Indian international prestige and presence (Jobelius, 2007: 4). Indeed, 'India's reform towards economic liberalisation, privatisation and globalisation of the country's foreign policy became also increasingly influenced by geo-economic considerations' (German Development Institute, 2009: 1).

The state-owned Export-Import Bank of India (also known as EXIM) has been a major agent of Indian financial support to Africa. For instance, the bank has lent money to the Common Market for Eastern and Southern Africa (COMESA) to be used to acquire capital goods from India (Beri, 2003) and has also financed Ethiopian sugar production, agricultural development in Botswana, and rural electrification and water provision in Ghana (Chaturvedi and Mohanty, 2007: 65). Such schemes make up around 30 per cent of total Indian aid to SSA (Agrawal, 2007: 7). EXIM generally extends credit to governments, parastatal organisations, commercial banks, financial institutions and to regional development banks to facilitate the export of commercial products on deferred payment terms utilising concessional interest rates of circa 4 per cent (German Development Institute, 2009: 2). EXIM also has a Focus Africa Programme, through which the financing of exports to ECOWAS states was facilitated (Beri, 2005: 387). These credit lines are not aid *per se*, as their purpose is not development but the advancement of Indian trade and investment opportunities and are rather state-supported export credits (Sinha, 2010).

Additionally, EXIM was a driver behind the $1 billion Pan-African e-Network Project. This is a good example of India's expertise in technical assistance, which makes up about 60 per cent of Indian aid (Agrawal, 2007: 7). In 2002, India approved an initial $100 million for the programme (Mawdsley and McCann, 2010: 88) which aims to provide facilities for telemedicine and education. The pilot scheme, launched in 2007, provided satellite linkages with Indian schools and hospitals, offering live teleconsultations. So, for example, Ethiopia's Black Lion and Nkempte hospitals were linked with the Care Hospital in Hyderabad and patients had consultations with Indian doctors. Following the success of the pilot scheme, the e-Network has now been linked to 53 African countries.

Human resource development remains at the core of India's development efforts in Africa. Notably, at the second Africa–India Forum summit in 2011, Manmohan Singh announced the establishment of a number of new institutions aimed at technical assistance. These included an India–Africa Food Processing Cluster, an India–Africa Integrated Textiles Cluster, an India–Africa Centre for Medium-Range Weather Forecasting, an India–Africa University of Life and Earth Sciences and an India–Africa Institute for Rural Development. Singh also proposed the establishment of an India–Africa Virtual University and pledged 10,000 scholarships for Africans to attend it. On top of these, Singh announced 400 new scholarships for African graduates and 500 more training positions under the Indian Technical and Economic Cooperation Programme (ITEC). A total of 2,500 ITEC training positions every year are now available. 'Our total commitment for the next three years by way of scholarships to African students will stand at more than 22,000', Singh was reported as declaring (*Times of India*, 25 May 2011).

ITEC has a reputation as one of the most prominent and longest-standing technical assistance programmes and 'the flagship programme' of New Delhi's technical cooperation efforts, 'not only because of its wide geographical coverage but also for innovative forms of technical cooperation' (ITEC, 2010). Established in 1964, the programme and its corollary, the Special Commonwealth Assistance for Africa Programme (SCAAP), cover training (both civilian and military), feasibility studies and consultancy projects, the worldwide deputation of Indian experts, study tours, equipment donations and aid for disaster relief. New Delhi sees ITEC and SCAAP as 'a visible symbol of India's role and contribution to South–South cooperation' (ibid.). Nigeria, Ethiopia, Sudan, Kenya, Tanzania, Uganda, Zimbabwe and South Africa have all benefited from ITEC, which has overall provided civil training to 14,500 trainees, mainly from Africa (Beri, 2003: 222). It is interesting to note that the main African beneficiaries of ITEC (with the exception of Ethiopia), are Commonwealth nations, reflecting the resilience of shared imperialist histories in modern international relations.

An important public relations success with regard to Indian technical assistance has been the activities of the 'Barefoot College', or Social Work and Research Centre in Rajasthan. The policy of the College is to take rural poor women and train them to become professionals without requiring them to read or write. Since 2004, the Barefoot College has trained over 140 women from 21 African countries as solar energy engineers (*Daily Nation*, Nairobi, 24 May 2011), with women coming from isolated villages in Benin, Cameroon, Malawi, Rwanda, Sierra Leone, Sudan and Zambia, among others. The College receives funding from diverse sources: the African energy programme saw the solar equipment funded by UNDP, whilst airfares and six-month training fees for women coming from Africa were paid for by India's Ministry of External Affairs. Though the project is non-governmental, the involvement of the Indian state grants New Delhi presence and prestige in a widely seen and effective aid programme.

Of note, unlike the West and China, India funds projects directly rather than supplying grants (Agrawal, 2007), a non-transferable method of aid that is arguably open neither to abuse nor conditionalities (Jobelius, 2007: 3). Indeed, Indian assistance generally does not offer up to predatory African regimes an option to avoid governance reform (ibid.: 5). Some analysts aver that emanating from the world's largest democracy, aid from New Delhi reinforces good governance and accountability when there is political space to do so (Vines and Sidiropoulos, 2008). This may be true, although we should be aware that India has 'attached more weight to solidarity with fellow developing countries and the defence of its own national security interests without a reference to ideology at the operational level' (Mohan, 2007). In other words, outright democracy promotion is not yet embedded in India's foreign policy, largely because of Nehruvian notions regarding state sovereignty, which does however appear to be changing slightly (Price, 2011: 19–20).

Interestingly, it does appear that '[i]f India is not currently feeling the heat of Western opprobrium to the extent of China in Sudan, it is most likely only because India is hiding behind China to the extent that it is a smaller investor and trader, it is a democracy and considered more multi-lateral in its foreign policy. India may one day face the same pressure and the same dilemmas as China over the balance between sovereignty and, for instance, concern for human rights' (*BBC News*, 24 May 2011). Also of course, 'India's democratic credentials leave it less exposed than China to Western criticism, although it professes non-interference in its inter-national relations. Reflecting the duality of Western perceptions of India and China, the former escaped criticism from the West for its presence in Sudan during the Darfur conflict, whereas the latter did not' (Rampa et al., 2012: 249). It can be stated that dual standards *are* in operation when (primarily Western) actors critique Chinese activities in Africa whilst overlooking Indian – or others' – behaviour.

Indian aid to Africa is not an expression of philanthropy and, like all other countries, New Delhi leverages its development assistance to promote specific political objectives. Indian aid not only helps to facili-tate an increase in Indian economic activity across Africa, but also serves to project the country as a major power and gain a support constituency as a means of 'increasing the leverage and influence of its global position … and promoting a new international order' (Naidu, 2007: 2). As has been noted, New Delhi views Africa as the source of potentially vital support (and important voting power) in international institutions and as part of this, its diplomacy encourages the belief that India is a long-time supporter of Third World interests. Here, policymakers are looking to posture New Delhi as the largest, wealthiest, and most diverse non-Western democracy (Bava, 2007: 2). Yet 'emerging economies' aid programmes are driven by vital national interests (e.g. energy security) and commercial considera-tions (e.g. market penetration). *This is no different from the way in which traditional donors worked in the past*' (Rampa et al., 2012: 251, emphasis added). In fact: 'Commercial and political self-interests dominate India's aid allocation … the importance of political interests, proxied by the voting alignment between donor and recipient in the United Nations, [is] significantly larger for India than for all traditional DAC donors' (Fuchs and Vadlamannati, 2013: 111).

Conclusion

An emerging India within the international system is of great significance for Africa. In tandem with other developing nations, India is increasingly pushing for a reconfiguration of some of the institutions of global govern-ance. In this regard, African states are seen as useful allies and a valu-able support constituency for New Delhi's aspirations; notably, almost all African countries back India's bid for a permanent seat at the United Nations. However, this process is taking place 'at a time when as a rising power India is integrating with the US-led neoliberal economic system, both as a producer and consumer of commodity capitalism' (Thussu, 2012: 441). The stability of this development model for India in the long-term is itself open to question. As Chandrasekhar (2012: 28) notes that,

> for much of India's population[,] growth seems to make little difference to their standard of living. That is a severe indictment of the strategy of growth, especially when the growth rate figures are remarkably high, as was true in India for a period after 2003, and those figures are used to argue that India is a successful nation en route to great power status. However, such reasoning serves two purposes. First, it provides the propaganda to make India an attractive site for speculative global capital, the entry of which triggers the speculative run that delivers expected profits for a period of time. Second, it helps divert attention from the predatory nature of the regime of accumulation that has come to prevail in the age of finance. However, the economic success involved here is necessarily transient. That is the realisation that slowly dawns as evidence of a crisis even of neoliberal growth surfaces in India.

Whilst in no way suggesting a 'coming collapse of India' thesis, the above *does* raise some questions and undermines the argument that India, as one of the BRICS, poses an alternative path of development which Africa may somehow copy. In fact, the 'hegemonic bloc that rules Indian society is well integrated into the rationale of dominant capitalist globalisation and so far none of the various political forces through which it is expressed challenges it' (Amin, 2005: 12). This points to a fundamental reality about the BRICS in Africa that has already been noted: they are *not* proposing any particular qualitative alternative (or even adjustment) to the domi-nant economic paradigm. Political and economic cooperation (as well as aid) in exchange for increased economic interaction and political support for India's rise on the global stage help us to understand current Indo–African ties. As one analysis put it:

> India is … cultivating a global relationship with the United States, and it is interacting in Africa with other global powers such as China. Africa is still a relatively small part of India's foreign policy, far less significant in commercial or political terms than the Middle East or Southeast Asia. But as India cultivates its global role, this is an area where it can position itself as a leader, a supplier of investment, and an aid donor. (Haté, 2008: 3)

This fits with another analysis, which argued that 'Since India lacks the foreign reserves to match the chequebook diplomacy of China, it is futile to imagine that economic munificence alone can give New Delhi traction in Africa. If credit lines and infrastructure construction become the sole pillars of India's strategy in Africa, it will end up second best forever vis-à-vis China' (*The Economic Times*, India, 24 May 2011). The question here then, is whether India is a 'scrambler or a development partner' (Corkin and Naidu, 2008). Whilst Indian academics forcefully assert that it is a true partnership (see Sharma, 2007), the answer to such a question remains very much open. The key issue is how can (or will) African leaders seek to leverage the newfound Indian interest in Africa so that Africa's place in global trade networks becomes more proactive and beneficial to the continent's citizens? It is certainly true that India is becoming heavily involved in the continent. This *may* offer up opportunities for African heads of state to negotiate a better deal with external actors. Much will depend upon African agency. African governments *could* use the opportunity of increased Indian corporate presence in Africa to source appropriate technology, skills and advice for economic development. Given that New Delhi generally prefers the roll-out of practical projects rather than ideological posturing, this is a possibility. Equally, the capacity-building programmes do have potential if graduates are subsequently supported and nurtured upon their return to society. As ever, it remains a priority for African elites to 'accelerate efforts at getting [their] own house in order and to implement the policies, institutions, and trade-enabling physical infrastructure that will be the critical foundations' for future development (Corkin and Naidu, 2008: 115).

Importantly, Indian economic involvement in Africa is not controlled by New Delhi, but by Indian corporate actors. Such activity is thus less influenced by normative concerns. Thus it is imperative for African states to recognise that whilst Indian official policy towards Africa talks the rhetoric of solidarity, Indian corporations generally only pursue the bottom line. A feature of current Indian policy towards Africa is that 'rather than concentrating on state-led development assistance, the Indian government has acted as an enabler for its private sector' (Price, 2011: 9). This, though, has potential downsides. New Delhi's ability to direct Indian engagement in Africa is, as is the case with Beijing's surveillance of Chinese actors on the continent, unreliable. There is in fact a need for New Delhi to strike a balance between its diplomatic rhetoric of South–South mutual cooperation and the commercial needs of Indian private sector actors. This will remain difficult as long as India's diplomatic expertise remains hidebound: New Delhi's External Affairs Ministry consists of about 750 diplomats – a fraction of China's 6,000-strong diplomatic corps (*Los Angeles Times*, 25 May 2011).

India is a middle-income nation and New Delhi's experience in how to navigate a post-colonial environment is arguably of more relevance to African states than any policy advice emanating from Western capitals. Thus the experience of a country such as India operating in Africa and seeking out some sort of 'partnership' potentially holds more for the continent in terms of demonstration effects and learning (Norbrook and van Valen, 2011: 23–24). However, African policymakers and academics need to be cautious here. There are plenty of very critical studies of India's developmental trajectory under neoliberalism. Indeed, other than the abstraction that India has seen growth under the past two decades of liberalisation, the idea of India as a 'model' (just as with China) needs a great deal of circumspection.

Controlling and managing Indo–Africa relations is crucial for the continent if it is to benefit from the opportunities that an increased Indian attention to Africa affords. Indian commentators like to assert that there 'exists enormous goodwill for India in Africa and India should take advantage of it to further strengthen ties through a new partnership' (Beri, 2003). Thus far, it is true that Indian actors have largely avoided the sorts of criticism from rights groups and the West that China has endured. However, the central question in Indo–African relations, just as with all of Africa's international relations, is the key challenge for the continent: poor governance and high levels of corruption coupled with dependency. It is up to Africans to negotiate with Indian actors to ensure that the benefits accrued from Indo–African ties are evenly shared and that Indian interest in the continent, alongside others, may help serve as a catalyst for economic revitalisation. How this plays out very much depends on the political leadership in each and every individual African country.

5

China
in Africa

The huge growth of Chinese political and business interests in Africa is conceivably the most significant development for the continent's international relations since the ending of the Cold War. Published trade figures alone bear evidence to the speed by which the Chinese economic presence in Africa has developed over the last ten years or so: China is now Africa's largest bilateral trading partner. A massive surge in Chinese economic interests in Africa has seen the value of China's trade with Africa increase from US$4 billion in 1996 to US$155 billion in 2011 (du Venage, 2012). China–Africa trade is estimated to have surpassed $200 billion in 2012 (*China Daily*, 18 February 2013). Much of this expansion is underpinned by a desire to obtain sources of raw materials and energy for China's on-going economic growth. New export markets for Chinese producers and traders, obliged to seek new markets by domestic dynamics within China's economy, also propels the economic connections (see Taylor, 2009a). Trade between Africa and China began to conspicuously accelerate around 2000, and between 2001 and 2006, Africa's exports to China increased at an annual rate of over 40 per cent (Wang Jianye, 2007: 5). Since 2003 alone, Sino–African trade has increased by nearly 500 per cent. Notably, back in 1990, no African countries traded amounts with China above 5 per cent of their GDP; by 2008, nearly two dozen had passed this benchmark figure.

Regarding broad Chinese foreign policy, there are contradictory signals. On the one hand Beijing generally supports the global order and makes no meaningful demands for change other than around technical issues: 'despite displeasure with certain aspects of the international order, China has mostly accepted that order and decided to fix its problems by reforming it from the inside' (Glosny, 2010: 116). Though at times it may express dissatisfaction with specifics, Beijing offers up no alternatives, something which many African elites seem to have overlooked in their enthusiasm for Sino–African relations and the putative notion of a Chinese 'model'. On the other hand, within its neighbourhood Beijing enunciates dissatisfaction and wants change: the situation in the South China Sea being a prime example. China might be regarded as a dissatisfied reformist – happy with the extant order but at times pressing (and demanding) for adjustment in areas of immediate concern, particularly regarding notions of territorial integrity and security.

Consequently, China might be said to have a personality disorder in the sense that it already is a great power, yet claims to be still a developing country. This contradiction is played out in a variety of ways and depends upon the context. Beijing is at times cautious and anxious to downplay any notion of the 'China threat', wary of being seen to be straying too far from the developing world and avoiding being cast as some sort of junior partner to the United States at the global level (hence its cool reaction to the notion of the G-2). At other times, it adopts a more pro-active stance. Under popular pressure to assume its 'rightful place', this China asserts that the global political economy has shifted in a way that empowers China and encourages more activity in defending Chinese interests overseas in places as diverse as Darfur, Libya, the Somali pirate crisis, etc. Finally, an internationalist China adopts the stance that Beijing is already a global power, which compels it to practise 'creative involvement' in a world where the decline of the West is inevitable and where new sites of authority are emerging. This stimulates China to enter into issue-based alliances that are fluid and dependent on context i.e. the BRICS:

> [A]s China regains its former global status it is increasingly a conflicted rising power possessing a series of competing international identities that try to satisfy a variety of international (and domestic) constituencies. This may consequently help to explain why China's foreign policy exhibits diverse – sometimes conflicting, sometimes complementary – emphases and policies simultaneously. (Shambaugh and Ren Xiao, 2012: 36–37)

Thus China may be said to have four broad identities at the international level: as a developing country; as an emerging power; as a global power; and as a quasi-superpower (Breslin, 2013). China's membership of BRICS enables Beijing to project these different identities at different times and in different contexts, granting it a degree of flexibility and adaptability, although clearly BRICS fits most closely with the identity as an emerging power. China's developing country credentials are best exemplified in China's links with Africa and the Forum on China-Africa Cooperation (FOCAC) summits, where a spirit of fraternal commonalities is ostentatiously expressed. As a global power, China's membership of the G-20 and the United Nations Security Council are emblematic, whilst the quasi-superpower status, which Beijing is probably the least comfortable with, is rarely articulated and when it is (such as with the G-2 appellation), is speedily rejected. Underpinning each of these identities however is one consistent element: China's anti-normative normative agenda. Briefly, this position advances the argument that each country should be able to choose their own path and be free from the imposition of others' values and positions. Essentially a reification of sovereignty, this stance is popular in Africa amongst its elites and undermines Western attempts to enforce conditionalities, even extend influence. It is in this realm of Chinese foreign policy that Beijing has been most heavily criticised by Western commentators, although the Chinese (and Africans) point out that this is simply adhering to the UN Charter and the global norm of non-interference and respect for sovereignty. As this frustrates the Western elites' ability to exert authority however, it is of little surprise that such a position most often clashes with Western policies. Within BRICS, Brazil and India escape such censure; a more assertive Russia increasingly attracts condemnation, whilst South Africa is somewhat overlooked.

China's Africa policies

With the abandonment of Maoism and the return to the capitalist road (see Fang Kang, 1978), reform-era China has been based on 'an unwritten social contract between the party and the people, where the people do not compete with the party for political power as long as the party looks after their economic fortunes' (Breslin, 2005: 749). When projected abroad, 'foreign policy that sustains an international environment supportive of economic growth and stability in China serves these objectives' (Sutter, 2008: 2). The developing world has long been a spatial area where Beijing's foreign policy has been pursued energetically, using the development of 'common interests' with the South to raise China's global stature. Africa specifically has emerged as a relatively significant component in Chinese calculations at diverse levels, whether state, provincial, municipal or individual. Whilst political considerations are important, the economics of the relationship are in in the driving seat.

Chinese engagement with Africa is longstanding (see Duyvendak, 1949; Hutchison, 1975; Taylor, 2006a), even if not the two or three thousand years of continuous interaction that Chinese spokesmen habitually claim. In the political realm, the continent has been of significance for China since around the late 1950s, when Chinese diplomacy began to emerge from out of the shadow of the Soviet Union (Han Nianlong, 1990: 138–9). During the Maoist period, China's role in Africa was ideologically motivated and included support for liberation movements fighting against colonial and minority-rule, as well as direct state-to-state aid, most noticeably with Tanzania. By the mid-1970s, China in fact had a greater number of aid projects in Africa than the United States (Brautigam, 1998: 4), although the Cultural Revolution incurred reputational costs amongst Africa's elites that undercut much of the prestige that may have accrued from such largesse.

However, as the 'Socialist Modernisation' programme picked up under Deng Xiaoping from the late 1970s onwards, there was an associated reduction of interest in the continent, although Chinese policymakers and many academics refute this (see Taylor, 1997). The decline in interest in Africa can in part be explained in this way:

> Africa's failure to develop its economies efficiently and open up to the international market militated against Chinese policy aims, and the increasing extraneous role the continent played in global (read superpower) geopolitics resulted in a halt to closer Chinese involvement. Essentially, Beijing not only viewed Africa as largely immaterial in its quest for modernisation, but also saw that the rationale behind its support for anti-Soviet elements in the continent was no longer valid. (Taylor, 1998: 443–4)

The accumulation model, based on attracting global capital into China to take advantage of the very low wage levels simply did not fit with an active Africa policy. Neglect of Africa by China got to a point where African students in Beijing demonstrated against China's declining interest in Africa and held aloft banners saying 'Remember the United Nations in 1971' – a reminder that it was African nations which helped China's entry into the UN (*Agence France-Presse*, 19 June 1986). In contrast to the Maoist past, ties with Africa were based on the dispassionate 'realities' of profit a.k.a. 'socialism with Chinese characteristics' (*Jianshe you Zhongguo tesede shehuizhuyi*). This 'great reversal' (Hinton, 1991) was traumatic in some quarters in Africa, where Maoist China had been seen as a stalwart of the post-colonial struggle.

However, an event and two processes – one within Africa and the others within China – came together to promote the current interest of Chinese actors in Africa. Firstly, the consequences of the events of June 4, 1989 in and around Tiananmen Square led to Beijing undergoing a critical re-evaluation of its policies. Whilst Tiananmen Square occasioned a short-lived crisis in China's relations with the capitalist West, the reactions by many of Africa's elites were far more subdued, if not supportive. As the former Chinese foreign minister, Qian Qichen (2005: 200), put it: 'it was ... our African friends who stood by us and extended a helping hand in the difficult times following the political turmoil in Beijing, when Western countries imposed sanctions on China'. Indicatively, the foreign minister of Angola expressed Luanda's 'support for the resolute actions to quell the counter-revolutionary rebellion' (*Xinhua*, 7 August 1989), whilst Namibia's Sam Nujoma dispatched a telegram of congratulations to the People's Liberation Army (*Xinhua*, 21 June 1989). As one commentator later remarked, 'the events of June 1989 ... did not affect the PRC's relations with the Third World as it did with the Western world ... what changed [was] the PRC's attitude towards the Third World countries, which ... turned from one of benign neglect to one of renewed emphasis' (Gu Weiqun, 1995: 125).

As a consequence, the developing world was raised up in Chinese policy reckoning to become a 'cornerstone' of Beijing's foreign policy.

Post-1989, the 1970s rhetoric of China being an 'all-weather friend' (*quan tianhou pengyou*) of Africa was dusted off and employed with enthusiasm, something which has endured to this day (Taylor, 2004). This posture of mutual affirmation was a restatement of the Five Principles of Peaceful Co-existence, initially articulated in 1954: mutual respect for each other's territorial integrity, non-aggression, non-interference in each other's internal affairs, equality and mutual benefit, and peaceful co-existence. These Principles are now mediated through capitalist practices and norms.

The aforementioned two macro-processes were, firstly, Chinese actors began to see in Africa great potential economically, partly as a result of neoliberal economic programmes that had gained momentum on the continent as the 1990s progressed through the imposition of reforms by the International financial institutions (IFIs). Beijing came to believe that African countries had implemented a raft of measures to advance privatisation, open up the domestic economy to international investment and sign a variety of bilateral and multilateral trading agreements that 'locked-in' the restructuring. This was ripe for exploitation. Chinese actors subsequently sought to take advantage of such developments and, in support of this, Beijing officially encouraged economic penetration at multiple levels. The mid-2000s policy to 'go global' *(zouchuqu)*, which encouraged Chinese corporations to invest overseas and play a role in international capital markets (see Hong Eunsuk and Sun Laixiang, 2006) was in many respects an attempt by Beijing to catch-up with a growing awareness regarding the interconnectedness of the international and domestic settings. This was expressed in the slogan *yu guoji jiegui,* or 'linking up with the international track' (Wang Hui, 2003).

Such an official standpoint couples with the faith held by many Chinese manufacturers and entrepreneurs that the sorts of products made by Chinese producers (household appliances, garments and other domestic goods) have great potential in Africa, where the economy is relatively underdeveloped and where the consumer base is identified as being more receptive to the kind of inexpensive products that a segment of Chinese manufacturers characteristically generate. That the domestic markets of many African countries are comparatively small and that there is relatively little competition means that market share can be substantial almost from day one of operations. Additionally of course, the African continent is seen by both the Chinese government *and* by Chinese companies to be abundant in natural resources, many of which are needed by China's burgeoning economy.

The above dynamics then link up with the second macro-process, namely that China's fast developing economy in itself pushed forward Sino-African commerce. Obviously, China's growth in recent years has been remarkable and does not need repeating here. Yet what is often disregarded in deliberations on Sino-African ties is that the significance of China to Africa has to be understood in terms of Beijing's own development path. China's real economic growth – on average just under 9 per cent annually for the last 30 years – has been based on export figures that have grown by an average of over 17 per cent per year. However, growing saturation of China's existing export markets as well as a precipitous rise in the price of imported unprocessed materials into China (due in the main to Chinese demand) makes the African continent increasingly valuable to China's economy. Certainly, as the growth in the net worth of Chinese exports declines, Beijing has to support domestic economic growth through the addition of more Chinese 'content' to its exported goods (*Business Day*, 22 February 2007). Sourcing raw materials to do this is fundamental and is where Africa fits centrally into both Chinese foreign policy *and* domestic necessities. This is where the dangers of entrenching African dependency loom largest.

On the political front, although preserving cordial ties with Washington is absolutely central to Chinese foreign policy, the developing world is more and more significant. Since the demise of the Cold War, Beijing has often articulated anxiety about the existence of an unchallenged superpower and the hegemonism (*baquanzhuyi*) that this stimulates. Consequently, Chinese official policy has been to argue that it is essential that China and the developing world elites assist each other and work together to somehow counteract an overweening United States. This policy is then set alongside an accommodation – but also hedging – with Washington (Foot, 2006).

The above posture then feeds into the long-held position by Beijing that it is the *de facto* leader of the developing world (formerly, the 'Third World'). Characteristically, when in South Africa in early 2007, President Hu Jintao asserted that whilst 'Africa is the continent with the largest number of developing countries', 'China is the biggest developing country' (*Xinhua*, Beijing, 8 February 2007). This is a common refrain, as is the assertion that 'Western powers, not China, colonised Africa and looted resources there' [*sic*] (*China Daily*, 26 April 2006). This construction of history is then linked to the notion that China and Africa are 'natural' partners; 'as developing regions that ... once suffered the oppression and exploitation of imperialism and colonialism, China and the African countries ... easily understand each other's pursuit of independence and freedom and ... have a natural feeling of intimacy' (Qian Qichen, 2005: 200). Although only a minor sideshow these days given the number of African states that still recognise Taipei (Burkina Faso, São Tomé and Príncipe, and Swaziland), competition for recognition with the Republic of China also played a role in Chinese policy in Africa up until around the mid-1990s (Taylor, 2002).

At the global level, as China's leadership has increasingly integrated China into the global capitalist economy, and plays more and more by essentially Western-derived rules and norms – epitomised by Beijing's membership of the World Trade Organization (WTO) – they have worked towards intensifying political ties with the developing world, not least in Africa. This can, in part, be seen as a hedging strategy to balance the international order, construct a defensive diplomatic shield and develop a support constituency. This milieu can then be deployed when appropriate, if and when China's growing internationalisation threatens domestic interests. Such policies are basically accepting of the extant world order, but require avenues where technical resistance to some negativities may be possible. This reality reflects the overall stress in China's diplomacy of practising both engagement *and* a certain distance *vis-à-vis* the global order (Breslin, 2007). This posture, and the instinct to 'restore' China to its 'rightful place' in the world (Scott, 2007), in part by being understood as some sort of mentor of the developing world, whilst equally acting as a 'responsible power' (*fuzeren de daguo*), are important rationales influencing Chinese foreign policy. Such coalition building partly explains the fresh diplomatic developments in Chinese links to Africa, so vividly demonstrated by the Sino-Africa Forums that have been held every three years since 2000. BRICS might be seen as another example.

Forum on China–Africa Cooperation (FOCAC)

The first Forum met in October 2000 in Beijing and was attended by nearly 80 ministers from 44 African countries. The second Ministerial Conference was held in Addis Ababa, Ethiopia, in December 2003 and passed the *Addis Ababa Action Plan (2004–2006)*. The FOCAC Summit and the third Ministerial Conference were held in Beijing in November 2006; the fourth met in Sharm el-Sheikh, Egypt, in 2009, whilst the fifth returned to Beijing in 2012.

The background to FOCAC I can be traced to the visit by Chinese Premier Jiang Zemin to Africa in 1996. In early 1996, Jiang Zemin toured Kenya, Ethiopia, Egypt, Mali, Namibia and Zimbabwe and, during this tour, President Jiang unveiled a new and emerging Chinese approach to Africa. The main theme of Jiang's pronouncements was to strengthen solidarity and cooperation with African countries. According to a Chinese report, '[t]he guiding principle that China follows in developing relations with African countries in the new situation is: "to treat each other as equals, develop sincere friendship, strengthen solidarity and cooperation, and seek common development"' (*Xinhua*, 22 May 1996). Interestingly, Chinese sources claim that it was African leaders who initiated and asked for a summit. In his diplomatic memoirs, Tang Jiaxuan, foreign minister of China from 1998 to 2003, wrote that in 1999, Madagascar's foreign minister, who was visiting Beijing at the time, proposed that China and Africa establish a mechanism to strengthen relations. After a feasibility study, China decided to follow up on the suggestion and proposed to hold the first Forum in 2000 (Tang Jiaxuan, 2011: 529). In October 1999 Jiang wrote to all heads of African states, as well as the Secretary-General of the OAU, to formally propose the convening of a forum. In his letter he outlined principles for carrying out consultation on an equal footing, enhancing understanding, increasing consensus, promoting friendship and furthering cooperation. When this was met with a favourable reception, the Chinese established a preparatory committee comprised of 18 ministries. The Ministry of Foreign Affairs and Ministry of Foreign Trade and Economic Cooperation (MOFTEC) were assigned the role of anchormen. In October 2000, a Forum on China–Africa Cooperation Ministerial Conference in Beijing was then held.

The meeting in October 2000 was the first gathering of its kind in the history of China–Africa relations and was attended by 80 ministers charged with foreign affairs and international trade and economic development from 45 African states. Representatives of international and regional organisations also attended, as did delegates from two African countries that did not then even have diplomatic ties with China (namely, Liberia and Malawi). Discussions at the conference were organised into four separate work sessions: trade, economic reform (with China's programme being showcased as a model), poverty eradication and sustainable development, and cooperation in education, science technology and health care.

FOCAC II was held from 15 to 16 December 2003 in Addis Ababa. This summit produced the *Addis Ababa Action Plan*, which envisioned an acceleration of Chinese involvement in promoting development on the continent. Apart from the Chinese role in infrastructure building, the document promised to expand agricultural support to states in Africa via training and technical support and advice. Linked to the issue of development was the question of Sino–African trade, which had, by the time of FOCAC II jumped by more than 400 per cent since FOCAC I. Problematically for Beijing, this increase in trade was hugely in favour of China. For instance, the trade relationship between Ethiopia and China was 80 per cent in favour of China, helping to prompt a recall of Ethiopian ambassadors and diplomats to attend a 10-day orientation on economic diplomacy, held by the Ministry of Trade and Industry and the Export Promotion Agency (*Addis Fortune*, 8 August 2004). In order to tackle such trade imbalances, the agreed document advocated the granting of zero-tariff treatment to various commodities from the least developed countries on the continent, whilst promoting investment.

However, it was the 2006 meeting in Beijing that arguably marked a climax in Sino–African ties, following on from the decision in 2005 to upgrade FOCAC to the status of an official summit between Chinese and African leaders i.e. a meeting of high-level political leaders with a definite programme of action on the agenda. Such a decision reflected the growing seriousness China's elites held Africa and was part of a wider decision-making process that decided to make 2006 the 'Year of Africa' for China. This began with the release of China's African policy document in January 2006, aimed at presenting 'to the world the objectives of China's policy towards Africa and the measures to achieve them' (Ministry of Foreign Affairs, 2006: 1).

The document, the first of its kind in Beijing's diplomatic history with the continent, was the equivalent of a White Paper and the Chinese government put forward its proposals for cooperation with Africa in various fields. Repeated references to the 'unequal' relationship that Africa has had with 'the West' were included, contrasting China's concrete support for 'African countries' independent choice of the road of development' (Ministry of Foreign Affairs, 2006: 2). In addition, Beijing advanced a new style of association with Africa, asserting that, 'China will unswervingly carry forward the tradition of China–Africa friendship, and, proceeding from the fundamental interests of both the Chinese and African peoples, establish and develop *a new type of strategic partnership with Africa*, featuring political equality and mutual trust, economic win-win cooperation and cultural exchange' (ibid.). Hours after the White Paper was released, Chinese Foreign Minister Li Zhaoxing set out on a nine-day tour of Africa that took him to Cape Verde, Senegal, Mali, Liberia, Nigeria and Libya. Later, in April 2006, President Hu Jintao toured Nigeria, Kenya and Morocco, giving Hu an opportunity to propose a five-point plan to forge what he called a 'New Type of China–Africa Strategic Partnership' (*Xinhua*, 27 April 2006). Subsequently, in June 2006, Premier Wen Jiabao took part in the World Economic Forum held in Cape Town, and then proceeded to visit Angola, Congo-Brazzaville, Egypt, Ghana, Tanzania and Uganda. This flurry of activity and official visits was to set the scene for FOCAC III, held in Beijing in November 2006.

The summit adopted an action plan on China–Africa cooperation for 2007–2009, in which both sides 'resolved' to bolster their companies' joint energy exploration and exploitation under the principle of reciprocity. The document was endorsed by the leaders of China and those of 48 African states attending the summit. The outcomes of FOCAC reflected the increased priority China's leadership placed on Africa. In the three-year plan, China pledged to double aid to Africa by 2009 (to about $1 billion); set up a $5 billion China–Africa development fund to encourage Chinese companies to invest in Africa; provide $3 billion in preferential loans and $2 billion in preferential buyer's credits to African countries; cancel all debt stemming from Chinese interest-free government loans that matured by the end of 2005 for the 31 highly indebted and least developed countries (LDCs) in Africa that have relations with China (an amount estimated at around $1.4 billion); further open China's markets to exports from African LDCs by increasing from 190 to 440 the number of products receiving zero-tariff treatment; train 15,000 African professionals, double the number of Chinese government scholarships given annually to Africans (to 4,000) and send 100 senior agricultural experts and 300 youth volunteers; build 30 hospitals, 30 malaria treatment centres and 100 rural schools (*Africa Renewal*, 19 January 2007). Stemming from FOCAC III, a formal strategic dialogue mechanism was established between China and the AU, with the first China–AU strategic dialogue being held in Addis Ababa in November 2008.

Equally, the China–Africa Development Fund was officially launched in June 2007 as China's prime investment vehicle in Africa. Established by the China Development Bank (which itself is under the direct jurisdiction of the State Council), by late 2009, the Fund had a $5 billion fund. However, it has been reported: 'The Fund is finding it increasingly challenging to fund infrastructure programmes in most African states because of the lack of essential facilities, including sound telecommunications systems'; and Wang Yong, the Fund's Managing Director for the Eastern Africa Investment Department stated: 'We find that they (prospective business partners) expect countries to have basic technology and sufficiently operational ports, airport and roads ... unfortunately these facilities are not necessarily available in some countries on the continent' (*Business Day*, 31 August 2009). Consequently, Fund personnel have begun touring Africa actively seeking investment sites.

The fourth Ministerial Conference was held in Sharm el-Sheikh, Egypt, November 8–9, 2009. In comparison to the festivities associated with FOCAC III in Beijing in of 2006, FOCAC IV was more muted. According to one Chinese source, the conference had two major tasks to perform. One was to review the implementation of the follow-up actions of the Beijing FOCAC Summit of 2006 and the other was to draw up a new plan of action for cooperation between China and Africa. FOCAC IV was, like all previous FOCACs, a bonanza of developmental assistance projects and loans. Yet according to one Chinese commentator, Liu Haifang of the Institute of West Asian and African Studies in Beijing, 'the most dramatic change in the new Sharm el-Sheikh Action Plan from the previous Beijing Action Plan [was] the absence in the new plan of any equivalent to the eye-catching pledge in the 2006 document to double China's aid assistance to African countries' (quoted in *Xinhua*, 17 December 2009). Instead, $10 billion in preferential loans was inserted and devoted specifically for infrastructure, highlighted as a key priority for Sino–African cooperation. Whilst the constraints of the financial crisis no doubt helped explain aspects of this development, Liu noted that the reason for this also sprang from domestic Chinese processes:

> After the 2006 Summit, a common theme in the extensive literature on China's aid assistance to Africa, was criticism of what was seen as inadequate transparency in the application of funds, and questioning of the apparent ambiguity between seeking economic profit and providing development assistance and aid. This may well have led to reflection and readjustment of the definition of China's official development assistance. It seems likely that a deliberate decision has been taken to avoid conspicuous words such as 'double aid' that were used in the previous plan and which stimulated too much close attention. (ibid.)

A further commentator in fact noted:

> Examination of these commitments shows how important it is to clarify the nature of Chinese aid to Africa and to specify its amounts. Indeed, the announcement of a doubling (in flow) of the aid between 2006 and 2009 does not refer to any baseline. The lack of clarity surrounding this announcement is a double-edged sword for the Chinese: on one hand it makes it impossible to critically monitor how well commitments are being met, but it also creates expectations from recipient African nations. While each country knows what it receives and might expect the doubling of aid on a bilateral basis, the promise of doubling has been made at the continent scale. The issue of aid allocation per country has never been settled and Chinese arbitrations start to make some African countries unhappy. (Guérin, 2008: 5)

Much of the problem stems around the issue of sustainability and the unrealistic expectations of African governments *vis-à-vis* China. It has become quite clear that some elements of African opinion have already entered into a dependency mind-set with regard to China's rise in Africa. Their 'vision' seems to be to replace dependency on the ex-colonial powers with dependency on China. In response, during his 2009 tour to Africa, whilst Hu Jintao sought to reassure the continent about Beijing's determination to fulfil its FOCAC III commitments, Wen Jiabao played the role of seeking to fend off the ever-increasing expectations of new aid pledges. The burden of these extremely high expectations, where China is presumed – uncritically – to be the new messiah in Africa, is a very heavy load for Beijing to shoulder.

Economic relations

The legitimacy of the Communist Party of China (CPC) and the political system it manages is today based upon the CPC's ability to sustain economic growth. Intimately linked to this, Beijing is faced with a long-term decline in domestic oil production (Taylor, 2006b). China's policymakers are actively encouraging national companies to aggressively pursue oil and other natural resources in Africa. China is currently the world's second largest oil importer and the second largest consumer of African resources. The abundance of natural resources in Africa has thus led Chinese corporations to seek long-term deals with African governments in order to ensure continued access to all varieties of raw materials and energy in Africa. As China's national oil companies are largely excluded from the majority of Middle Eastern oil supplies and as Beijing wishes to limit vulnerability on the international oil market, there is a policy to encourage investment in Africa, courting states that the West have overlooked. This resource-based foreign policy has, by its very nature, 'little room for morality' (Zweig and Bi Jianhai 2005: 31).

The interest in ensuring its resource security and economic growth through involvement in Africa is by no means restricted to oil, and encompasses all natural resources. From investment in copper in Zambia, platinum interests in Zimbabwe to supporting fishing ventures in Gabon and Namibia, Chinese corporations have vigorously courted and pursued the political and business elite in Africa to guarantee continued access, often lubricated with sweetener deals provided by central government. One of the benefits of Chinese interest in African resources is that it has dramatically increased demand and has revitalised industries such as Zambia's copper industry. However, the influx of capital into weak and authoritarian governments also has long-term consequences for Africa as leaders may be tempted to neglect necessary reforms, bolstered by newly perceived economic security from Chinese (and other emerging economies') interest (see Taylor, 2010):

> On the one hand, the high prices of some commodities, which are driven by China's growth and demand, may be detrimental for the exporters of these commodities as they create strong incentives for remaining within the existing pattern of exports, although this pattern is a major factor of vulnerability to external shocks and fluctuations of prices and demand. This entrenching of the specialisation of SSA in commodity exports is driven not only by China but also by other emerging countries (e.g. India, Brazil): the composition of SSA's exports to other developing countries over the 2000s has shifted towards primary products at the expense of manufactures. On the other hand, these commodities' high prices harm the African countries that do not export them and need to import them (e.g. oil or food importers), as they cause a deterioration of the trade balance. (Sindzingre, 2013: 36)

Obviously, this potential negative outcome is not a problem that can be specifically associated with Chinese engagement with Africa. It is in fact intimately linked to the nature of the state in much of Africa and the colonial inheritance. In short, African politics must be understood as the utilisation of patronage and clientelism and operates within neopatrimonial modes of governance. 'Political instability is ... rooted in the extreme politicisation of the state as an organ to be monopolised for absolute power and accelerated economic advancement' (Fatton, 1988: 35). In this context, the idea that resources should be channelled towards the nebulous concept of 'national development' is out of the question in many African states. Productive economic activities and notions of long-term investment are side-lined in favour of immediate consumption, display and resource diffusion (Chabal and Daloz, 1999). In this regard, Chinese policy is vulnerable to the claim that in dealing only with the state and rigorously adhering to its 'non-interference' strategy, Beijing exacerbates existing structural faults in the political economies of a number of African states. Until and unless African elites themselves advance transparency, pro-development policies and equitable growth (and are prepared and competent enough to put them into force), China at present does little to press them on such issues.

One must note that with the exception of oil exports to China, Sino–African trade is generally lopsided in favour of Chinese exporters who are penetrating African markets with cheap household products. Such imports into Africa have been criticised as doing little to encourage indigenous African manufacturing. Certainly, it is the historic failure of African economies to industrialise and develop that means that they produce very few processed goods. They are thus a natural target for Chinese exporters. Yet, such Chinese engagement reifies Africa's status as an exporter of raw materials whilst being an importer of manufactured goods, something which has consigned the African continent to under-development and a reproduction of Africa's historical relationships with the external world.

Complicating this milieu is the fact that many of the products manu-factured in China, but which are sold in African markets, are not actu-ally brought into the continent by Chinese but by African traders. There are now quite elaborate trading networks linking China and Africa and much of this is centred in the southern province of Guandong where a relatively large population of African entrepreneurs now live and make deals. The point of this is crucial: Chinese traders are *not* 'flooding' the African market with cheap Chinese goods. Rather, African actors are actively facilitating the penetration of Africa by Chinese-made products in conditions where local African industrial capacity is low/non-existent. This is somewhat ironic given that condemnation by many African trade unions and civil society organisations of the 'Asian tsunami' in cheap products lays the blame squarely on 'the Chinese'. Yet, given this, serious concern must be expressed that a dependent relationship is being further entrenched. Even if we accept the symbiotic nature of the partnership between the external and domestic, the fact remains that a relationship of dominance and subordination, with strong dependent features exists. That a certain nonchalance on the part of China regarding such dynamics exists is apparent.

A Chinese model?

Politically as well as economically, China's presence in Africa has been based on the premise of providing an alternate development model for African states and leaders. In fact, 'the rise of China compelled an unholy alliance of normally opposed views from across the political spectrum – "Left" neoliberals, statists and progressives/socialist of various stripes – all in the end little concerned whether China is or is not socialist or has or has not fully imbibed market reforms, yet all upholding China as a model of successful Third World development' (Westra, 2012: 147). Regrettably, there has been a 'blind idealisation of how China manages growth by blending political authoritarianism and market liberalisation' (Lin Chun, 2013: 82).

According to Naidu and Davies (2006: 80), China is seen as a 'refreshing alternative to the traditional engagement models of the West ... African governments see China's engagement as a point of departure from Western neocolonialism and political conditions'. Of course, this 'refreshing alternative' suits incumbent elites. How it may affect and is received by citizens in autocratic African countries is another matter. Thus far, the emphasis China places on respect for state sovereignty and non-inter-ference in its diplomatic rhetoric has meant a willingness to deal with states that have been ostracised by the West. This may appear attractive to some repressive African leaders, but it profoundly challenges the claimed Western vision of a flourishing Africa governed by liberal democracies. In Zimbabwe, for instance, '[r]umors abound that China has sold Zimba-bwe's internal-security apparatus water cannons to subdue protesters and bugging equipment to monitor cell phone networks' (*New York Times*, 25 July 2005). A Zimbabwean analyst commented: 'It is important to note ... that Chinese "non-interference" policy cannot be permanent. The Chinese are well aware of this themselves. Where deals are signed with unpopular dictatorial regimes that could later be revised by a new government, it becomes necessary for the Chinese to protect such regimes' (Karumbidza, 2007: 88–9). Despite Chinese protestations to the contrary, supplying governments with equipment to suppress their own citizens *does* consti-tute a political decision to interfere.

This brings us to the very notion of an alternative Chinese model in Africa. Dirlik (2006) notes that the 'Beijing Consensus' draws its meaning and appeal not from some coherent set of economic or political ideas *à la* Ramo (2004), but from its intimation of an alternative pole, from which those opposed to Washington and, by extension 'the West', can draw inspiration. Certainly, 'China's alternative path is partly attractive because of the apparent success of the experience of economic reform. Other developing states might also lean towards the Chinese way not just because China's leaders don't attach democratising and liberalising conditions to bilateral relations, but also because China is coming to provide alternative sources of economic opportunities (with non-democ-ratising strings attached)' (Breslin, 2007: 2). But this does not yet mean that a coherent alternate has emerged.

First, conceptions of Chinese 'soft power' built on 'the appeal of China as an economic model' (Kurlantzick 2006: 5) overstate the ability of China to project and promote an alternative economic type (Yan Xuetong, 2006). It is true that economically liberalising whilst preserving an author-itarian political system might be appealing to some African autocrats. China's sustained growth has taken place with no reference to democracy or transparency. Yet, China's extraordinary economic growth has come about, certainly initially, within the broader context of a capable state and in a region that is itself economically dynamic. Rapid economic growth without democratisation as per the East Asian model often required a strong developmental state. Analysis of China within this vein generally confirms such a proposition (Ming Xia, 2000) though with certain caveats (Breslin, 1996).

Contrast such a milieu with Africa. Granted even the relative declining reach of the Chinese state as liberalisation progresses (Wang Hui, 2003), the type of comparative internal strength and concomitant stability that Beijing is able to enact is beyond the ambition of most – if not all – current African leaders. This of course assumes that development is on the agenda. Ake (1991: 319) noted: 'One of the most amazing things about the literature on development in Africa is how readily it assumes that everyone is interested in development and that when [African] leaders proclaim their commitment to development and fashion their impressive development plans and negotiate with international organisations for development assistance, they are ready for development and for getting on with it'.

Furthermore, any notion of a Chinese model wrenched from its historical context is fallacious. Discussion of a model must be based on 'a collective appreciation of the historicity and fundamental justice of the Chinese communist revolution' (Lin Chun, 2013: 84). The China of today did not begin in 1978 with 'The Four Modernizations', or Deng Xiaoping's 1992 southern tour, but is built on the decades of fundamental restructuring that China's socio-economic formation underwent, *under revolutionary conditions*. Mao Zedong (1961/2000: 65) noted: 'Historical experience is written in iron and blood'. Ignoring this fundamental reality and instead revering an ahistorical 'model' severed from its past foundations and experience is unproductive and ridiculous. The China of today would not exist – could not exist – without the post-1949 experience. It is doubtful if current African elites would embrace the model in all its historical totalities.

Besides, the irony is that those who applaud alternatives to Western dominated IFIs often – sometimes perhaps without realising so – end up in a position where they not only support the authoritarian milieu in some African states, but also the emerging leadership of China. Opposition to American hegemony – something that has considerable appeal – can result in the promotion not of social democracy, nor even Keynesian liberalism, but of illiberal authoritarianism. As Zha Daojiong notes (2005), within China itself there is a debate as to whether or not the Latin American fate of social polarisation, international dependency and economic stagnation is China's future fate unless appropriate policies are implemented. These debates often question the capitalist direction of Beijing's current course, again undermining the notion of a 'model' (see Wang Chaohua, 2003; Wang Hui, 2003). Analyses of the so-called 'China miracle' (Wu Yanrui, 2003), which offer up more sober interpretations, seem to have been missed by those advocating the Chinese model.

Indeed, although the idea of a China model of development built around strong state control of the economy has gained considerable interest in recent years, captured in the 'Beijing Consensus' debate, Huang Yasheng (2011) recaps that for much of the post-Mao period the emphasis has been on the introduction of the market rather than its suppression. What we have seen is a fusing of macroliberalisation with a selective continuation of state discretion and sectoral regulation (Hsueh, 2011: 3–4). Although pragmatism might be the key characteristic of the Chinese experience and a lesson for others to learn (although how they might learn from an ad hoc, unique, non-model model is unstated!), this pragmatism has entailed accepting, rather than nullifying, key elements of the neoliberal paradigm; 'on questions of trade, FDI and regulation, China's actual reform experience is pretty much in line with the policy prescriptions attributed to the Washington Consensus' (Karp, 2009: 204). If the question of dependency is brought in, the notion of a Chinese model that Africa might emulate is radically destabilised, for 'as the Chinese state continues to lose its planning and directing capability, and the country's resources are increasingly incorporated into foreign networks largely for the purpose of satisfying external market demands, the country's autonomous development potential is lost' (Hart-Landsberg, 2013: 87).

Breslin (2013: 629) argues: 'A strong argument can ... be made that China has been one of the main national beneficiaries of the spread of a post-Fordist form of neoliberal globalization that is typically associated with Western and capitalist power and interests. And this is not just a "passive" acceptance of existing norms and processes – China was not dragged into WTO membership against its will'. Those who argue that China offer an alternative economic model may wish to explain then how China differs from the West, other than possessing a somewhat stronger residual role for the state: 'In contrast to the pre-reform period, almost all economic activity is now market determined. And, while the state continues to dominate in many strategic sectors, such as finance, energy, and transportation, the great majority of value added in the all-important manufacturing sector is now produced by profit-seeking, private firms (Hart-Landsberg, 2010: 17).

Debates around China's contemporary political economy have been increasingly polarised. One school of thought contends that China is a benevolent and progressive rising power which is qualified to transform the neoliberal world by somehow making it more compassionate and diverse, given Beijing's alleged regime based on Confucian principles of social harmony and balance. Whilst Arrighi's (2007: 24) thesis that 'the nature of development in China is not necessarily capitalist' can be dismissed out of hand, more nuanced arguments suggest that China has either rejected neoliberalism (Rucki, 2011) or challenged it through global governance institutions (Strange, 2011). As, it is claimed, a 'myth that the Chinese ascent can be attributed to an alleged adherence to the neoliberal creed' (Arrighi, 2007: 353), Beijing in this reading is see as representing a robust challenge to the hegemony of neoliberalism (Lo and Zhang, 2011). However, it seems apparent that Mao's fear of the capitalist roaders restoring capitalism upon his death has indeed occurred. In this restoration, Deng Xiaoping and his successors instrumentalised the Chinese state to play a leading role in this process by being 'highly active in reorganising social relations commensurate with the restoration of capitalism' (Hart-Landsberg and Burkett, 2004: 26). Through a Gramscian passive revolution (Gray, 2010), an 'increasingly hierarchical and brutal form of capitalism' has developed in China that is heavily inclined to the propensities of the policy paradigm of neoliberalism (Hart-Landsberg and Burkett, 2004: 26). Lin Chun (2013: 56) notes: 'The erosion of socialism in China is undoubtedly ... the work of a "peaceful evolution" [a passive revolution, in other words] through capitalist integration'.

Whilst recognising the particularities of the Chinese adoption of market principles (what Harvey (2005) characterises as neoliberalism 'with Chinese characteristics'), it is clear that the Chinese regime of accumulation has been dominated by transnational capital (Hart-Landsberg and Burkett, 2005) and that 'China's rise as an export powerhouse is primarily due to its position as the final assembly platform for transnational corporate cross-border production networks' (Hart-Landsberg, 2013: 46). Indeed, 'by 2005 more than 70 percent of the value-added profits of China's electronics and information industry, 90 percent of the production and market of its motor industry, and 80 percent of the management of its machinery and chemical industries had been controlled by foreign capital' (Lin Chun, 2013: 58).

Beijing's elites have consciously enmeshed China's economy into the American-dominated structures of global capitalism, whilst at times protecting key policy tools, such as capital controls (Vermeiren and Dierckx, 2012). Important factions now in fact join the transnational elite, with all the interest and agendas so entailed (Breslin, 2004). The claim that the rise of China will challenge – or even displace – global neoliberalism is inconsistent with objective reality.

Instead, rather, China now plays the role of 'America's head servant' within the extant order, supporting American monetary dominance through the recycling of FDI-driven export incomes in dollar-denominated assets (Hung, 2009). China itself has been moving 'unmistakably toward the market doctrines of neoclassical economics, with an emphasis on prudent fiscal policy, economic openness, privatisation, market liberalisation and the protection of private property' (Yao, 2010). The idea that China does not support the neoliberal order needs to answer the question why Beijing joined the WTO (and was accepted) and the fact that China has not employed its mounting position as a creditor to either question the current neoliberal underpinnings of the international financial system or push for any serious reform process within the G-20.

In fact, 'Chinese political and business leaders continue to enjoy record profits, so they have little reason to press for a change in economic policy' (Hart-Landsberg, 2013: 65). When it is stated that 'Chinese political and business leaders continue to enjoy record profits', this is meant literally: 'The net worth of the 70 richest delegates in China's National People's Congress … rose to 565.8 billion yuan ($89.9 billion) in 2011, a gain of $11.5 billion from 2010 … That compares to the $7.5 billion net worth of all 660 top officials in the three branches of the US government' (Forsythe, 2012). Why would this capitalist nobility rock the boat?

Beijing's stance seems to be to take advantage of the US-guaranteed world order, with the benefits that this accrues for China's elites whilst trying to downplay any rise in responsibility: 'China's strategy towards the BRICS stems from this perspective: play the game of integrating into the capitalist system without assuming the political consequences' (Laïdi, 2012: 620). Consequently, China as an alternative – and possible challenger to the capitalist world order lacks serious credibility. China is both an active participant and tacit co-manager of the established global order. Through this, Beijing lends credibility to the system whilst at the same serving to play an important role as an intermediate actor bridging the ongoing world system, dominated as it is by the capitalist heartland and emerging 'rising' actors.

Conclusion

Chinese foreign policy in Africa has been based on several key aims. Beijing has focused on ensuring its regime security through access to crucial resources. By portraying itself as an advocate for the developing world and emphasising the rhetoric of South–South cooperation, China has arguably sought to offer itself up as an alternative model to Western dominance. However, to achieve its policy goals, Beijing has equally been prepared to defend autocratic regimes, some of which commit gross human rights abuses, such as Sudan and Zimbabwe. In this way, China's interactions with the continent fit the pattern of most external actors' intercourse with Africa: beneficial to the ruling elite.

It must be emphasised that China's policies towards Africa are evolving and maturing and Beijing is going through a steep learning curve. Recent developments suggest that China is starting to realise that like all other actors in Africa, Beijing needs stability and security in order for Chinese investments to flourish and for its connections with the continent to be coherent. The history and development of Sino–African relations thus far suggests certain patterns, but the relationship is fluid and ever changing. Indeed, it has to be said that in relative terms, the exponential increase in Chinese trade with Africa from the start of this century means that we are in the very early stages of a solidified Sino–African relationship. At present the picture appears mixed – there are instances where the Chinese role in Africa is positive and appreciated. The laying down of infrastructure is one such area. Equally, there are issues where Beijing is, at present at least, playing an equivocal role which arguably threatens to unravel some of the progress made in Africa in recent times on issues of good governance and accountability. Also, there are dynamics which are negative, such as the reification of Africa's dependent status within the global political economy.

Problematically, the continent lacks a consistent and unified collective policy to connect with Beijing. As a Kenyan report put it, 'China has an Africa policy. Africa doesn't have a China policy' (*Daily Nation*, 12 June 2006). At FOCAC III for instance, Africa was unsuccessful in developing a combined negotiating approach that might have shaped the debate and been advantageous to the continent. As one commentary at the time noted, 'Whereas the FOCAC declaration present[ed] a genuine platform for pragmatic co-operation, to Africa's advantage, Africa's failure to form a unified voice could seriously hamper its ability to determine the terms and general direction of the interaction [because] rather than work as a bloc, Africa continues to negotiate with China on a country-by-country basis' (*Business in Africa*, 20 December 2006). Remarkably, there is in fact no official AU view on Sino–African ties whether positive or negative. This is partly because China prefers bilateral dealings, which makes constructing a single 'China policy' difficult, but also reflects the lumpen nature of the comprador African elites' total lack of any vision for the continent. Most African governments' reactions to the rise of Chinese activity on the continent have been unreflexive and uncoordinated, grasping onto an objectified 'China' as the latest fad.

Where there is coherence in Sino–African relations, a key intention enunciated by Beijing is to encourage Chinese corporations to invest overseas, play a role in international capital markets and to aid in putting into action the policy of ensuring regime security through access to crucial resources. A Chinese Ministry of Commerce statement has in fact averred that Africa is 'one of the most important regions for carrying out our "go outward" strategy' (quoted in Gu Xuewu, 2005: 8). The resulting hike in commodity prices has been skewed to only certain economies. South Africa provides iron ore and platinum whilst the DR Congo and Zambia supply copper and cobalt. Timber is sourced from Gabon, Cameroon, Congo-Brazzaville and Liberia, whilst various west and central African nations supply raw cotton to Chinese textile factories. It is however the extractive industries that remain China's biggest commercial interest in Africa.

According to one source (TRALAC, 2013: 1), the top 20 products imported by China from Africa in 2012 accounted for 96 per cent of China's total imports from *all* African countries, with the top five import products accounting for 89 per cent of total African imports for the year. China's imports from African countries are *highly* concentrated. In 2012, Beijing's main imports from Africa in 2012 were mineral products (55 per cent); other unclassified goods (26 per cent); base metals (4 per cent); precious stones and metals (3 per cent) and textiles and clothing (1 per cent). Given the nature of these industries globally – but particularly in Africa – criticism of Chinese activities is largely to be expected.

Framed within a wider analysis of Africa's structural position in the global economy, obvious problems become apparent.

At the same time, the novelty of China's approach to Africa is becoming less clear as market logics permeate Beijing's interactions with the continent. This can be most evidently seen in the plethora of private Chinese actors engaging with Africa, but can also be seen in official relations. The aid sector is one such example, where the use of the private sector, including industrial and business enterprises, for development efforts has increasingly characterised Chinese aid. Indeed: 'The recent use of domestic tendering processes for foreign aid project selection in China, as well as of import and export credits, has encouraged China's private sector to engage in development efforts. Whereas prior to 1978 all businesses were State Owned Enterprises, there is now a growingly large and dynamic array of private enterprises. Even China's COMPLANT [China National Complete Plant Import & Export Corporation] is now listed on the stock exchange' (Warmerdam, 2012: 234). Such realities again destabilise the notion that the 'China model' is radically distinct from that of the West. In fact, the role of diverse Chinese actors in Africa reproduces much that has already been seen before. A problem here is that it appears that many African elites and commentators are seemingly blind to such realities.

Yet equally, sensationalist accounts of Chinese neo-colonialism are nonsensical. It should not need to be said, but there is no evidence of China seeking colonies, using prisoners as cheap labour or any of the other lurid accusations made against 'the Chinese' in Africa. Chinese commercial activities in Africa are straightforward transactions (Brautigam, 2011) and as Beijing's Special Representative on African Affairs, Zhong Jianhua, asserted, 'China is neither bad nor good. China is a combination of these things' (quoted in *Africa Research Bulletin*, 6 August 2013). It is 'Commodity scarcity at home, not imperial ideology, [that] compelled China to venture abroad' (Chu, 2013: 209). Whilst the effect may be to help reify some African countries' status in the global division of labour, this cannot be seen either as a deliberate plot by Beijing, nor that Chinese actors are any more rapacious or more damaging than the traditional exploiters of Africa's wealth i.e. Western capitalism.

6

'Africa Rising' | Jobless Growth
& Deindustrialisation

The BRICS are not a cohesive group and differences exist in how they approach the African continent, despite extravagant claims that they are 'rapidly morphing into a more coherent power grouping that reflects the shifting balance of power in the global economy' (*Financial Times*, 25 March 2013). The question arises: are the BRICS any more than a rather self-conscious attempt to bring the ostensible (and in some cases, self-appointed) managers of tomorrow to today's agenda? Currently, they seem little more than emerging/re-emerging states acting and voting in their own interests, which just happen to (occasionally) coincide. The quest for higher representation and political voice regarding global governance and the ongoing world order is probably the most important attribute that contributes to the relevance of the BRICS (Keukeleire et al., 2011: 16ff). Beyond that, there is precious little substance and a lot of the hype about the rise of the BRICS seems to stem from the declinist literature and mood in the West rather than in any sober evaluation of what the BRICS actually are.

Whilst not exaggerating them, we should note the weaknesses that the BRICS individually and collectively exhibit. This is likely to have implications for Africa in the long-term – certainly if African elites wish to construct alliances with these 'new' actors as a means to lessen political dependence on the West. 'Since its inception, the BRIC concept has been founded on economic growth projections, with no reference to other parameters such as political/social development and inclusivity, let alone sustainability, as these dimensions are entirely neglected by GDP' (Centre for the Study of Governance Innovation, 2013: 3). Furthermore, the member states of BRICS differ geographically, politically and militarily, and despite being perhaps credibly anointed as leading developing economies, their differences are in fact so plain that a meaningful alliance beyond rhetoric is very difficult (Jacobs and van Rossem, 2013). Tensions between the various members are obvious:

Besides the inherent GDP-link uniting these five nations, there is little else they have in common. Politically, the BRICS comprise three democracies (including the largest in the world, India), a totalitarian regime (China), and a nation characterized by significant authoritarian tendencies (Russia). China and India have been forced to an uneasy cohabitation, due to longstanding geopolitical rivalries, including territorial disputes over Tibet. The two countries are also divided with respect to Pakistan. China has also been opposed (or at least luke-warm) to India's bid to join the permanent members of the UN Security Council. Although trade between the two giants has been growing rapidly, Indian authorities have been vocal against the slow pace in opening Chinese markets, while China has accused the Indian government of carrying out a containment policy through its outreach to East Asian nations such as Japan, Indonesia and South Korea. As continental powerhouses, South Africa and Brazil have been ambivalent as to how to combine their regional commitments with their membership in BRICS. In addition, while Brazil, India and South Africa have traditionally supported a progressive human rights agenda, both China and Russia (the only two permanent members of the UN Security Council among the BRICS) have systematically opposed it. (Centre for the Study of Governance Innovation, 2013: 3)

As a result, other than the summits, actual BRICS cooperation is almost exclusively bilateral, rather than pentalateral. In addition, each state has a varying relationship with the United States, albeit all accept the logic and norms of an American-dominated world order.

Brazil currently is going through a period of turmoil that raises questions as to its future trajectory. Though it has an overabundance of natural resources, growing by the day, and a degree of human capital that is the envy of the others, it is relatively geographically isolated and economically remains reliant on its agricultural and oil sector. Its key weaknesses are in terms of atrocious income inequalities and a dire national infrastructure that needs immediate but costly investment. Ongoing and widespread popular unrest is a manifestation of such realities. Indeed, whilst Brazil's elites have celebrated their country's 'rise', deep rooted social issues are mostly left unaddressed, increasingly exploding in popular indignation. During the good times, Brazil relied heavily on commodity prices, propelled by China. When this declined, a stagnant economy was the result, further stimulated by credit-driven consumerism. The FIFA World Cup for 2014, awarded to Brazil in 2007 during the height of hubris about the emerging economies, was intended to draw attention to the growing economic power of Brasília (de Almeida et al., 2013). Instead, current developments suggest the contrary, with a distinct 'bread and circuses' feel to the forthcoming event.

For its part, Russia has proven to be among the most vulnerable to the effects of the crisis and recession in the core. An autocracy sitting astride what is effectively a military-petroleum complex, Russia has the least interest in Africa. Its overdependence on oil and natural gas are likely to be problematic for Moscow's long-term economic growth and development. Unafraid to use coercion to intimidate consumers of Russian commodities, Moscow's key interests in Africa are to diversify the sources of its main basis for political power. Ambivalent about the South, Russia is eager to join the OECD and be seen as 'developed' and 'modern'. If measured against the other BRICS, Russia is an unreliable ally of Africa in the sense that its foreign policy does not even pretend to advance the interests of the Global South. Like Brazil, Russia is mainly a commodity brokerage economy which expands or declines in line with commodity prices. Both countries will remain as middle-income states, lacking global competitiveness.

India's liberal democracy grants it a vibrant civil society but this can at times act to constrict policymakers. Equally, this democracy is likely to slow down – if not reverse – the current neoliberal experiment being promoted by key Indian elites. The state-society complex in India is fragile, with obscene income inequality, extensive and entrenched corruption, and a desperate infrastructure in urgent need of renewal and/ or replacement. Only around 100–150 million (out of 1.2 billion) drive the economy and although a great deal of hype has been circulated (often centred around the curious notion that India's out-of-control population automatically makes it a superpower), it is difficult to see how India will structurally change from its current status as an agrarian society with a sprinkling of a service sector and an insignificant manufacturing base. Though reforms have been advanced since 1991, domestic entrepreneurship remains restricted by a notorious bureaucracy and foreign direct investment (FDI) is relatively weak. A model built on outsourcing – with a concomitant neglect of manufacturing – serves as a weak platform for long-term growth. Domestic insecurity as well as a fractious neighbourhood also poses problems. In terms of Africa, India is likely to remain interested, but at a lower level than China.

Regarding China, there are plenty of signs that the economy is overheating. Excessive financial bubbles stimulated by easy credit have formed, with the real estate market particularly vulnerable. Indeed, 'in China the sheer size of nonperforming loans relative to the overall size of the economy is much greater than the size of the subprime market was to the US or European Union economies' (Karabell, 2010: 199). If a rapid crisis in China's economy occurs, growth will likely be depressed, with possible political outfall. Already, the Chinese authorities are battling over 100,000 euphemistically-termed 'disturbances' annually, mostly over land rights and the abuse of power by government authorities. Serious demographic and ecological challenges exacerbate an already problematic situation. Although one need not subscribe to any 'coming collapse' thesis, China *does* face mounting domestic problems, which are likely to distract the government away from foreign matters. Indeed, the financial crisis has already made it evident that the earlier optimism about China emerging as the alternative engine of growth for Africa (and by extension, the world economy) was perhaps inappropriate, given the decline in China's exports from late 2008. This then led to overcapacity. Quite simply, China's over-reliance on FDI and exports fuelled rapid growth in some sectors before 2008, but when global demand plummeted and domestic production costs climbed, overcapacity appeared alongside falling profits. Problematically for China, economic history suggests a strong relationship between overcapacity and economic crises.

Expanding African reliance?

According to Gammeltoft (2008), the BRICS expansion into Africa is merely a reflection of a third wave in outward-flowing FDI from developing economies (see also Dunning et al., 1998). The first wave was stimulated by market- and efficiency-seeking factors. Investments were predominately in other developing countries, usually neighbouring states. This first wave of FDI came primarily from – and was located in – Latin America. Corporations from the region internationalised and invested within the region in merchandise production that had already satiated growing domestic markets. In the second wave, strategic asset-seeking became an additional motivation and developed and developing countries beyond the investor's own region became more important targets for investments. This wave was dominated by Asian corporations and complemented the export oriented industrialisation strategies of the Asian Tigers. Latin American outward FDI was less noticeable during this period, beginning in the 1980s, which was characterised by expansion into the fast growing markets of other Asian emerging economies. Additionally, outward FDI sought to take advantage of cheap labour costs in developing countries.

The current period is marked by 'the emergence of a third wave, which is not confined to Latin America but applies to outward investment flows from emerging and developing countries in general' (Gammeltoft, 2008: 5). This wave is increasingly global in scope and more geographically diverse in terms of the country origins of outward FDI. It is marked by the upsurge of the BRICS (see Sauvant, 2005). The total value of BRIC outward FDI rose from less than $10 billion a year in the late 1990s to about $147 billion in 2008 before declining to $100 billion in 2009 (IMF, 2011: 13). The upsurge in outward FDI from the BRICS has been monumental (Gammeltoft et al., 2010: 258).

However, Jacobs (2012: 60) notes: 'Foreign direct investment has increased – both in volume and in geographical spread – but as a result, volatile commodity prices are becoming increasingly difficult for Africa to manage'. Consequently, 'the BRICS are not building an economically and politically more solid Africa' (ibid.). This really is the key question in analysing the effect of the BRICS on Africa. Currently, 'South–South FDI flows are highly concentrated in the infrastructure and extractive sectors' (Gammeltoft, 2008: 10). It is of course true that some investment from the BRICS countries (particularly China and India) are going into manufacturing and production and that such developments do hold potential (Brautigam, 2009). It would be a caricature to suggest that actors from the BRICS are *only* interested in resources. However, the overall pattern of the emerging relationships does suggest that the historic economic relationship between Africa and the world is being reified. Besides, as Southall (2009: 14) notes:

> while the hope of the development literature has been that higher rates of inflow of capital investment will have downstream effects on African employment (through increased government revenues and spending alongside an injection of consumer wealth into local economies), there is little evidence that this will take place on a substantial scale. The fundamental reason for this is that the new scramble rests heavily on the engagements of foreign governments and corporations with African elites. While Western governments and international financial institutions take considerable efforts to control and discipline wayward African regimes through 'good governance', these strictures systematically fall away when serious access to profits and valuable resources are at stake. In any case, the 'good governance' paradigm is currently under severe challenge by Chinese foreign policy, which curries favour with African governments by elevating the principles of non-interference and sovereignty.

The implications for Africa's continued dependency on primary commodities, particularly in the energy and minerals sector is a worry for the continent's future development trajectories: 'countries continue to be natural resource exporters whose products do not compete directly with the manufactured exports of the developed North. Interdependence of this sort "is a code word for continued dependence of the developing South"' (Roy, 1999: 119). This is a historic situation and has been long held up as one of Africa's key development challenges. As new centres of accumulation develop in the historic South, this dependence is arguably being diversified, but not rectified.

Recent events confirm this reality and the last ten years have highlighted just how unstable commodity prices are. The aggregate trend in prices for all primary commodities for the period 1995–2010 declined from 1995 to 2001, with prices down by one third. From 2001, which coincided with the big upsurge of interest in Africa by the BRIC, commodity prices started to climb at accelerating speeds. This was stopped in its tracks by the 2008 crisis, with prices tumbling by nearly 40 per cent by the year end. Clearly, any sense of planning depending on receipts from commodities is extremely problematic, given that international commodity prices are especially volatile. This trend has only increased as the world has become more economically integrated: 'In the past 30 years, there have been as many price shocks across the range of commodities as there were in the preceding 75 years' (Brown, 2008).

Commodity dependence is typically measured by the share of export earnings of the top single commodity (or top three export commodities) in GDP, in total merchandise exports, and in total agriculture exports. The percentage of people occupied in commodity production or the share in government revenue accruing from commodities are also important measurements (South Centre, 2005). 'Examining trends in the share of primary commodities in total exports for the period 1995–2009', which coincides with the increase in interest in Africa by, among others, the BRICS, 'shows that despite a contraction between 1995 and 2000, the share of primary commodities in total exports rose rapidly between 2000 and 2009' (UNDP, 2011: 60). This development had particular implications for the African continent: 'The share of primary commodities in exports increased across all regions of the developing world ... Africa – the region most dependent on primary commodity exports throughout the period – became even more commodity-dependent (the share of primary commodity exports was 72 per cent in 1995 and rose to 81 per cent by 2009)' (ibid.). Put another way, 'dependence on external markets, as measured by the export-to-gross domestic product (GDP) ratio ... doubled from 26 per cent in 1995 to 51 per cent in 2007' (Dembele, 2012: 183). This super cycle was largely – though not exclusively – driven by growth and industrial demand within the BRICS. As Miguel (2009) has shown, economic relationships with the BRICS (particularly China) and rising commodity prices were the main drivers behind the recent economic improvements in Sub-Saharan Africa (SSA), adding nearly 2.5 percentage points to the growth of the typical African economy by the mid-2000s (Collier, 2007).

Using the United Nations Conference on Trade and Development (UNCTAD) secretariat calculations, themselves based on its *UNCTAD Stat*, a diversification index can be calculated that signals whether the structure of exports by product of a given state or group of countries differ from the structure of export products of the world. The index ranges from 0 to 1 and shows the extent of the differences between the structure of trade of a country or country group and the world mean. In other words, are countries/groups of countries more or less diversified than the world average? The figures demonstrate that Africa continues to be much less diversified than the rest of the world (UNCTAD, 2013). Indeed, exports from Africa have become even more concentrated, with an increase in the aggregate concentration ratio from 0.35 in 2000 to 0.48 in 2008 (Ancharaz, 2011).

'African economies exhibit very low level of diversification. By all measures and accounts, there has been limited diversification of exports by the African economies. Over the last 25 years or so, there has been very little change towards improved diversification in the African economies in general' (Ben Hammouda et al., 2006: 593). What diversification that has occurred has been volatile. This is extremely problematic given that African economies have become more concentrated, whilst according to the United Nations Economic Commission for Africa (UNECA): 'The diversification of African economies is one way through which the recent economic growth achievements could be sustained ... diversification is a *prerequisite* to achieving positive development in the continent' (UNECA, 2007: 115, emphasis added).

A working paper from the OECD claims that 'China's and India's growing demand for commodities has served to diversify export clients away from OECD countries' (Avendaño et al., 2008: 8). However, as the above diversification index shows, what has actually happened is that Africa has more or less remained undiversified in its exports, remaining dependent on primary commodities. In some respects, this is history repeating itself, with commodity booms being initially held by some to be positive for Africa. Hone (1973) asserted (off the back of the then-latest commodity boom): 'The trade prospects for the developing world are [now] considerably better in 1973 than they were in 1951 or even in 1960'. We all know what actually happened. Indeed, 'several countries [in Africa] have the dubious distinction of having been among the fastest growers in one decade, then the slowest in another. For example, half the fastest ten growers in the 1960s were among the slowest in at least one of the subsequent decades' (Weeks, 2010: 3).

Half of the countries in Africa derive over 80 per cent of their merchandise export income from commodities. In Middle and West Africa, the ratio of commodity exports to total merchandise exports was an astonishing 98 per cent and 93 per cent respectively. As a whole, the latest available figures (2009–2010) reveal that Africa's export profile in terms of commodities is made up of fuels (69 per cent), minerals, ores and metals (16 per cent), and agricultural products (7 per cent) (UNCTAD, 2012a: 21). The total share of fuels and mining products in Africa's total merchandise exports increased from 48.4 per cent in 2003 to 70.6 per cent in 2008. Although in 2011 it was down to 64 per cent in 2011, what this shows is that the upsurge of interest in Africa by the BRICS and other emerging economies has coincided with – and possibly exacerbated – the continent's increased dependency on primary products, particularly mineral products (WTO, 2012: 51). UNECA notes: 'The growth spurt of the first decade of the twenty-first century ... was driven largely by primary production and exports'. Problematically, although Africa seems to have fared better than some regions since the recent global crisis, 'the risk of similar events reversing its modest gains calls into question the sustainability and reliability of a strategy based on exports of primary commodities' (a strategy embedded in structural adjustment programmes (SAPs) and the neoliberal development policies of the post-SAP era). (UNECA, 2012a: 66).

The International Monetary Fund (IMF) comments that the 'BRICs' economic growth and rising demand for primary commodities have been key factors behind the growth of world trade and booms in international trade of primary commodities' (IMF, 2011: 12–13). Resource-based commodities form the bulk of African exports to the BRICs. Whilst this has certainly led to an increase in income for some African countries (or their elites), '[b]y diverting resources from non-raw material sectors and contributing to real exchange-rate appreciation, a price boom runs the risk of locking developing-country commodity exporters into what Leamer called the "raw-material corner", with little scope for industrial progress or skills advancement' (Avendaño et al., 2008). Leamer's argument came from his illustrating both relative factor endowments and relative factor intensities with three factors and any number of goods (Leamer, 1987). Given Africa's factor endowments being concentrated in commodities and the export profile and sector concentration being in the same, the raw material corner has been the continent's broad fate:

> During colonisation and the period immediately after, the structure of external trade of African countries were mainly determined by the needs of the colonial masters. African countries mainly exported natural resources such as timber and minerals and imported manufactured goods. About six decades later, this structure of trade has not been significantly altered. Invariably, African countries have continually and consistently not managed to diversify trade into manufactured products. (Afari-Gyan, 2010: 63)

The result has been what Shivji (2009: 59) terms 'structural disarticulation', where Africa exhibits a 'disarticulation between the structure of production and the structure of consumption. What is produced is not consumed and what is consumed is not produced'. Ake (1981) has convincingly demonstrated that this disarticulation is a major feature of Africa's political economy and a key factor behind the continent's underdevelopment.

While low commodity prices foster palpable problems, even high commodity prices can generate major problems and fashion a trap of sorts, obliging countries and producers to decide between immediate profits (highly attractive for unstable and predatory regimes) and future long-term sustainability. For instance, both Algeria and Nigeria 'have fallen prey to over optimistic spending habits during commodity booms, using current and expected profits to finance social and/or politically motivated projects. Such programmes can quickly become unsustainable when commodity prices drop, but are typically very tricky for politicians to cut, and so tend to get funded out of borrowed money, adding to a country's debt burden' (Brown et al., 2008).

There is no doubt that the exponential growth of the BRIC economies has helped stimulate the global commodity booms witnessed in the first decade of this century (Wang, 2007). This is important given that labour-intensive agricultural and manufactured goods do not feature significantly in the exports of African countries to the BRICS. This dependence is a two-edged sword. Countries with the highest economic integration with the BRICS generally managed to sustain growth during the global downturn, compared to a contraction observed in countries with the least ties. Interestingly, the risk analysis company Maplecroft released in 2011 its *Emerging Powers Integration Index Series*, assessing the economic integration of 180 countries with each of the BRICS (Maplecroft, 2011). According to this, the countries most integrated with the BRICS are resource-rich developing economies, which provide the raw materials to fuel economic growth back in the BRICS domestic economies. Of these many are located in Africa. Zimbabwe was ranked joint 1st, Liberia 5th, Guinea-Bissau 6th, Zambia 7th, DR Congo 10th, Mozambique 12th, Mauritania 15th, Congo-Brazzaville 18th and Sudan 20th. Whilst the data showed which countries stood to gain most from the economic rise of the BRICS, it also revealed just how exposed some countries were to economic contagion should the growth of the BRICS falter. As Alyson Warhurst, CEO of Maplecroft noted: 'Should growth in the BRICs economies falter or lead to internal unrest and repression, we could see contagion spread to those countries that are most highly integrated with the emerging powers' (ibid.). Clearly,

> [T]he positive effect of the world business cycle suggests that the economic performance of African countries is sensitive to world markets. Specifically, this result provides strong support for the hypothesis of the dependence of African countries' economic growth on the economic growth of industrialised nations. This implies that a relatively high degree of integration of African countries with the world economy carries some benefits in as far as the industrialised countries continue to grow. However, should industrialised countries suffer economic setbacks, this could have adverse impacts on the African economies. (Bangwayo-Skeete, 2012: 312)

The same can be equally applied to the BRICS economies and is clearly something which African policymakers need to address if they are thinking that latching onto the BRICS will be an eternal Good Thing.

Exports from Africa to the BRICS broadly exhibit a very clear and continuous pattern in terms of commodity structure, which is consistent with Africa's Ricardian advantage in commodity production, with extractive commodities dominating (see Straffo and Dobb, 1986). In turn, Africa's imports from the BRICS are dominated by manufactured goods. The emergence of China and India and other emerging economies has clearly reinforced Africa's comparative advantage in the production of resource-based commodities and this runs the risk of intensifying the continent's resource dependence (Goldstein et al., 2007). Indeed, as the IMF (2011: 15) warns:

> [T]he prominence of commodities in LICs [low income countries]' exports to BRICs has heightened concerns about the pattern of special-

isation of many LICs and implications for growth over the medium to long term. These concerns are not new but may now appear more daunting given BRIC-induced commodity booms. They are typically expressed as a fear that commodity exports exert upward pressures on real exchange rates and make manufactured exports uncompetitive – a standard 'Dutch disease' effect ... or a worry that, contrary to diversification into manufacturing or new business services, specialisation in primary commodities does not allow for strong productivity gains that will sustain high growth rates. Some have also raised concerns that for some commodities, demand from China and India is mainly for unprocessed goods (compared to demand from advanced economies where satisfying production standards implies a need for more value-added), adding to the risk that LICs could be trapped into low value-added production structures.

In short, such processes are simply the diversification of dependency (the IMF calls it 'the pattern of specialisation'), with Africa being further trapped into low value-added production structures. This is hardly a credible alternative development model for the continent. Instead, such processes rather reflect 'a significant spatial reorganisation of global capitalism, together with intensified processes of primitive accumulation' (Ayers, 2013: 13). It is this reality that evidences the symptoms of economic growth and talks of the 'new scramble for Africa' (see Carmody, 2011).

Indeed, since the upsurge of interest in Africa by the BRICS (amongst others), there have been very few signs of social transformation in Africa and in fact there have been signs of *deindustrialisation*. The growth and governance models being pursued in Africa are based on facilitating market-based actors' profit-making and capital accumulation, but generally ignore conditions that enhance production; the existing growth model is based on a simplistic raising of national GDPs (Hamilton, 2003). Governments 'focus their attention heavily on the main tables, especially the gross domestic product (GDP), and the international agencies reinforce this bias' (Kpedekpo and Arya, 1981: 208). As noted previously, in the context of the 'Africa Rising' trope, this is massively problematic, given the accuracy of statistics on Africa.

GDP growth is routinely used as *the* major benchmark against which success is considered. This is then used to argue that Africa has turned a corner and is the 'next Asia'. This fixation on growth stems from developments within the discipline of Economics. 'From the 1960s on, GDP conquered the political scene and affirmed itself as the supreme indicator of modernity and progress. Everything else (e.g. environmental sustainability, social justice, poverty eradication) were sacrificed on the altar of economic growth' (Fioramonti, 2013: 51). This measurement of one indicator of the economy as being *the* yardstick to measure progress and enable pundits to pronounce on the trajectories of, for example the BRICS or 'Africa Rising', was bolstered in the early 1990s:

In 1992, the GNP was superseded by GDP ... Traditional GNP referred to all goods and services produced by the resident of a given country, regardless of whether the 'income' was generated within or outside its borders. This meant that, for instance, the earnings of multinational corporations were attributed to the country where the firm was owned and where the profits would eventually return. With the introduction of the gross 'domestic' product, this calculation changed completely. GDP is indeed territorially defined, which means that the income generated by foreign companies is 'formally' attributed to the country where it is generated, even though the profits may very well not remain there. This conceptual evolution ... was by and large responsible for the economic boom of many developing nations. Yet, it is obvious that the gains it revealed were more than apparent than real (Fioramonti, 2013: 41).

Given the capital-intensive nature of much investment in the resource sectors of Africa by foreign corporations (BRICS-originated or otherwise) one can imagine how distortionary the effect is on reporting Africa's growth based on GDP rather than GNP. Yet it is precisely the GDP figures that are bandied about.

Furthermore, little or no consideration is paid to the long-term implications of how these growth rates have been accomplished. Minerals resource extraction is, by definition, non-renewable and in the current milieu of dependent relations, Africa's wealth is being taken out of the continent at an exponential rate by an ever-diversifying array of actors. All the while, this is being celebrated as Africa's gain. In fact, 'the continent is actually losing a net 6% of the gross national income each year, thanks to the Resource Curse writ large' (Bond, 2014: 237). 'GDP calculates such exports as a solely positive process (a credit) without a corresponding debit on the books of a country's natural capital' (Bond, 2011: 39), despite the fact that there is an actual 'decline in "natural capital" that occurs *because the minerals and petroleum are non-renewable* and lost forever' (Bond, 2014: 237). The World Bank itself recommended in 2006 that subtracting the value of non-renewable resources through extraction gave a superior indicator of actual gains made through trade. This was termed 'genuine saving' (GS) and is a measure of net investment in produced, natural and human capital: 'Genuine saving provides a much broader indicator of sustainability by valuing changes in natural resources, environmental quality, and human capital, in addition to the traditional measure of changes in produced assets. Negative genuine saving rates imply that total wealth is in decline' (World Bank, 2006: 66).

This has *massive* implications for the 'Africa Rising' narrative, given that the majority of this 'rising' has been built on non-renewable extraction and that resource-rich countries are historically the poorest genuine savers (Atkinson and Hamilton, 2003). In fact, '[w]ith the exception of Algeria and Guinea, for whom GS was just above zero for the period 1970–

2001, every country with an average share of fuel and mineral exports in total exports of over 60% had negative GS' (Dietz et al, 2007: 35). As Bond (2011: 40) notes in his critique of the whole 'Africa Rising' trope, using GS as the measurement,

> Africa's most populous country, Nigeria, fell from a GDP in 2000 of $297 per person to negative $210 in genuine savings, mainly because the value of oil extracted was subtracted from its net wealth. Even the most industrialised African country, South Africa, suffer[ed] from the resource curse: instead of a per person GDP of $2,837 in 2000, the more reasonable way to measure wealth results in genuine savings declining to negative $2 per person that year.

Obviously, GDP is not calculated making deductions for the depreciation of fabricated assets or for the depletion and degradation of natural resources. Thus a country can have very high growth rates calculated using GDP indicators, whilst embarking on a short-term and unsustainable exploitation of its finite resources. Consequently, the idea of GS traces its roots back to the work of economists such as Solow (1974) and Hartwick (1977), whose work sought to model a development path where social welfare did not deteriorate in economies based on the exploitation of non-renewable resources. GS or adjusted net savings thus measures the true rate of savings in an economy, after taking into account investment in human capital, the decline in asset values through the extraction of natural resources and damage caused by pollution. Persistently low or negative GS are indicators that a country's trajectory is unmaintainable, whilst negative adjusted net saving rates in themselves demonstrate that the total wealth of a country is in decline.

Table 3 shows a representation of both GDP growth rates (the indicator used to celebrate 'Africa Rising') and the adjusted net saving rates. The year 2000 is the start date, for comparison with the latest available data (2008). Of interest is the comparison (and contrast) between the two different indicators. Equally, the difference between the 2000 and 2008 figures using the GS statistics shows the sustainability (or otherwise) of African countries' development paths.

Such unsustainability is missed in standard GDP measurements, despite the fact that the 'policy implications of measuring genuine savings are quite direct: persistently negative rates of genuine savings must lead, eventually, to declining wellbeing' (Hamilton and Clemens, 1999: 352). Beyond this depletion of finite resources and a subsequent negative debit on a country's stock, inequality has been re-inscribed during this boom: 'There is evidence that economic disparities in resource-rich countries are rising with economic growth, dampening the potential for poverty reduction' (Africa Progress Panel, 2013: 27). According to one source, three ongoing crises currently exist: Africa is affected via reduced demand and lower prices for their exports, reduced financial flows and falling remittances; climate change remains unchecked; and malnutrition and hunger

Table 3 GDP Growth vs. Adjusted Net Savings

	GDP Growth Rate (%) 2000	Adjusted net savings 2000	GDP Growth Rate (%) 2008	Adjusted net savings 2008
Algeria	2.2	16.02	2.4	21.36
Angola	3.0	−32.75	13.8	−42.63
Benin	4.9	2.58	5.0	..
Botswana	5.9	48.79	3.7	37.17
Burkina Faso	1.8	−1.00	5.8	..
Burundi	−0.9	−7.55	5.0	..
Cameroon	4.2	2.93	2.6	..
Cape Verde	7.3	..	6.2	..
CAR	−2.5	1.12	2.0	−4.59
Chad	−0.9	0.58	−0.4	−49.89
Comoros	1.4	4.90	1.0	7.04
Congo, DR	−6.9	−12.51	6.2	−2.49
Congo-B	7.6	−40.75	5.6	−57.11
Djibouti	0.4	−2.52		..
Egypt	5.4	8.50	7.2	2.06
Equ. Guinea	12.5	−7.08	16.8	−38.45
Eritrea	−3.1	−2.22	−9.8	..
Ethiopia	6.1	1.29	10.8	8.94
Gabon	−1.9	0.13	1.0	3.56
Gambia	5.5	6.33	5.7	3.87
Ghana	3.7	5.96	8.4	−6.55
Guinea	2.5	3.15	4.9	−11.31
Guinea-Bissau	3.6	−10.45	10.5	16.63
Ivory Coast	−3.7	5.37	2.3	1.68
Kenya	0.6	6.96	1.5	10.21
Lesotho	5.1	15.25	5.7	19.41
Liberia	25.7	..	10.5	..
Libya	3.7	..	3.8	..
Madagascar	4.8	1.67	7.1	6.99

	GDP Growth Rate (%) 2000	Adjusted net savings 2000	GDP Growth Rate (%) 2008	Adjusted net savings 2008
Malawi	1.6	4.41	8.3	25.06
Mali	3.2	9.21	5.0	..
Mauritania	−0.4	−15.12	3.5	..
Mauritius	9.0	18.13	5.5	8.48
Morocco	1.6	18.83	5.6	19.83
Mozambique	1.1	2.55	6.8	−4.58
Namibia	3.5	20.81	3.4	9.87
Niger	−1.4	−3.44	9.6	..
Nigeria	5.4	..	6.0	..
Rwanda	8.3	5.06	11.2	20.08
São Tomé		..	9.1	..
Senegal	3.2	..	3.7	12.21
Seychelles	4.2	..	−1.9	..
Sierra Leone	6.7	−11.26	5.3	−0.96
Somalia		..		..
South Africa	4.2	4.75	3.6	−3.45
Sudan	8.4	−10.32	3.0	−13.13
Swaziland	1.8	7.40	2.4	7.14
Tanzania	4.9	12.58	7.4	..
Togo	−0.8	−8.94	2.2	..
Tunisia	4.7	16.94	4.6	6.98
Uganda	3.1	1.89	8.7	3.27
Zambia	3.5	−9.73	6.0	−0.71
Zimbabwe	−3.1	5.32	−17.7	..

(Source: World Bank)

are on the rise, propelled by the recent inflation in global food prices (Addison et al., 2011). This would remain unknown if the 'Africa Rising' narrative was taken at face value and the celebration of the arrival of the BRICS in Africa was uncritically digested.

In addition, not only has this model of growth promotion so far been unsuccessful in generating sustainable developmental outcomes, it has made things worse regarding issues such as equality, the environment and Africa's dependent status within the global political economy. As Jerven (2010b: 146) notes, '[t]he most recent period of economic growth did not entail the large improvements in human development that were the case from 1950–1975 ... Furthermore, the latest period of economic growth has not been associated with much industrial growth.' Even the Africa Progress Panel, which is invariably Pollyanna-ish in its assessment of Africa, admits that:

> After a decade of buoyant growth, almost half of Africans still live on less than $1.25 a day. Wealth disparities are increasingly visible. The current pattern of trickle-down growth is leaving too many people in poverty, too many children hungry and too many young people without jobs. Governments are failing to convert the rising tide of wealth into opportunities for their most marginalised citizens. Unequal access to health, education, water and sanitation is reinforcing wider inequalities. Smallholder agriculture has not been part of the growth surge, leaving rural populations trapped in poverty and vulnerability. (Africa Progress Panel, 2012: 8)

This has gone hand in hand with no serious structural change in the continent's economies, as has been pointed out; indeed, the two factors are linked. The share of Africa in global manufacturing value added (MVA) actually *fell* from 1.2 per cent in 2000 to 1.1 per cent in 2008 whilst there has been no substantial change in the region's share of global manufacturing exports in recent years, i.e. the years when the upsurge in Africa has been most pronounced. In 2000, manufacturing made up 12.8 per cent of GDP in Africa, but by 2008 it accounted for only 10.5 per cent. Looking at Table 4, it is apparent that with the exception of Eastern Africa, manufacturing is in decline across the continent. Note that the share of mining and utilities has hugely increased over the last few decades and that within the manufacturing sector, resource-based manufacturing accounted for about 49 per cent of total MVA in Africa.

This fact of manufacturing underdevelopment in Africa is also apparent at the global level. Manufacturing exports represent a low percentage of total African exports and, more importantly, the share has declined over the years. While the share of manufactures in Africa's exports was 43 per cent in 2000, it fell to 39 per cent in 2008. Problematically, what manufacturing that does take place is generally resource-based. However, it is in low technology manufacturing where labour-intensive, job creating opportunities are created. Table 5 reveals that this sector of manufac-

Table 4 Manufacturing and Mining as Share of Africa's GDP, 1970–2008

	% share of GDP	1970	1980	1990	2000	2005	2008
Africa	Manufacturing	6.3	11.9	15.3	12.8	11.6	10.5
	Mining	4.8	19.3	15.2	18.4	23.0	25.8
Eastern Africa	Manufacturing	1.7	4.9	13.4	10.4	10.3	9.7
	Mining	0.8	1.5	3.3	3.1	3.6	3.7
Middle Africa	Manufacturing	10.3	11.8	11.2	8.2	7.3	6.4
	Mining	19.1	21.2	18.9	39.3	47.9	50.5
Northern Africa	Manufacturing	13.6	9.7	13.4	12.8	11.3	10.7
	Mining	15.7	33.0	17.2	19.5	28.2	29.8
Southern Africa	Manufacturing	22.0	20.9	22.9	18.4	17.9	18.2
	Mining	12.0	24.0	14.3	11.7	11.2	13.1
Western Africa	Manufacturing	13.3	16.8	13.1	7.8	6.0	5.0
	Mining	7.7	21.3	18.8	29.3	27.7	29.6

(Source: UNCTAD, 2011: 15)

turing is relatively small (to very small), as the key contributor to the MVA in Africa.

In fact, 'fewer than 10% of African workers are currently in manufacturing of any kind and only about 1% in modern companies with advanced technology' (*Africa Confidential*, 2014: 1).

In short, as has been repeatedly indicated, the much-vaunted recent economic growth in Africa is based on trade in resources, not production. Such growth is problematic given that 'production is the key to accumulation since the profits of all capital, even merchant capital that operates exclusively in the sphere of circulation, originate in the sphere of production' (Kay, 1975: 71). The economic advantages of current trade accrue to the accumulation centres outside of Africa. The result is that the role of Africa is being reified as a source of cheap raw materials, exported to feed external economies and/or processed up the value chain into finished products. 'Since the surpluses that could lead to industrial investments are not forthcoming, the peripheral nations seem condemned to be producers of raw materials in perpetuity. The economic landscape then is weak industrial development, chronic balance of payment problems all under the management of a neocolonial comprador class' (Amaizo, 2012: 127). This is a chronic problem for Africa, given that building up capabilities in manufacturing and improving the productivity of agriculture are the levers to wealth creation, with suitable pro-poor policies aimed at equitable and sustainable development at the heart of long-term poverty reduction.

Of course, not all BRICS involvement in Africa revolves around commodities; that would be a crude caricature. But Table 6 shows that commodities certainly dominate BRICS-Africa trade.

Table 5 Manufacturing as Contributor to the MVA in Africa

Country	Resource-based manufacturing share of MVA (2009)	Low technology manufacturing share of MVA (2009)	Medium/ high technology manufacturing share of MVA (2009)
Algeria	67	20	13
Angola	46	41	12
Cameroon	75	24	2
CAR	76	16	8
Congo-B.	81	6	13
Egypt	37	16	48
Ethiopia	67	20	13
Gabon	76	16	8
Ghana	86	7	6
Ivory Coast	70	13	17
Kenya	68	19	13
Lesotho	36	55	9
Libya	81	8	11
Madagascar	79	13	7
Malawi	38	48	14
Mali	28	61	11
Mauritius	35	48	16
Morocco	45	30	25
Nigeria	26	53	21
Senegal	80	6	14
South Africa	52	17	31
Sudan	84	9	7
Tanzania	68	6	26
Tunisia	51	26	22
Uganda	58	29	13
Zambia	74	11	15
Zimbabwe	44	44	12

(Source: UNCTAD, 2011: 27–8)

Table 6 Key Product Composition of BRICS Imports from Africa (% share, 2010)

	Brazil	*Russia*	*India*	*China*	*South Africa*
Mineral fuels, oil, etc.	85		71	65	76
Ores, slag, ash		3	2	14	
Precious stones, metals	1		13	4	6
Copper				6	3
Fertilisers	5		1		
Edible fruit and nuts		29	2		
Cocoa		16			
Tobacco		9			
Inorganic chemicals	1	8	4	1	

(Source: Fundira, 2012b: 11, 18, 24, 31, 38)

Such a situation *further* reinforces and helps underpin the overall structure of Africa's insertion into the global economy. The BRICS certainly did not create this milieu, but their current trade profile with the continent promotes the reification of existing and ongoing developments. Here it is fruitful to note Shaw's (1985: 63) separation of structural and superficial features of Africa's economies. The superficial features can be identified in the GDP figures, industry, prices, debt levels and exchange, etc. 'The *structural* features are, however, less apparent and more profound: Africa's changing place in the effective international division of labour'. There is no evidence thus far to suggest that BRICS–Africa engagement will result in any qualitative change in Africa's structural profile.

Some writers have focused on textile investment from the BRICS (specifically China and India) as being areas of hope; it appears that this possibility is now over. To avoid quotas imposed on Asian producers under the WTO Multifibre Arrangement (MFA) (1974–2004) and to exploit incentives created by the United States' African Growth and Opportunities Act (AGOA), it is true that companies from Asia established factories across Africa. However, since the end of the MFA and the conclusion of American quotas on Chinese goods in 2008, the investment flows have effectively tapered off. Such investment that came from Asia was opportunistic, with companies setting up production in Africa, engaging in minimal assembly tasks and then exporting their products to the American market.

Whilst AGOA temporarily boosted trade in manufactures between the USA and Africa, the upsurge ended soon after the MFA ended. The goals ostensibly inscribed in AGOA – to generate long-term manufacturing growth and spill-over effects for Africa – failed to appear. What links with the local economy that did take place were transitory. In fact, even though cotton can be sourced in Africa, many of the Asian investors derived the bulk of their inputs from back home. What linkages with the local that were established consisted in low skills areas such as in assembly, packaging and shipping. Of course, such minimal investment made it easier for the factory owners to quickly shut up shop once the temporary advantages opened up by AGOA and the MFA finished. This is precisely what occurred (see Rotunno et al., 2012).

Problematically, 'Sub-Saharan Africa's international competitiveness in individual industries, especially in manufacturing and agro-processing, has seen little improvement over the last two decades. Its exports remained undiversified and their growth was overwhelmingly accounted for by natural resources. Sub-Saharan Africa's world market share in processing industries is not only low but has remained virtually unchanged' (World Economic Forum et al., 2011: 15). Indeed, as has been noted, there is evidence of *deindustrialisation*. Sub-Saharan Africa's overall share of light manufacturing world exports declined from 1.2 per cent in 1980, to less than 0.9 per cent in 2008. Meanwhile, heavy manufacturing saw an infinitesimal increase of 0.1 per cent between 1995–97 and 2008, during which it produced 0.3 per cent of world exports. Agribusiness saw a similarly tiny development, from 1.5 to 1.7 per cent between 1995–97 and 2006–08 (ibid.: 15, 19). In other words, all areas where value might be added and production relatively enhanced are either stagnant or in decline. Instead, mining represented 73 per cent of Africa's export growth between 1995 and 2008 (ibid.: 4):

> Africa's current pattern of growth is that it has been accompanied by de-industrialisation as evidenced by the fact that the share of manufacturing in Africa's gross domestic product (GDP) fell from 15 per cent in 1990 to 10 per cent in 2008. The most significant decline was observed in Western Africa, where it fell from 13 per cent to 5 per cent over the same period. Nevertheless, there has also been substantial de-industrialisation in the other sub-regions of Africa. For example, in Eastern Africa the share of manufacturing in output fell from 13 per cent in 1990 to about 10 per cent in 2008 and in Central Africa it fell from 11 to 6 per cent over the same period. Furthermore, in Northern Africa it fell from about 13 to 11 per cent and in Southern Africa it fell from 23 to 18 per cent. The declining share of manufacturing in Africa's output is of concern because historically manufacturing has been the main engine of high, rapid and sustained economic growth (UNCTAD and the United Nations Industrial Development Organisation … The declining share of manufacturing in Africa's output is of concern because historically manufacturing has been the main engine of high, rapid and sustained economic growth. (UNCTAD, 2012b: 2–3)

Notably, 'Africa – the region most dependent on primary commodity exports' has become even more commodity-dependent since the upsurge in interest in the continent by the emerging powers. The share of primary commodity exports was 72 per cent in 1995 but had risen to 81 per cent by 2009' (UNDP, 2011: 60). This has historical antecedents and was a feature of the recent upsurge in African growth on the back of the global commodities boom of 2003–2007, bouncing back in 2009. Indeed:

> the twenty-first century global growth pattern structurally resembles the post-war era when industrialising countries (rather than private consumption) drove world demand, with high prices for commodities; except now the industrialisers are in Asia ... the terms of trade noted by structuralist and dependency economists from Prebisch to Emanuel (rising prices for manufactured goods, declining prices for raw materials) produced growing unequal exchange; but this time with China as the world's leading factory economy. (Nederveen Pieterse, 2012: 4)

This intensification of commodity dependence can be seen quite clearly when comparing data from Africa between 2000 and 2012. What is apparent, as seen in Table 7, is that there has been deindustrialisation *alongside* the entrenchment of dependency on primary products.

Table 7 Commodity Composition of Africa's Total Exports (by percentage, 2000–2012)

Commodity	Years	North Africa	Sub-Saharan Africa
Food, live animals, beverages and tobacco	2000	4.5	11.1
	2012	4.1	9
Crude materials (fuels excluded)	2000	2.8	7.9
	2012	2.5	10.3
Mineral fuels, lubricants	2000	68.2	47.9
	2012	72.3	54.2
Chemicals	2000	4.7	3.0
	2012	5.5	2.3
Machinery and transport equipment	2000	3.5	5.6
	2012	5.4	5.8
Other manufactured goods	2000	16.0	18.9
	2012	9.4	12.3

(Source: UNSD, 2013)

Uncomfortably, the 'basis of recurring growth in African has always been strong external demand. Growth has not been triumphant and the end of growth periods has ended with a combination of predatory rent-seeking and depressed external markets. The recent boom was one-sided, based on external market demand for natural resources' (Jerven, 2010b: 146).

This is a serious issue: 'The risks are that Africa–BRICS engagement could lock African countries into specialising in primary commodities, crimping the strong productivity gains needed to sustain high growth and sharpening socio-economic inequalities' (UNECA, 2013a: 3).

Without serious and credible policies, the diversification of dependency towards the BRICS and other emerging powers may lead to negative outcomes for Africa, with history repeating itself. Certainly, 'African economies are as dependent on external forces as ever', whilst the 'dependency of African economies on export volumes and prices makes their development path one of recurring growth and recession' (Jerven, 2010b: 147). It is thus imperative that 'mineral-abundant countries should be aware of the medium term cycles in commodity prices, and develop policies to take advantage of the expansionary phases and take precautionary action against the contraction phases … [Furthermore] the stepwise deterioration in real non-oil commodity prices with each super-cycle mean being lower than the previous one underlines the importance of diversifying toward the production of manufactured goods and services' (Erten and Ocampo, 2013: 28).

'Economic development usually refers to sustainable economic growth accompanied by significant structural change in production patterns and generalised improvement in living standards' (Whitfield, 2012: 241). Relationships based on extraction have not historically worked as a catalyst for this outcome. This is perhaps why the governor of the Nigerian Central Bank, Sanusi Lamido Sanusi, asserted at the World Economic Forum in Davos in January 2013 that Nigeria should not content itself with only being the producer of only raw materials for China. 'How can we move up the value chain?' he asked. 'China still uses raw materials from Africa, and Africa still buys Chinese manufactured products … We have to get China to produce products on African soil. We have to take advantage of the Chinese market' (quoted in *Financial Times*, 29 January 2013). Sanusi noted that unless Nigeria and other African countries start manufacturing products themselves, it would be stuck with 5 to 6 per cent growth at best, a growth rate that would never allow Africa to develop.

Also present in Davos was Yi Gang, deputy governor of the People's Bank of China. Indicating that China had no policy in this regard, Yi merely asserted that 'as labour cost increases, some manufacturers will move to Africa and elsewhere. And we would love to see more manufacturing in Africa' (ibid.). This hardly constitutes an active policy of promoting African diversification. Some analysts already state that China's engagement with Africa will not result in any radically different outcome from previous actors' activities on the continent, as Beijing does not encourage diversification or value-added industrialisation, or even the redistribution of economic rents (Mohan and Power, 2009: 28). It would be somewhat unfair to pick out China in this regard – their (non-)position on moving Africa up the value chain characterises the rest of the BRICS.

Furthermore, as the African Development Bank's *African Economic*

Outlook 2012 demonstrated, the high growth figures for Africa have not translated in any way into employment and a key characteristic of the continent's growth trajectory has been jobless growth.

> The current pattern of Africa's economic growth is particularly worrisome given the fact that the region has a young and growing population and will, according to the United Nations Population Division, account for about 29 per cent of the world's population aged 15–24 by 2050. Furthermore, population projections indicate that the working age population in Africa is growing by 15.3 million people per annum, and this number is expected to increase over the coming decades. While having a young and growing population presents opportunities in terms of having an abundant labour supply with much creative potential, it also means that African countries will need to engage in growth paths that generate jobs on a large scale to absorb the additional labour. In particular, they will need to move away from jobless growth strategies and towards inclusive growth paths that are labour-intensive and create learning opportunities for young people. (UNCTAD, 2012b: 3)

The World Bank estimates that around only one quarter of Africa's young will find salaried jobs over the next ten years (*Africa Confidential*, 2014: 1). The remaining three quarters will be unemployed, underemployed or subsisting on small-scale farming or the informal sector.

The idea of development has commonly been an alternative word for industrialisation, and economic history proves that unless economies are moving up the value chain, they will be stuck in the rut of trading on commodities that simply provide diminishing returns in the medium- to long-term. Unless an economy is engaged in activities that deliver increasing returns over time (as found in manufacturing production), then the economy is not developing – it is just growing. The problem is that neoliberal economists argue that economies must integrate into the global economy using their notional comparative advantages. If these mean focusing on primary commodity extraction, then so be it. In this (entirely erroneous) reading, the simple existence of upward GDP growth and flourishing trade volume (not the quality thereof) are seen as evidence of success. This is on what the discourse about 'Africa Rising' is based upon. But growth and trade in commodities do not equate to development and in fact may simply be the manifestation of an intensification of dependency. Indeed, industrialisation develops countries, extraction exploits them (Bond, 2006). The vast majority of Africa's countries that are said to be on the rise are still locked into primary commodity sectors and evidence very little progress towards engaging in value-added industrial production.

Bhagwati recently argued that economic growth was the guaranteed way – if not the only way – to reduce poverty and promote development: 'growth [will] pull the poor into gainful employment, thereby helping to lift them out of poverty ... and that higher incomes [will] enable them to increase their personal spending on education and health' (Bhagwati, 2011).

This orthodox fetishisation of growth and the neglect to link this to industrialisation means that the sort of far-fetched comparisons between 'Africa Rising' and the experience of the East Asian Tigers is wholly specious. The World Bank (2011: 4), for example, claimed that 'Africa could be on the brink of an economic take-off, much like China was 30 years ago'. Yet this sort of approach 'centres on economic growth without asking whether growth necessarily translates into development' (Shivji, 2009: 14).

Whilst not denying that there have been some improvements in Africa, as mentioned above, the majority of African economies are either stagnating or de-industrialising:

> The share of MVA [manufacturing value added] in Africa's GDP fell from 12.8 per cent in 2000 to 10.5 per cent in 2008, while in developing Asia it rose from 22 per cent to 35 per cent over the same period. There has also been a decline in the importance of manufacturing in Africa's exports, with the share of manufactures in Africa's total exports having fallen from 43 per cent in 2000 to 39 per cent in 2008. In terms of manufacturing growth, while most have stagnated, 23 African countries had negative MVA per capita growth during the period 1990–2010, and only five countries achieved an MVA per capita growth above 4 per cent. (Rowden, 2013)

Growth in absolute terms *vis-à-vis* African manufacturing has been concentrated in but a select few countries: South Africa, Egypt, Tunisia, Morocco, Mauritius and Algeria (seven of the top ten African manufacturing companies are South Africa, the other three Egyptian). Even here, Africa remains at the lower end of production processes – the most sophisticated product South Africa exports in any sizeable amount to China is steel (African Development Bank, 2012).

Commodities did not drive East Asian development, industrial policies did (along with massive transfers of capital from the United States and Japan in a crusade against the threat of 'communism'). Rajadhyaksha (2012) notes that 'the Asian experience tells us that no country can banish mass poverty unless it creates millions of new jobs a year in manufacturing and services'. Resource-based exports can only promote development *if* there are strong and credible domestic policies to promote industrialisation *alongside* commodity extraction. Development is, after all, 'fundamentally about structural change' (Rodrik, 2007) and it is at the heart of any true independence project. Commodity-dependent countries are exposed to repeated price shocks and their domestic policies are de-linked from growth rates: growth may just stem from the 'good luck' of possessing resources and not from 'good policies' (Easterly et al., 1993).

Obviously, countries moving up the value chain through industrialisation and diversification do not simply abandon their natural resource assets. What matters for developmental realisation is *not* whether a country continues to export commodities but rather what policy initiatives it introduces, in conjunction with such exports, to promote manufactures. Yet whilst prices for commodities are currently high, for manufactured goods they are low (due in large part to the depression of prices due to oversupply by the emerging economies, particularly China). This means that the exporters of commodities and energy can quickly accumulate capital (entrenching dependency), but that nascent manufacturing sectors and net energy importers suffer. True, African consumers benefit with cheap imported products, but this is hardly a sustainable developmental model.

The story of 'Africa Rising', bolstered by demand from the emerging economies (such as the BRICS) is just that, a story. In this discourse, where growth-for-growth's sake is a manifestation of development and progress, the agenda of industrialisation and moving Africa up the global production chain has been abandoned. Instead, reporting and analysis has been hypnotised by the stellar growth rates recorded recently (setting aside, of course, the fact that these are starting from very low bases). It is true that growth in non-minerals sectors have been recorded, driven largely by agricultural sectors, but in most African countries these are mainly subsistence-based with low levels of productivity and basic, if not primitive, technologies. Minimal scaling-up and commercialisation characterises these sectors, with little value added. The service sector in parts of Africa has also grown, particularly in the much-vaunted telecommunications sector, as well as wholesale and retail trade. But these do not provide sufficient wage employment. The telecommunications sector demands specialised skills, often provided by expatriates, whilst the actual wage employment base is tiny.

In order to understand Africa's growth predicament, one needs to understand the economic constraints imposed by the absence of a real manufacturing sector. Currently, Africa's manufacturing sector only represents 12.9 per cent of its GDP (OECD, 2011). Compare that to the strong manufacturing sectors in other emerging economies, where structural change has already occurred and where millions have been lifted out of poverty as a result: manufacturing contributes 20 per cent of GDP in Brazil, 34 per cent in China, 30 per cent in Malaysia, 35 per cent in Thailand and 28 per cent in Indonesia. Notably, 'Between 1995 and 2008, manufacturing growth in developing economies was more than 6 per cent per year, in Africa it was about 3 per cent' (Page, 2011: 1). In fact, since 1980, industry in Africa has declined as a share of both global production and trade (UNIDO, 2009), and today, Africa's industrial sector is in many ways less advanced than in the first decade following independence (ibid.):

> Africa's industrialization has been weak and inconsistent. In 1980–2009, the share of manufacturing value added to GDP increased marginally in North Africa, from 12.6 per cent to 13.6 per cent, but fell from 16.6 per cent to 12.7 per cent in the rest of Africa. Some African countries have managed to develop manufacturing activities on the

back of preferences in third-country markets, but most of these have limited scope and size, and are vulnerable to erosion of trade preferences as trade liberalizes further in destination markets. (UNECA, 2013b: 74)

Sub-Saharan Africa's share of manufacturing in GDP is less than one half of the average for all developing countries and, in contrast with developing countries as a whole, it is declining (Page, 2012). What is clearly missing from Africa's growth story is structural change. There is little evidence that significant changes in structural variables underpinned more rapid growth between 1995 and 2005 (Arbache and Page, 2009). Like the 1995–2005 growth turnaround, the region's post-crisis recovery has been driven primarily by fewer mistakes, commodity prices and the recovery of domestic demand. Without major changes in economic structure Africa remains vulnerable to shocks and to a long-run decline in commodity prices. (Page, 2011: 2). Indeed, how and why Africa can be said to be rising when a majority of its countries export commodities (but have to import almost everything else) is reflective of the neoliberal fixation on global 'integration' and economic growth as an indication of the robustness of a country's economic situation.

Furthermore, it continues to be the case that 47 per cent of the population of Sub-Saharan Africa still lives below the $1.25-a-day poverty line and between 1981 and 2008, the percentage of the continent's poverty rate declined only 4 percentage points. Indeed, 'although Africa's growth exceeded the world average in the 2000s, it did not translate into commensurate poverty reduction at a time when poverty elsewhere fell heavily' (UNECA, 2013b: 9). By contrast, East Asia saw dramatic drops in poverty, from 77 per cent of the population in 1981 to 14 per cent in 2008, with South Asia recording the percentage of its population in poverty decline from 61 per cent to 36 per cent. Data from the 2008–2011 African Economic Research Consortium (AERC) Collaborative Growth–Poverty Nexus project was analysed, using data from African economists in 11 countries: Benin, Burkina Faso, Cameroon, Chad, Ethiopia, Ghana, Guinea, Kenya, Malawi, Nigeria and Senegal. The key findings included that, with the exception of Ghana and Senegal, poverty reduction was modest or fluctuated, with poverty sometimes increasing. Yet among the five countries that provided information on severe poverty Senegal's figures declined by 2.8 per cent between 1995 and 2007, whilst Ghana's were reduced by only 2.1 per cent. Ghana, which is routinely held up as a 'success story', experienced an *increase* in inequality during this period. Whilst some development indicators were positive, almost all were relative and from a very low base (McKay, 2013). Yet the 'ruling ideological design of development is that the corporations will deliver us from poverty by raising the rate of economic growth. The IMF, the World Bank, and the Asian Development Bank propagate tirelessly this ideology in various guises' (Bhaduri, 2010: 44).

7
Conclusion Diversifying Dependency?

Emerging countries' trade structures with Africa do not exhibit any exceptionalism and are comparable to the relationships established by the capitalist core since the colonial period, following the model of the 'small colonial open economy' (Hopkins, 1973). The trade between the BRICS and Africa is clearly dominated by the exportation of commodities. 'For all the three emerging economies, Africa is a major supplier of natural resources. Mineral fuels account for 70% of Africa's exports to China, 80% of exports to India and 85% of exports to Brazil. This is comparable to African exports of mineral fuels to the US that account for over 83% of the total export basket' (WTO, 2013: 18). It is not *impossible* that accrued revenues may help implement constructive change, perhaps in the direction of the welfare reforms pursued by some Middle Eastern oil producers. It is just unlikely.

Problematically, developments elsewhere may well push Africa further down the energy dependency road as, paradoxically, exports to the West (particularly the United States) decline. In the past few years, a radical change in the forecasts for growth in American oil production and oil reserves has taken place. This has sprung from light tight oil (LTO), which includes both crude oil and condensate in all tight formations, including shale basins (LTO is frequently referred to as 'shale oil'). Currently, the global oil industry is considering LTO's potential and its likely implications for oil supply and demand. Oil companies have started to develop unconventional hydrocarbons, successfully bringing to the market several large and under-exploited oil and natural gas liquid resources. American shale/tight oil, Canadian tar sands, Venezuela's extra-heavy oil, and Brazil's presalt oil are the main examples. This has meant that the fear of a decline in oil supplies (the 'peak oil' thesis), which would then prompt concerns about energy shortages and propel oil prices upwards, possibly leading to 'oil wars' has been quietly shelved. There is now little doubt that unconventional resources through the 'energy revolution' will satisfy global demand. Instead, the debate now revolves around the speed and price at which these resources can be extracted.

The U.S. Energy Department forecasts U.S. production of crude and other liquid hydrocarbons will average around 11.4 million barrels per day (bpd) by 2014, which would place the United States just below Saudi Arabia's expected output for 2013 of 11.6 million bpd. Several forecasts put American production at 13–15 million bpd by 2020, with the International Energy Agency (2012b), suggesting that the United States may supplant Saudi Arabia as the world's largest producer. It should be said at this juncture that Saudi oil is cheaper to tap than tight oil and LTO needs a price above $70 per barrel to be profitable (break-even prices of most tight oil are in the range of $40– $60 per barrel). However, the recent turnaround in the United States' crude oil production is extraordinary and will have major implications for Africa (and the world). As the United States meets more of its current and future demand for oil from indigenous supplies, imports from traditional suppliers will inevitably fall. This has already started to happen in dramatic fashion, as shown in Table 8.

Table 8 U.S. Imports of Total Crude Oil and Products from Africa, 2010–2012 (in thousands of barrels)

	2010	*2011*	*2012*
Algeria	186,019	130,723	88,487
Angola	143,512	126,259	85,335
Cameroon	19,728	13,921	12,356
Chad	11,312	18,473	11,004
Congo-B	26,276	19,275	11,341
DRC	3,225	3,999	137
Equ. Guinea	21,063	8,500	15,100
Gabon	17,022	12,557	15,886
Ghana	215	3,832	313
Ivory Coast	17,022	12,557	15,886
Liberia	–	20	1
Libya	25,595	5,542	22,281
Nigeria	373,297	298,732	161,558

(Source: U.S. Energy Information Administration)

In its Medium-Term Oil Market Report for 2013, the International Energy Agency (2012b) asserted that LTO and other aspects of the energy revolution will acts as a 'supply shock' to the global oil market, that will be 'as transformative to the [energy] market over the next five years as was the rise of Chinese demands in the last 15 years'. Already, exports of Nigerian oil to the US almost halved between 2011 and 2012. In the late 2000s, Nigeria was regularly exporting around one million barrels a day of crude to the US, but by the end of 2012 that number was just 405,000 barrels a day. Nigeria has experienced difficulties in finding alternative destinations for its crude and it has had to cut prices. Indeed, at the start of 2013, weak demand forced Nigeria to sell some cargoes of its oil below the official selling price. This would see Nigeria lose $380,000 on a typical cargo (*Wall Street Journal*, 6 March 2013).

Such a scenario is obviously very serious for Nigeria. Addressing the Nigeria Economist's Group Summit in May 2013, Diezani Alison-Madueke, Minister of Petroleum Resources, gave a rather pessimistic outlook for the future. In her speech, she asserted that:

> US dependence on oil imports is expected to continue declining over the next 10 years reaching a share of about 43% of total oil consumption by 2020 from 67% in 2005 ... Between 2007 and 2011, US shale gas share of total gas supply increased from 8% to 32%; consequently pipeline & LNG import share of total gas supply declined from 16% and 3% in 2007 to 12% & 1% respectively. As a result of shale gas production, it is projected that U.S. will become a net exporter of natural gas in the year 2020. This is already evident in the decline of Nigeria's LNG exports to the US from 12% in 2007 to 1% in 2011 (Alison-Madueke, 2013).

Consequently, '[u]nprecedented growth in USA gas reserves inevitably *eliminates* USA as a destination for Nigerian gas' (ibid., emphasis added). In addition, the growth in gas reserves helps re-establish the United States as a major producer of industries such as petrochemicals, fertiliser etc., in effect slashing the market options for such products from Nigeria.

How this all fits into discussions about the BRICS and 'Africa Rising' is that declining North American imports from African countries will likely create a new alignment in the global oil market. For countries that rely on oil exports for the majority of total annual government revenue and foreign exchange earnings, this is highly problematic. One key way in which such countries may seek to avoid the implications of declining exports to the traditional importers is to shift attention to the emerging economies, specifically Asian buyers (especially China and India). This may not all be smooth however, as African producers that produce light sweet crude may not have large enough market in Asia as several Asian refiners already process heavy crude produced by OPEC members in the Persian Gulf. However, the Asian option seems to be the only one available: the oil minister of Angola, Jose Maria Botelho de Vasconcelos, has in fact argued that '[e]merging markets like India and China have been growing, and they have absorbed a large part of Angolan exports', (quoted in *E&P Magazine*, 22 July 2013). But the 'solutions' to the energy revolution thus far simply imply a further intensification of an over-reliance on primary commodities, with the hope that, through such a diversification of dependency, the effects of new developments in the oil industry may be mitigated: hardly a sustainable or visionary response.

Indeed, rentier strategies rather than developmental strategies tend to be negative – as the history of Africa's petro-states testify. What is a more likely scenario is one that reifies a situation that Julius Nyerere commented on over 30 years ago, when he noted that 'we are all, in relation to the developed world, dependent – not interdependent – nations. Each of our economies has developed as a bi-product and a subsidiary of development in the industrialised North, and is externally oriented. We are not the prime movers of our own destiny' (Nyerere, 1979: 58). A key issue here is that 'the production of primary goods for export creates a demand for other activities, notably transport, construction and services, which is incompatible with balanced development and channels the meagre proceeds from the foreign sale of these commodities into expenditures which do not stimulate the rest of the economy' (Tschannerl, 1976: 14).

Africa needs to rethink its strategies and find ways and means to make them more compatible with the objective of sustainable development. 'To sustain economic growth, Africa will need to enhance productivity and competitiveness through investing in infrastructure, technology, higher education and health; broadening the range of and adding greater value to exports; and making the necessary investments in productive sectors and trade facilitation. All these measures require collaboration among stakeholders under the leadership of the developmental state' (UNECA, 2012b: 66). A redefinition of growth to include structural transformation is needed *á la* Kuznets' definition of a country's economic growth being 'a long-term rise in capacity to supply increasingly diverse economic goods to its population, this growing capacity based on advancing technology and the institutional and ideological adjustments that it demands' (1971). Such a definition puts to shame the crass celebration of Africa's recent growth rates as symbolising some sort of watershed event for the continent.

To end with and to return to the issue of the BRICS and 'Africa Rising', it takes more to be a global power than pure economic resources, however impressive some of the BRICS growth trajectories have been of late. As a bloc to be taken earnestly as some sort of alternative to the North and which may affect Africa's place in the world, the BRICS require a developed, intelligible, vision for the global order. This, and the political will to use their capacities to work at this, are the minimum necessary conditions. But here we run into problems if we are to take seriously some of the more excited claims about the BRICS and the way they are supposedly changing the world. Thus far, the enthusiasm for global leadership – once it is realised that this comes with costs and responsibilities – seems highly constrained. Rhetoric only goes so far, until practical action and practical alternative plans are demanded. There is clearly no current new international economic order on the table. Furthermore, '[b]eyond annual meetings on presidential and ministerial level, BRICS' cooperation is not institutionalised in a formal way. Other multilateral gatherings as well as bilateral negotiations are reflecting existing asymmetries and differences within BRICS and are to some extent undermining the BRICS-concept' (European Parliament, 2012: 9).

Instead, the BRICS states seem content to engage in helping to legitimise the ongoing order, improving it here and there in line with their own interests and requesting *some* more roles in various decision-making functions. These are technical, problem-solving activities and do not question – let alone threaten – the hegemonic order. Given that much analysis places some of the blame for Africa's ongoing condition on this very same world order, the BRICS emerge as disappointing advocates for the continent – or at least those elements that are dissatisfied with the extant situation. Indeed, the notion that the BRICS pose a potential counter-hegemonic force needs to be discounted. In looking at world order, Cox wrote: 'A counter hegemony would consist of a coherent view of an alternative world order, backed by a concentration of power sufficient to maintain a challenge to core countries' (1981: 150–151) It is clear that the BRICS do *not* offer a 'coherent view of an alternative world order', beyond appeals to a stricter adherence to state sovereignty norms.

The BRICS have a massive stake in the contemporary order and so wish to be involved in shaping and stabilising it. Anand (2012: 70) notes: 'the Western states can no longer push ahead their agenda unilaterally. However, one can see that this co-option is a disciplinary move and see the rise of the non-Western powers as a victory of the West ... It is by working within the existing system, by focusing on the market economy, by adopting vehemently Western political ideas of state and sovereignty though not necessarily democracy, that the non-Western powers have become resurgent.' A stable external environment is vital for the emerging economies and the option of being bystanders is no longer possible. In this regard, the BRICS *does* provides a platform for debates regarding the fairness of the global order and issues related to representation in bodies such as the United Nations Security Council, World Bank, International Monetary Fund, etc.

Furthermore, by promoting multilateral solutions to global governance issues, the BRICS can push for closer adherence to UN normative values, particularly around sovereignty. This is an agenda that enjoys the support of African elites, given that sovereignty is routinely defined by them as the right to rule unhindered and which endows them with the agency through which to manage external ties (see Brown, 2013). Yet there is no real overall alternative agenda and there are no broad principles – other than greater representation – that underpin the BRICS. As Otero-Iglesias notes, specifically regarding Brazil, but which could easily be applied to the other BRICS, 'it is very difficult to know what the Brazilian government actually wants other than more voice in global governance' (2012: 5).

Due to this failure to develop any credible vision beyond securing seats at the top table, there is a real danger that the BRICS as an institutionalised expression of select emerging economies will be co-opted by the capitalist core, whilst at the same time the BRICS will be expected to contribute to the costs and burden-sharing of maintaining the extant global order – an order that ultimately disproportionally benefits elites from the capitalist heartlands and which continues to underdevelop Africa. This brings with it a tension within the BRICS set-up. The more it institutionalises whilst accepting the hegemonic order, the greater the chance that it will be co-opted.

Conversely, if the BRICS lack institutionalisation, then their coherency is weakened and they are reduced to a mere talking shop. In other words, if the BRICS simply becomes a forum for big regional integration centres to converse, its value-added is limited. This reality is a profound contradiction that the BRICS members must face and may influence the eventual fate of the grouping along the lines suggested by Martynov (2011: 74):

> [T]he redistribution of votes in the international financial institutions in favour of BRICS, as well as the proposed reform of the Security Council, still comes across as the BRICS countries fighting to achieve their own tactical goals, which have nothing to do with the proclaimed long-term strategy. Once those goals have been achieved, BRICS could enter a period of stagnation and slow decline, having outlived its usefulness or it could rapidly disintegrate, unable to cope with growing trade and economic rivalry between its member states. The short-term nature of the goals pursued by the BRICS members is quite obvious. It is equally obvious that the strategic aspirations of the BRICS organisation must be much more substantial and long-term than the tactical goals of its individual members.

Here of course the reality of many Africas re-emerges, just as does the issue of the 'Global South'. What is the Global South today? What *are* its substantial and long-term goals? Related to this, which Africa are we talking about when discussing any given position? This is indeed a problem for any notion that the BRICS speaks for the South and for any analysis that the BRICS may or may not help Africa. The short answer is: it depends on both the structural position of each African economy in the global system and the needs and interest of the population versus the interests of dominant elites. As has been noted, 'using the positive image of South–South cooperation to assuage international (development) critics, [BRICS engagement] disproportionately benefits African elites' (Jacobs, 2012: 77). Indeed, increased demand for Africa's primary resources 'has been based upon a reinforcement of alliances between international capital and political elites in resource rich territories, entrenching patterns of patronage, corruption and informalised economy' (Southall and Comninos, 2009: 380).

Yet as has also been noted, the current pattern of growth in Africa, spurred on in a key way by the BRICS, is neither inclusive nor sustainable:

> There are various reasons for this. Firstly, African countries are heavily dependent on natural resources as drivers of economic growth. But most of these resources – fossil fuels, metallic and non-metallic minerals – are non-renewable and are being depleted at a very rapid rate with negative consequences for future growth and sustainability. The dependence on resource-based growth is also of concern to African policymakers because commodity prices are highly volatile and subject to the caprices of global demand. Such price instability has negative consequences for investment and makes macroeconomic planning challenging. (UNCTAD, 2012b: 2)

In addition, 'higher resource rents are conducive to more corruption' (Arezki and Gylfason, 2013: 3) which will likely further stimulate numerous neopatrimonial regimes across Africa.

Problematically, the upsurge in interest in Africa and the concomitant diversification of its political relationships may make unity more and more difficult. Constructing a pan-African agenda is already extremely difficult and continental responses (rather than bilateral) are likely to become more and more difficult to sustain as the diversity of Africa's political and economic relations intensifies. This is problematic given that much of the 'new' interest in Africa is hinged upon economic activities that threaten to deepen the continent's dependent position in the global economy:

> Africa's terms of (mal)integration in the global political economy have not been fundamentally restructured with the rise of China and other 'emerging economies', or their increasing footprint within Africa. Overwhelmingly, Africa continues to be incorporated within the global economy and international division of labour on a subordinate neocolonial basis, coerced for the most part into primary commodity production ... As such, the BRICs' burgeoning [economic role] in Africa reproduces, and arguably intensifies, Africa's inveterate and deleterious terms of (mal)integration within the global political economy. (Ayers, 2013: 23)

Furthermore, a by-product of this upsurge in interest in Africa is the deepening of uneven development across the continent. Given that the BRICS' interest in maintaining the liberal order appears central to their efforts, it appears that externally-oriented African factions are the most likely to share some basic agreement with the BRICS. Obviously, the strength of each faction in each African country depends on the balance of forces within each state-society complex, but overall it does have to be said that apart from a few countries, this faction is rarely dominant in Africa, other than as a manifestation of compradorism (see Amin, 2011a). These elites benefit handsomely from rents paid to them by actors wishing to access resources, but do little else (Shivji, 2009), hardly an element with which progressive forces can identify.

At the same time, the West ostensibly emphasises social development such as education and health, whilst the BRICS emphasise infrastructure development. The latter is supported by African elites over and above the Western agenda as it does not threaten to upset the regimes that underpin the African state. This is also problematic as the dominant political culture in Africa remains an important Achilles' heel for the continent's advancement. Communal and narrow elite interests trump those of the civic public realm. Again, hardly progressive.

'The BRICS picture is now clear. It is a rapidly institutionalising political framework that has not yet reached the status of a fully-fledged international organisation. Even minimal permanent structures, such as an international secretariat, are still missing' (Tudoroiu, 2012: 36). Indeed, the 'claim that the joint actions of the five countries already concern a broader, political domain cannot be supported with solid arguments. Presently there are no signs of such generalised cooperation. Furthermore ... diverging interests will most likely prevent it in the future' (ibid.: 38). Currently, 'few observers believe that well-choreographed encounters, handpicked initiatives or lofty plans mean that diverse and potentially antagonistic states are either willing or able to translate their combined economic prowess into collective geopolitical clout' (Brütsch and Papa, 2012: 1). If this is the case, where does that leave those African leaders who seem to have identified in BRICS an alternative bloc to counter Western hegemony?

In addition, the 'BRICS countries are not yet able to assume the role of economic drivers for the world's economy. In 2011, overall economic dynamism slowed in all BRICS countries except Russia' (Erber and Schrooten, 2012: 16–17). In this regard, it is vital to acknowledge 'challenges [to] the counter-position that the rise of China and other emerging powers is beneficial to 'developing' countries and will overcome the contradictions and dysfunctions of the contemporary US-led capitalist world order' (Ayers, 2013: 10). Besides, questions as to the long-term ever-upward trajectory of the BRICS have been tentatively asked. Bardhan, for one, argues that both China and India's long-term fragility makes them giants with 'feet of clay' (Bardhan, 2010). More broadly, according to Sharma (2012: 2–3), context needs to be understood when looking at the BRICS:

> The unusual circumstances of the last decade made it look easy: coming off the crisis-ridden 1990s and fuelled by a global flood of easy money, the emerging markets took off in a mass upward swing that made virtually every economy a winner. By 2007, when only three countries in the world suffered negative growth, recessions had all but

disappeared from the international scene. But now, there is a lot less foreign money flowing into emerging markets. The global economy is returning to its normal state of churn, with many laggards and just a few winners rising in unexpected places.

In other words, the BRICS simply reflected the continuing law of uneven development, which has been seen before:

[U]nder capitalism the development of different undertakings, trusts, branches of industry, or countries cannot be *even*. Half a century ago, Germany was a miserable, insignificant country, as far as its capitalist strength was concerned, compared with the strength of England at the time. Japan was similarly insignificant compared to Russia. Is it 'conceivable' that in ten or twenty years' time the relative strength of the imperialist powers will have remained *un*changed? Absolutely inconceivable. (Lenin, 1917/1966: 119)

In Lenin's comparisons, replace Germany with Brazil, Japan with India, etc.

Returning to Africa, imagining that resistance to neoliberalism might be located in the elites of the continent is, to put it mildly, naïve. They are, for the most part, compradors sitting at the apex of dysfunctional neopatrimonial regimes. Here, the question of African agency comes to the fore and will be the deciding factor, as Ramos and Sunkel (1993: 8–9) put it:

It is not demand and markets that are critical. The heart of development lies in the supply side: quality, flexibility, the efficient combination and utilisation of productive resources, the adoption of technological developments, an innovative spirit, creativity, the capacity for organisation and social discipline, private and public austerity, an emphasis on savings, and the development of skills to compete internationally. In short, independent efforts undertaken from within to achieve self-sustained development.

In their analysis of Sino–African relations specifically, Ajakaiye and Kaplinsky warn:

A reincarnation of dependency theory, in which Africa was seen as a quivering victim of external forces, must be abandoned, both in order to understand better what is happening and why it is happening, and in helping Africa to make the best of the opportunities opened up by the rapid emergence of the Asian Driver economies and the consequent restructuring of the global order in the twenty-first Century. (2009: 482)

This is a crude distortion of analyses that recognise the dependent status of African post-colonial economies. Except for the most vulgarised reductions, few serious studies posit Africa as 'a quivering victim of external forces'. Rather, African agency is explicitly recognised, albeit this is conditioned by the class structure of post-colonial states and may express itself through the development of a lumpenbourgeoisie (Arrighi, 1970: 242). This is always dependent on context: 'the room for manoeuvre available to African actors is dependent on rather particular configurations of power and interests internationally' (Brown, 2012: 1903). Detailed analysis is required of each state–society complex within Africa and the opportunities and constraints that these engender when encountering external impulses. Through this, an avoidance of a 'voluntarist emphasis on agency alone', and 'structural pessimism' can be arrived at (ibid.). The outcome(s) 'will depend on on-going struggles and those to come: social struggles (local dominated classes against dominating classes) in all their political dimensions, international conflicts between the leading blocs in command positions of the states and nations. There are no evident prognoses and different ones are possible' (Amin, 2011b: 166–67). Given that capitalism is a global system, strategic manoeuvring necessarily must be both national and international.

A major issue with this regard is that in most African countries there is a real lack of any serious ideological debate about the type of social system that will engender development and ensure broad improvements in the standard of living of the people. Intellectuals who might critically contribute to this debate are generally marginalised, whilst the popular sphere is dominated by opportunists – many sourcing their funding from the West – who promote the discourse that there is no alternative to neoliberal reform. In this milieu there is minimal critique or profound economic analyses of capitalism: it is assumed as a given. Intellectual demobilisation has gone hand in hand with the pauperisation of African academia. Working class figures, intellectuals and/or political leaders who may provide a trenchant analysis of the situation beyond mere problem-solving are few and far between and where they exist are hopelessly overworked.

Politics in most of Africa lacks a class basis and political parties are led by individuals either at the head of neopatrimonial regimes or by actors who wish to replace them with themselves. Personalities and identity politics rule, rather than concrete alternative policies. If and when there is any discussion of a future dispensation, these are expressed through populist rhetoric: 'end corruption', 'promote development'. These are of course admirable notions in and of themselves, but unless situated within a wider structural context are mere abstractions. Where the political class recognises that the neoliberal model is inappropriate for sustainable development, the material rewards granted through collaboration with Western donors and the international financial institutions dampens any practical efforts to address the problem. Besides, within the logic of neopatrimonialism, issues of social welfare, broad upliftment in incomes and a reduction of inequalities do not appear high on the short-termist agenda of many African regimes. The reproduction of such systems is the end result. This is why assertions by the Africa Progress Panel that '[f]ar from being hostage to a non-curable resource curse, this generation of political leaders has an opportunity to harness resource wealth for a transformation in human development' lacks credibility (2013: 7). This is just wishful thinking, detached from the political economy of Africa. The role of the dismal science in this naivety cannot be overlooked – as the contributors to the bullish *Oxford Companion to the Economics of Africa* demonstrate throughout. Economic theories, when shorn of 'anomalies' such as politics, sociology, history, culture, etc., have the knack of appearing elegant. With the routine presentation of false assumptions as the established orthodoxy in economics, it is no wonder that the 'Africa Rising' trope is most enthusiastically propagated by those with no interest in, nor knowledge of, political economy. This is extremely problematic given that – as is well known by all serious students of Africa – 'A significant number of countries in SSA ... are characterised by nondevelopmental regimes that rely on predation and neopatrimonialism, making it unlikely that those governments will harness the opportunities for structural change that are offered by enhanced fiscal space and revenues. Such political economy is recurrent throughout SSA and ... aggravates the consequences of existing export structures' (Sindzingre, 2013: 45).

A starting point then is firstly, the correct analysis of Africa's political economy and then secondly, an accurate appraisal of exactly what the BRICS are – and what they are not. Regarding the BRICS, they are *not* a bloc (even putatively). Secondly, the potentiality of the BRICS as a site for a project that is anti-neoliberal is currently non-existent. Defending globalisation and the advancement of specific externally-oriented interests and values, whilst ameliorating the excessively negative aspects of this project, is the new message (Bond, 2013). The BRICS 'elites' want only to have a more regulated and balanced neoliberal order. They do not call for the creation of a new world order opposed to the existent' (Otero-Iglesias, 2009: 8). In fact, they are little more than an alliance of the dissatisfied.

With this in mind, African civil society needs to recognise that there is a quite definite contradiction between, on the one hand, supporting global free trade and, on the other, committing oneself to somehow changing the rules of the system to ensure greater equity. Instead, African progressive actors need to demand that external relations be subordinated to the logic of internal development and that national development should not be simply driven by the imperatives of worldwide capitalist expansion (Amin, 1990). Such a stance requires a model of development that is based on enlarging the opportunities for non-commodity production and a rejection of the tyranny of comparative advantage.

Ideally, the rise of 'new' actors in Africa such as the BRICS offer *potential* opportunities for the continent. Increasing competition for Africa's resources thereby reduces transaction costs and possibly improves Africa's capacity to gain access to goods and services for more acceptable prices. Second, the interest of the new actors in African markets potentially may boost the continent's economies. The new infrastructure being laid out by Chinese and other actors may help in this regard. After all, without sufficient infrastructure, African countries will never be able to employ the powers of science, technology and innovation to attain developmental goals.

Augmented receipts from commodities, new market opportunities and new financing mechanisms being made available *may* facilitate greater African agency. But *none* of this is automatic and whilst it varies from country to country, the prognosis thus far is not encouraging. Few state elites in Africa have the capacity (or will) in place to allocate some of the rents from commodity booms towards the goals of long-term development. This is not to say that Africa's future is foreclosed, just that the celebratory rhetoric of 'Africa Rising' needs ditching. A, or *the*, prerequisite for this, control over foreign economic relationships, is still lacking. As noted with regard to Nigeria, but which might equally be extended to all African states:

> [I]ndustrialisation policy of government must be necessitated by national expediency as against the quest to satisfy globalisation. Industrialisation that leans heavily on global dictates is bound to expose Nigerians to danger. This is not to imply that the nation must not align with global realities. The point is that local needs and local content – in terms of thoughts, social capital, manpower and technology – must be central. (Akanle, 2011: 13).

The patterns that have caught the attention and imagination of commentators regarding BRICS investment directed to resource extraction and infrastructure projects, deepened economic exchange between the BRICS and parts of Africa, the growth of trade volumes between the BRICS and Africa, etc., still do not indicate any fundamental break with the long-established patterns of asymmetrical economic relations that Africa has with the rest of the world. In fact, '[e]vidence is mounting that the traditional fault-lines of North–South interaction are being replicated in the burgeoning trade between Southern states' (Nel and Taylor, 2013: 1096). It is apparent that a very large part of the 'Africa Rising' story is the dependent status the continent has *vis-à-vis* external economies. The IMF puts it: 'Threats to the outlook from outside the region include (i) the possibility of several more years of economic stagnation in the euro area and (ii) a sharp drop in investment in major emerging market economies' (IMF, 2013: vii).

In other words, we are not witnessing auto-development, but rather high growth grounded firmly in the external, with all the vagaries and vulnerabilities that this brings. Consequently, this 'growth appears ... to be intrinsically fragile and based on distorted factors rather than on sound economic fundamentals. World trade is sensitive to global economic conditions, and the rebound in world exports after the 2008–2009 crisis may yet be threatened by the weak growth of the euro area' (Sindzingre, 2013: 34). With Africa's economies highly vulnerable to global business cycles, their export structures, invariably dominated by a few commodities, makes Africa extremely susceptible.

During the initial stages of growth, investment opportunities are abundant and capital inflows are arguably impervious to the economies of scale factor. This stage is relatively short-lived however. When these early investment opportunities are exhausted, capital flows start to respond sensitively to the size of markets, economies of scale in production and comparative advantages, all of which are highly dependent upon integrated infrastructure – something which Africa palpably lacks. It is then that the difference between short-term economic performance (however spectacular) and the long-term strategic needs of a sustainable development strategy becomes apparent. The 'Africa Rising' discourse has ignored this and simply latched onto the initial stages of growth as being indicative of a long-term change in Africa's position. Given the structural position of most African states and the asymmetrical relationship(s) that characterise the continent's political and economic external relationships, careful analysis is required. But this is often lacking. Emblematically, Rotberg's contribution to the 'Africa Rising' discourse starts off with the claim that '[a]lmost everywhere in [Africa] there is the exciting bustle of improvement and take-off' (2013: 1), but then later admits that 'Sub-Saharan Africa's economic development prospects almost entirely depend on continued Chinese demand' (ibid.: 151). The profound contradiction between these two statements – of talk of an 'Africa Rising', but then admitting this is wholly dependent on external demand – goes unremarked.

In Africa, 'excessive financial and trade integration into a volatile world economy, non-renewable resource extraction costs, the "ecological debt" (as well as other non-remunerated value transfers) and climate change damage, as well as internal features of economies suffering from "resource curse" and processes of extreme uneven and combined development' stake out the continent's political economy (Bond, 2011: 31). If the involvement of the BRICS (alongside other actors) is to intensify such structural features, celebration of the emerging economies as agents of change for Africa needs greater investigation, to say the least, particularly when framed within the 'Africa Rising' narrative.

It hardly needs stating that the diversification of dependency is *not* a coherent development project for the continent, even if the notion that the BRICS somehow facilitate an escape route from the historic relationships with the North is held. In short, the BRICS are potentially problematic vehicles upon which popular African hopes can be pinned on, unless there are serious and qualitative adjustments by the political class in Africa towards the goal of Africa's structural transformation. An exercise of African agency in this progressive direction is barely a necessary and certainly not a sufficient condition. Africa's resources must be taken control of by Africans and used to lessen inequality and promote sustainable development: 'autonomous and hence continuous development will only occur when the periphery can establish exchange relations ... which do not tie it into a system of dependency likely to perpetuate the underdevelopment created by ... subordination to the dominant institutions of international capitalism' (Brett, 1992: 13). With their rise and incorporation into the global structures of power and governance in accordance with the normative principles of capitalism, the BRICS have joined these 'dominant institutions'; South–South solidarity coming from this direction is likely to be voided of content. The 'Declaration of the Second BRICS Trade Union Forum' in 2013 explicitly recognised this, asserting that what was needed was a 'decisive shift in the current political and economic outlook of BRICS' and that 'effective and full participation of the working class in all institutions of BRICS' was required as only in that way 'will BRICS be different from existing multilateral institutions' (COSATU, 2013). This is unlikely to happen.

Policies must be put in place in Africa that 'meet[s] national needs; international economic relationships must be sufficiently diversified to promote this national economic development and control over economic growth must remain in national hands' (Green and Seidman, 1968: 79). The continent needs to have its eyes wide open in dealing with the BRICS (as with all other external actors) and certainly regard the rhetoric about 'win–win' partnerships as nonsense. After all, '[a]ccumulation of wealth at one pole is ... at the same time, accumulation of misery, agony of toil, slavery, ignorance and mental degradation at the other' (Marx, 1867/1976: 645). As the United Nations Economic Commission for Africa (UNECA) asserts, 'African countries ought to be able to adopt a ... strategy of integrating trade, financing and development considerations in their approach to the BRICS' (UNECA, 2013a: 32). This very much depends on the types of states and social formations that exist in individual countries. In some countries this may lead to optimal policymaking *vis-à-vis* the BRICS. In others, the pessimistic evaluation by UNECA that 'Africa does not appear to have established the necessary capacity to negotiate such outcomes' with the BRICS is probably correct (ibid.). It is surely obvious that an 'increase in trade (North–South or South–South) in and of itself does not lead to development' (Kwa, 2010: 9).

Of course, external conditions are not propitious to true development – the WTO makes sure of that with multiple agreements that criminalise industrial policy instruments used previously by the core to nurture domestic capacities. This is likely to lock in the dominant position of the core capitalist countries at the top of the world hierarchy of wealth, with the BRICS countries expressly hoping to join such elite status. This is but a modern version of List's 'kicking away the ladder' (Wade, 2003). In such circumstances, a 'rise' based on an intensification of resource extraction through diversifying partners, whilst inequality and unemployment increase and deindustrialisation continues apace, demolishes the 'Africa Rising' narrative. For the continent's part, there are no external heroes waiting to rescue the continent, the BRICS included: 'national liberation takes place when, and only when, national productive forces are completely free of all kinds of foreign domination' (Cabral, 1979: 143). That has to be the starting point for any true rise of Africa.

BIBLIOGRAPHY

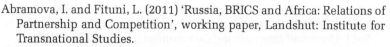

Abramova, I. and Fituni, L. (2011) 'Russia, BRICS and Africa: Relations of Partnership and Competition', working paper, Landshut: Institute for Transnational Studies.

Adamson, P. (2013) 'A Measure of Progress', *New Internationalist*, no. 460, March.

Addison, T., Arndt, C. and Tarp, F. (2011) 'The Triple Crisis and the Global Aid Architecture', *African Development Review*, vol. 23, no. 4.

Afari-Gyan, N. (2010) 'Transforming Africa's Structure and Composition of Trade after the Global Economic Crisis', *Global Trade Alert*, no. 5, May.

Africa Confidential (2013) 'Harsh Truths and High Growth', vol. 54, no. 1.

Africa Confidential (2014) 'Making the Best of the Boom', vol. 55, no. 2.

AfricaFocus Bulletin (2013) 'Africa: Whose "Africa Rising"?' October 18, 2013.

African Development Bank (2011a) 'The Middle of the Pyramid: Dynamics of the Middle Class in Africa', *African Development Bank Market Brief*, 20 April.

African Development Bank (2011b) 'Russia's Economic Engagement with Africa', *Africa Economic Brief*, vol. 2, no. 7.

African Development Bank (2012) *African Economic Outlook 2012*, Paris: OECD Publishing.

African Union (2009) 'African Union Signs Partnership Agreement With the Government of the Federative Republic of Brazil, on Social Development', Press Release No. 25, Sirte, Libya, 3 July.

African Union (2011) Press Release No. 08/Africa–India Forum Summit 'Second Africa–India Forum Summit Opens Tomorrow in Addis Ababa, 23 May', Addis Ababa: African Union.

Africa Progress Panel (2012) *Africa Progress Report 2012: Jobs, Justice and Equity: Seizing Opportunities in Times of Global Change*, Geneva: Africa Progress Panel Foundation.

Africa Progress Panel (2013) *Africa Progress Report 2013: Equity in*

Extractives: Stewarding Africa's Natural Resources for All, Geneva: Africa Progress Panel Foundation.

Aglietta, M. (2008) 'Into a New Growth Regime', *New Left Review*, no. 54.

Agrawal, S. (2007) *Emerging Donors in International Assistance: The India Case*, Ottawa: IDRC-Partnership and Business Development Division.

Ajakaiye, O. and Kaplinsky, R. (2009) 'China in Africa: A Relationship in Transition', *European Journal of Development Research*, vol. 21, no. 4.

Akanle, O. (2011) 'Post-colonial Nation Building, Global Governance, Globalisation and Development in Nigeria and Africa', *Africa Insight*, vol. 41, no. 3.

Ake, C. (1981) *A Political Economy of Africa* Lagos: Longman Nigeria.

Ake, C. (1991) 'How Politics Underdevelops Africa', in Adedeji, A., Teriba, O. and Bugembe, P. (eds) *The Challenge of African Economic Recovery and Development*, London: Frank Cass.

Akyüz, Y. (2012) *The Staggering Rise of the South?* Geneva: South Centre.

Albright, D. (1980) 'Moscow's African Policy of the 1970s' in Albright, D. (ed.) *Africa and International Communism*, London: Macmillan.

Alden, C. and A. Viera (2005) 'The New Diplomacy of the South: South Africa, Brazil, India and Trilateralism', *Third World Quarterly*, vol. 26, no. 7.

Alesina, A. and Dollar, D. (2000), 'Who Gives Foreign Aid to Whom and Why?' *Journal of Economic Growth*, vol. 5, no. 1.

Alison-Madueke, D. (2013) 'The Future of Nigeria's Petroleum Industry', ministerial keynote address by Diezani Alison-Madueke, Honorable Minister, Ministry of Petroleum Resources at the Nigeria Economist's Group Summit, Abuja, Nigeria, May 24.

Amaizo, Y. (2012) 'An Alternative African Developmentalism: A Critique of Zero-sum Games and Palliative Economics', *Africa Development*, vol. 37, no. 4.

Almeida, W. (2009) 'Ethanol Diplomacy: Brazil and U.S. in Search of Renewable Energy', *Globalization, Competitiveness and Governability*, vol. 3, no. 3.

Amin, S. (1974) *Accumulation on a World Scale: A Critique of the Theory of Underdevelopment*, New York, NY: Monthly Review Press.

Amin, S. (1990) 'The Agricultural Revolution and Industrialization' in Amara, H. and Founou-Tchuigoua, B. (eds) *African Agriculture: The Critical Choices*, London: Zed Books.

Amin, S. (2002) 'Africa: Living on the Fringe', *Monthly Review*, vol. 53, no. 10.

Amin, S. (2004) *The Liberal Virus: Permanent War and the Americanization of the World, New York*, NY: Monthly Review Press.

Amin, S. (2005) 'India, a Great Power?', *Monthly Review*, vol. 56, no. 9.

Amin, S. (2010) 'The Battlefields Chosen by Contemporary Imperialism: Conditions for an Effective Response from the South', *Kasarinlan: Philippine Journal of Third World Studies*, vol. 25, nos 1–2: 5–48.

Amin, S. (2011a) *Maldevelopment: Anatomy of a Global Failure*, Oxford: Pambazuka Press.

Amin, S. (2011b) *Ending the Crisis of Capitalism or Ending Capitalism?* Oxford: Pambazuka Press.

Amin, S. (2014) *Samir Amin: Pioneer of the Rise of the South*, Heidelberg: Springer.

Amoako, K. (2011) 'Transforming Africa: Start Now, We Can't Wait', *African Business*, vol. 45, no. 377.

Anand, D. (2012) 'China and India: Postcolonial Informal Empires in the Emerging Global Order', *Rethinking Marxism: A Journal of Economics, Culture and Society*, vol. 24, no. 1.

Ancharaz, V. (2011) 'Trade, Jobs and Growth in Africa: An Empirical Investigation of the Export-led Jobless Growth Hypothesis', paper presented at the ICITE 3rd Regional Conference on 'Trade, Jobs and Inclusive Development', Gammarth, Tunisia, September 22.

Arbache, J. and Page, J. (2009) 'How Fragile is Africa's Recent Growth?' *Journal of African Economies*, vol. 19, no. 1.

Arezki, A. and Gylfason, T. (2013) 'Resource Rents, Democracy, Corruption and Conflict: Evidence from Sub-Saharan Africa', *Journal of African Economies*, vol. 22, no. 4.

Arkhangelskaya, A. (2012) 'Images and Prospects of BRICS in Africa', paper presented at Congreso Ibérico de Estudios Africanos, Madrid, Spain, 14–16 June.

Arkhangelskaya, A. (2013) 'Africa–Russia: New Wave?' *Global Review*, Spring.

Arkhangelskaya, A. and Shubin, V. (2013a) 'Russia's Africa Policy', Occasional Paper no. 157, Braamfontein: South African Institute of International Affairs.

Arkhangelskaya, A. and Shubin, V. (2013b) 'Is Russia Back? Realities of Russian Engagement in Africa', in *Emerging Powers in Africa*, London: LSE Ideas.

Armijo, L. (2007) 'The BRICS Countries as Analytical Category: Mirage or Insight?' *Asian Perspective*, vol. 31, no. 4.

Armijo, L. and Burges, S. (2010) 'Brazil, the Entrepreneurial and Democratic BRIC', *Polity*, vol. 42, no. 1.

Arrighi, G. (1970) 'International Corporations, Labour Aristocracies and Economic Development' in Rhodes, R. (ed.) *Imperialism and Underdevelopment* New York: Monthly Review Press.

Arrighi, G. (2007) *Adam Smith in Beijing: Lineages of the Twenty-first Century*, London: Verso.

Aryeetey, E. and Asmah, E. (2011) 'Africa's New Oil Economies: Managing Expectations' in Brookings Institute *Foresight Africa: The Continent's Greatest Challenges and Opportunities for 2011* New York: Brookings Institute.

Aryeetey, E., Devarajan, S., Kanbur, R. and Kasekende, L. (2012) 'Overview' in Aryeetey, E., Devarajan, S., Kanbur, R. and Kasekende, L.(eds.)

Oxford Companion to the Economics of Africa, Oxford: Oxford University Press.

Atkinson, G. and Hamilton, K. (2003) 'Savings, Growth and the Resource Curse Hypothesis', *World Development*, vol. 31, no. 11.

Austen, R. (1987) *African Economic History*, London: James Currey.

Avendaño, R., Reisen, H. and Santiso, J. (2008) 'The Macro Management of Commodity Booms: Africa and Latin America's Response to Asian Demand', OECD Development Centre, Working Paper no. 270.

Ayers, A. (2013) 'Beyond Myths, Lies and Stereotypes: The Political Economy of a "New Scramble for Africa"', *New Political Economy*, vol. 18, no. 1.

Ban, C. (2012) 'Brazil's Liberal Neo-developmentalism: New Paradigm or Edited Orthodoxy?' *Review of International Political Economy*, vol. 20, no. 2.

Bangwayo-Skeete, P. (2012) 'Do Common Global Economic Factors Matter for Africa's Economic Growth?' *Journal of International Development*, vol. 24, no.3.

Barbosa, A., Narciso, T. and Biancalana, M. (2009) 'Brazil in Africa: Another Emerging Power in the Continent?' *Politikon: South African Journal of Political Studies*, vol. 36, no. 1.

Bardhan, P. (2010) *Awakening Giants, Feet of Clay: Assessing the Economic Rise of China and India*, Princeton, NJ: Princeton University Press.

Bava, U. (2007) 'New Powers for Global Change? India's Role in the Emerging World Order', *Dialogue on Globalization* Briefing Paper no. 4, New Delhi: Friedrich Ebert Stiftung.

Bayart, J-F. (2000) 'Africa in the World: A History of Extraversion', *African Affairs*, vol. 99, no.395.

Becker, U. (ed.) (2014) *The BRICS and Emerging Economies in Comparative Perspective: Political Economy, Liberalisation and Institutional Change*, New York and Abingdon: Routledge.

Ben Hammouda, H., Karingi, S., Njuguna, A. and Sadni Jallab, M. (2006) 'Africa's (Mis)fortunes in Global Trade and the Continent's Diversification Regimes', *Journal of World Investment & Trade*, vol. 7, no. 4.

Beri, R. (2003) 'India's Africa Policy in the Post-Cold War Era: An Assessment', *Strategic Analysis*, vol. 27, no. 2.

Beri, R. (2005) 'Africa's Energy Potential: Prospects for India', *Strategic Analysis*, vol. 29, no. 3.

Bhaduri, A. (2010) *Essays in the Reconstruction of Political Economy* Delhi: Aakar Books.

Bhagwati, J. (2011) 'Does Redistributing Income Reduce Poverty?' *Chazen Global Insights*, Columbia Business School, 3 November.

Bhattacharya, S. (2010) 'Engaging Africa: India's Interests in the African Continent, Past and Present', in Cheru, F. and Obi, C. (eds) *The Rise of China and India in Africa*, London: Zed Books.

Blades, D. (1975) *Non-Monetary (Subsistence) Activities in the National*

Accounts of Developing Countries, Paris: OECD.

Bond, P. (2004) 'The ANC's "Left Turn" and South African Sub-imperialism', *Review of African Political Economy*, vol. 31, no. 102.

Bond, P. (2006) *Looting Africa: The Economics of Exploitation*, London: Zed Books.

Bond, P. (2011) 'Africa's "Recovery": Economic Growth, Governance and Social Protest', *Africa Insight*, vol. 41, no. 3.

Bond, P. (2013) 'Sub-imperialism as Lubricant of Neoliberalism: South African "Deputy Sheriff" Duty within BRICS', *Third World Quarterly*, vol. 34, no. 2.

Bond, P. (2014) '"Africa Rising"? Afro-Optimism and Uncivil Society in an Era of Economic Volatility' in Obadare, E. (ed.) *The Handbook of Civil Society in Africa*, Heidelberg: Springer.

Bondarenko, D. (2012) 'The Image of Russia in Africa: The Soviet Legacy's Role', paper presented at 8th Iberian Conference on African Studies, Madrid, Spain, June 14–16.

Bonnett, D. (2006) 'India in Africa: An Old Partner, a New Competitor', *Traders Journal*, no. 26.

Boschi, R. (2014) 'Politics and Trajectory in Contemporary Brazilian Capitalism' in Becker (2014).

Boussena, S. and Locatelli, C. (2013) 'Energy Institutional and Organisational Changes in EU and Russia: Revisiting Gas Relations', *Energy Policy*, vol. 55, April.

Bracking, S. and Harrison, G. (2003) 'Africa, Imperialism & New Forms of Accumulation', *Review of African Political Economy*, vol. 30, no. 95.

Brands, H. (2010) *Dilemmas of Brazilian Grand Strategy* Carlisle, PA: US Army War College Strategic Studies Institute.

Brautigam, D. (1998) *Chinese Aid and African Development: Exporting Green Revolution*, Basingstoke and New York: Macmillan.

Brautigam, D. (2011) 'Aid "With Chinese Characteristics": Chinese Foreign Aid and Development Finance Meet the OECD-DAC Aid Regime', *Journal of International Development*, vol. 23, no. 5.

Brautigam, D. (2009) *The Dragon's Gift: The Real Story of China in Africa*, Oxford: Oxford University Press.

Bremmer, I. (2006) 'Taking a Brick out of BRIC', *Fortune*, 20 February.

Brenner, R. (2006) 'What Is, and What Is Not, Imperialism?' *Historical Materialism*, vol. 14, no. 4.

Breslin, S. (1996) 'China: Developmental State or Dysfunctional Development?' *Third World Quarterly*, vol. 17, no. 4.

Breslin, S. (2004) 'Globalization, International Coalitions, and Domestic Reform', *Critical Asian Studies*, vol. 36, no. 4.

Breslin, S. (2005) 'Power and Production: Rethinking China's Global Economic Role', Review of International Studies, vol. 31, no. 4.

Breslin, S. (2007) *China and the Global Political Economy*, Basingstoke: Palgrave Macmillan.

Breslin, S. (2013) 'China and the Global Order: Signalling Threat or

Friendship?' *International Affairs*, vol. 89, no. 3.

Brett, E. (1992) *Colonialism and Underdevelopment in East Africa: The Politics of Economic Change, 1919–1939*, Aldershot: Gregg Revivals.

Broadman, H. (2007) *Africa's Silk Road: China and India's New Economic Frontier*, Washington, DC: World Bank.

Broadman, H. (2008) 'China and India Go to Africa: New Deals in the Developing World,' *Foreign Affairs*, vol. 87, no. 2.

Brown, O. (2008) *From Feast to Famine: After Seven (Relatively) Good Years, What Now for Commodity Producers in the Developing World?* Regina, SK: International Institute for Sustainable Development.

Brown, O., Crawford, A. and Gibson, J. (2008) *Boom or Bust: How Commodity Price Volatility Impedes Poverty Reduction, and What to Do About it*, Regina, SK: International Institute for Sustainable Development.

Brown, W. (2012) 'A Question of Agency: Africa in International Politics', *Third World Quarterly*, vol. 33, no. 10.

Brown, W. (2013) 'Sovereignty Matters: Africa, Donors, and the Aid Relationship', *African Affairs*, vol. 112, no. 447.

Brütsch, C. and Papa, M. (2012) *Deconstructing the BRICs: Bargaining Coalition, Imagined Community or Geopolitical Fad?* Cambridge: Centre for Rising Powers, Working Paper no. 5.

Burges, S. (2005) 'Auto-Estima in Brazil: The Logic of Lula's South–South Foreign Policy', *International Journal*, vol. 60, no. 4.

Burges, S. (2009) *Brazilian Foreign Policy After the Cold War*, Gainesville, FL: University Press of Florida.

Burges, S. (2013) 'Brazil as a Bridge between Old and New Powers?' *International Affairs*, vol. 89, no. 3.

Burkett, M. and Hart-Landsberg, P. (2003) 'A Critique of "Catch-Up" Theories of Development', *Journal of Contemporary Asia*, vol. 33, no. 2.

Busani, B. (2010) 'Africa and Brazil to Cross-fertilize Agricultural Ideas', July 27, www.SciDev.net (accessed 2013, no specific date available).

Cabral, A. (1979) *Unity and Struggle: Speeches and Writings of Amilcar Cabral*, New York: Monthly Review Press.

Cabral, L. and Weinstock, J. (2010) *Brazilian Technical Cooperation for Development, Drivers, Mechanics and Future Prospects*, London: Overseas Development Institute.

Campbell, H. (2012) 'Africa and the BRICS Formation: What Kind of Development?' *Pambazuka News*, no. 581.

Captain, Y. (2010) 'Brazil's Africa Policy under Lula', *The Global South*, vol. 4, no. 1.

Cargill, T. (2011) *Our Common Strategic Interests: Africa's Role in the Post-G8 World*, London: Royal Institute of International Affairs.

Carlsson, J. (1982) 'The Emergence of South–South Relations in a Changing World Economy', in Carlsson, J. (ed.) *South–South Relations in a Changing World Order*, Uppsala: Scandinavian Institute of African Studies.

Carmody, P. (2011) *The New Scramble for Africa*, Cambridge: Polity Press.

Carmody, P. (2013) *The Rise of the BRICS in Africa: The Geopolitics of South–South Relations*, London: Zed Books.

Cason, J. and Power, T. (2009), 'Presidentialization, Pluralization and the Rollback of Itamaraty: Explaining Change in Brazilian Foreign Policy Making in the Cardoso-Lula Era', *International Political Science Review*, vol. 30, no. 2.

Centre for the Study of Governance Innovation (2013) *On the BRICS of Collapse? Why Emerging Economies Need a Different Development Model*, Pretoria: Centre for the Study of Governance Innovation.

Chabal, P. and Daloz, J-P (1999) *Africa Works: Disorder as Political Instrument*, Oxford: James Currey.

Chandrasekhar, C. (2012) 'India's Economy: The End of Neoliberal Triumphalism', *The Marxist*, vol. 28, no. 2.

Chaturvedi, S. and Mohanty, S. (2007) 'Trade and Investment: Trends and Prospects', *South African Journal of International Affairs*, vol. 14, no. 2.

Chhiba, P. (2011) 'The Return of the Kremlin: Cautious Optimism for Africa?' *Consultancy Africa*, 16 June.

Chiriyankandath, J. (2004) 'Realigning India: Indian Foreign Policy after the Cold War,' *Round Table*, vol. 93, no. 374.

Christensen, S. (2013) 'Brazil's Foreign Policy Priorities', *Third World Quarterly*, vol. 34, no. 2.

Chu, B. (2013) *Chinese Whispers: Why Everything You've Heard about China is Wrong*, London: Weidenfeld and Nicolson.

Clarke, D. (2012) *Africa's Future: Darkness to Destiny: How the Past is Shaping Africa's Economic Evolution*, New York: Profile Books.

Collier, P. (2007) 'Managing Commodity Booms: Lessons of International Experience', Oxford University, Centre for the Study of African Economies, Department of Economics, paper prepared for the African Economic Research Consortium.

Confederation of Indian Industry (2013) *India–Africa: South–South Trade and Investment for Development*, New Delhi: Confederation of Indian Industry.

Corkin, L. and Naidu, S. (2008) 'China and India in Africa: An Introduction', *Review of African Political Economy*, vol. 35, no.115.

Cornelissen, S. (2009) 'Awkward Embraces: Emerging and Established Powers and the Shifting Fortunes of Africa's International Relations in the Twenty-first Century', *Politikon : South African Journal of Political Studies,* vol. 36, no. 1.

COSATU (2013) 'Declaration of the Second BRICS Trade Union Forum', press release, 25 March.

Cox, R. (1981) 'Social Forces, States and World Orders: Beyond International Relations Theory', *Millennium: Journal of International Studies*, vol. 10, no. 2.

Dadwal, S. (2011) *India and Africa: Towards a Sustainable Energy Part-*

nership, Occasional Paper no. 75, Braamfontein: South African Institute of International Affairs.

da Silva, L. (2008), 'Brazilian Foreign Policy', www.brazemb-ksa.org/foreignpolicy.htm (accessed 2013, no specific date available).

Dauvergne, P. and Farias, D. (2012) 'The Rise of Brazil as a Global Development Power', *Third World Quarterly*, vol. 33, no. 5.

Dauvergne, P. and Neville, K. (2009) 'The Changing North–South and South–South Political Economy of Biofuels', *Third World Quarterly*, vol. 30, no.6.

Davies, M. (2013) 'The Emerging New World: The BRICS, South Africa and New Models of Development', Johannesburg: Frontier Advisory, January.

de Almeida, B., Bolsmann, C, Júnior, W. and de Souza, J. (2013) 'Rationales, Rhetoric and Realities: FIFA's World Cup in South Africa 2010 and Brazil 2014', *International Review for the Sociology of Sport*, 26 April.

de Almeida, P. (2007) 'Brazil as a Regional Player and an Emerging Global Power', Friedrich Ebert Stiftung Briefing Paper no. 8.

de Castro, M. and de Carvalho, M. (2003) 'Globalization and Recent Political Transitions in Brazil', *International Political Science Review*, vol. 24, no. 4.

Delfin, S. and Page, J. (eds) (2008) *Africa at a Turning Point? Growth, Aid, and External Shocks*, Washington, DC: World Bank.

de Lima, M. and Hirst, M. (2010) 'Brazil as an Intermediate State and Regional Power: Action, Choice and Responsibilities', *International Affairs*, vol. 82, no. 1.

Dembele, D. (2012) 'Africa's Developmental Impasse: Some Perspectives and Recommendations', *Africa Development*, vol. 37, no. 4.

Desai, M. (2012) 'Parties and the Articulation of Neoliberalism: From "The Emergency" to Reforms in India, 1975–1991' in Go, J. (ed.) *Political Power and Social Theory*, vol. 23, Bingley: Emerald Group Publishing.

Desai, R. (2007) 'Dreaming in Technicolour? India as a BRIC Economy', *International Journal*, vol. 62, no. 4.

Desfosses, H. (1987) 'The USSR and Africa', *Issue: A Journal of Opinion*, vol. 16, no. 1.

Devarajan, S. (2013) 'Africa's Statistical Tragedy', *Review of Income and Wealth*, vol. 59, No. S1.

Deych, T. (2012) 'BRICS in Africa: China and Russia Roles', paper presented at Congreso Ibérico de Estudios Africanos, Madrid, 14–16 June.

Dietz, S., Neumayer, E. and De Soysa, I. (2007) 'Corruption, the Resource Curse and Genuine Saving', *Environment and Development Economics*, vol. 12, no. 1: 33–58.

Dirlik, A. (2006) 'Beijing Consensus: Beijing "Gongshi". Who Recognizes Whom and to What End?' mimeo.

Doelling, R. (2008) 'Brazil's Contemporary Foreign Policy Towards

Africa', *Journal of International Relations*, vol. 10, no. 32.

Donaldson, R. and Nogee, J. (2005) *The Foreign Policy of Russia: Changing Systems, Enduring Interests*, New York, NY: M.E. Sharpe.

Dowd, D. (1967) 'Some Issues of Economic Development and of Development Economics', *Journal of Economic Issues*, vol. 1, no. 3.

Drèze, J. and Sen, A. (2013) *An Uncertain Glory: India and its Contradictions*, London: Allen Lane.

Dubey, A. (2010) *Indian Diaspora in Africa: A Comparative Perspective*, New Delhi: MD Publications.

Dunn, K. and Shaw, T. (eds) (2001) *Africa's Challenge to International Relations Theory*, Basingstoke: Palgrave Macmillan.

Dunning, J., van Hoesel, R. and Narula, R. (1998) 'Third World Multinationals Revisited: New Developments and Theoretical Implications' in Dunning, J. (ed.) *Globalization, Trade and Foreign Direct Investment*, London: Pergamon.

du Venage, G. (2012) 'China as a Vital Force for Africa', *Asia Times*, 8 June.

Duyvendak, J. (1949) *China's Discovery of Africa*, London: Probsthain.

Easterly, W. (2003) 'Can Foreign Aid Buy Growth?' *Journal of Economic Perspectives*, vol. 17, no. 3.

Easterly, W., Kremer, M., Pritchett L. and Summers, L. (1993) 'Good Policy or Good Luck? Country Growth Performance and Temporary Shocks', *Journal of Monetary Economics*, vol. 32, no. 3.

Elliot, L. (2006) 'Africa Calls on Brown to Block IMF Reforms', *The Guardian*, August 31.

Erber, G. and Schrooten, M. (2012) 'Germany Profits from Growth in Brazil, Russia, India, China, and South Africa – But for How Much Longer?' *DIW Economic Bulletin*, vol. 2, no. 10.

Ernst & Young (2011) *It's Time for Africa: Ernst & Young's 2011 Africa Attractiveness Survey*, London: Ernst & Young Global.

Ernst & Young (2012) *Africa by Numbers: Assessing Market Attractiveness in Africa: Ernst & Young's 2012 Africa Attractiveness Survey*, London: EYGM.

Ernst & Young (2013) 'EY launches Africa Global Tax Desk Network in Beijing', press release, London: Ernst & Young Global, 14 January.

Erten, B. and Ocampo, J. (2013) 'Super Cycles of Commodity Prices Since the Mid-Nineteenth Century', *World Development*, vol. 44, April.

European Parliament (2012) *The Role of BRICS in the Developing World*, Brussels: European Union.

Fang Kang (1978) 'Capitalist Roaders are the Bourgeoisie Inside the Party' in Lotta, R. (ed.) *And Mao Makes 5*, Chicago, IL: Banner Press.

Fatton, R. (1988) 'Bringing the Ruling Class Back In: Class, State, and Hegemony in Africa', *Comparative Politics*, vol. 20, no. 3.

Fatton, R. (1999) 'Civil Society Revisited: Africa in the New Millennium', *West Africa Review*, vol. 1, no. 1.

Ferguson, J. (2006) *Global Shadows: Africa in the Neoliberal World Order*,

Durham, NC: Duke University Press.

Fidan, H. and Aras, B. (2010) 'The Return of Russia–Africa Relations', *Bilig*, no. 52, Winter.

Fihlani, P. (2012) 'Could Chicken Row Threaten Brazil–South Africa Friendship?' *BBC News*, 3 October.

Fioramonti, L. (2013) *Gross Domestic Problem: The Politics Behind the World's Most Powerful Number*, London: Zed Books.

Fioramonti, L. (2014) *How Numbers Rule the World: The Use and Abuse of Statistics in Global Politics*, London: Zed Books.

First, R. (1970) *The Barrel of a Gun: Political Power in Africa and the Coup d'Etat*, London: Allen Lane.

Fonseca, G. (2011) 'Notes on the Evolution of Brazilian Multilateral Diplomacy', *Global Governance*, vol. 17, no. 3.

Foot, R. (2006) 'Chinese Strategies in a US-Hegemonic Global Order: Accommodating and Hedging', *International Affairs*, vol. 82, no. 1.

Ford, N. (2006) 'Indian Connection Gathers New Momentum: With the Emergence of China and India, Africa's Traditional Trading Partners are Changing', *African Business*, vol. 235, 1 November.

Forrest, T. (1982) 'Brazil and Africa: Geopolitics, Trade, and Technology in the South Atlantic', *African Affairs*, vol. 81, no. 322.

Forsythe, M. (2012) 'China's Billionaire People's Congress Makes Capitol Hill Look Like Paupers', *Bloomberg.com*, February 27.

Foster, J. (2007) 'No Radical Change in the Model', *Monthly Review*, vol. 58, no. 9.

Freemantle, S. and Stevens, J. (2009) 'Tectonic Shifts Tie BRIC and Africa's Economic Destinies', *Standard Bank Economics: BRIC and Africa*, 14 October.

Freemantle, S. and Stevens, J. (2010) 'Private Players to Lead the Next Phase of Brazil–Africa Ties', 8 November, www.howwemadeitinafrica.com (accessed 2013, no specific date available).

French, H. (2012) 'The Next Asia Is Africa: Inside the Continent's Rapid Economic Growth', *Atlantic Monthly*, 21 May.

Frynas, J. and Paulo, M. (2007) 'A New Scramble for African Oil? Historical, Political, and Business Perspectives', *African Affairs*, 106, no. 423.

Fuchs, A. and Vadlamannati, K. (2013) 'The Needy Donor: An Empirical Analysis of India's Aid Motives', *World Development*, vol. 44, no. 1.

Fundira, T. (2012a) *Brazil Africa Relations: 2011 Highlights*, Stellenbosch: TRALAC.

Fundira, T. (2012b) 'Trade at a Glance: The BRICS and Japan's Engagement with Africa', Stellenbosch: TRALAC.

Galeotti, M. (1995) *The Kremlin's Agenda: The New Russia and its Armed Forces*, Bracknell: Jane's Information Group.

Gall, N. (1977) 'The Rise of Brazil', *Commentary*, vol. 63, January.

Gallagher, K. and Porzecanski, R., (2010) *The Dragon in the Room: China and the Future of Latin American Industrialization*, Redwood City,

CA: Stanford University Press.

Gammeltoft, P. (2008) 'Emerging Multinationals: Outward FDI from the BRICS Countries', paper presented at the IV Globelics Conference at Mexico City, Mexico, 22–24 September.

Gammeltoft, P, Pradhan, J. and Goldstein, A. (2010) 'Emerging Multinationals: Home and Host Country Determinants and Outcomes', *International Journal of Emerging Markets*, vol. 5, nos 3/4.

Ganguly, S. and Pardesi, M. (2007) 'India Rising: What is New Delhi to Do?' *World Policy Journal*, vol. 24, no.1.

German Development Institute (2009) 'India's Development Cooperation – Opportunities and Challenges for International Development Cooperation', Briefing Paper, 3/2009.

Ghosh, A. (2006) 'Pathways Through Financial Crisis: India', *Global Governance: A Review of Multilateralism and International Organizations*, vol. 12, no. 4.

Giles, K. (2013) *Russian Interests in Sub-Saharan Africa*, Carlisle, PA: Strategic Studies Institute and U.S. Army War College.

Glosny, M. (2010) 'China and the BRICs: A Real (but Limited) Partnership in a Unipolar World', *Polity*, vol. 42, no. 1.

Goldman, M. (2008) *Petrostate: Putin, Power, and the New Russia* Oxford: Oxford University Press.

Goldstein, A., Pinaud, N., Reisen, H. and Chen Xiaobao (2005) *The Rise of China and India: What's in it for Africa?* Paris: OECD Development Centre Studies.

Gramsci, A. (1971) *Selections from the Prison Notebooks*, London: Lawrence and Wishart.

Gray, K. (2010) 'Labour and the State in China's Passive Revolution', *Capital & Class*, vol. 34, no. 3.

Green, R. and Seidman, A. (1968) *Unity or Poverty? The Economics of Pan-Africanism* Harmondsworth: Penguin.

Guérin, E. (2008) 'Chinese Assistance to Africa: Characterization and Position Regarding the Global Governance of Development Aid', IDDRI, *Idées Pour le Débat*, no. 3.

Guan, E. (2010) 'Understanding Brazil's Oil Industry: Policy Dynamics and Self-Sufficiency', *Journal of Emerging Knowledge on Emerging Markets*, vol. 2.

Gu Weiqun (1995) *Conflicts of Divided Nations: The Cases of China and Korea*, Westport, CT: Westview.

Gu Xuewu (2005) 'China Returns to Africa', *Trends East Asia*, no. 9.

Hamilton, C. (2003) *Growth Fetish*, London: Allen and Unwin.

Hamilton, K. and Clemens, M. (1999) 'Genuine Savings Rates in Developing Countries', *World Bank Economic Review*, vol. 13, no. 2.

Han Nianlong (1990) *Diplomacy of Contemporary China*, Hong Kong: New Horizon Press.

Harris, D. (1975) 'The Political Economy of Africa: Underdevelopment or Revolution', in Harris, D. (ed.) *The Political Economy of Africa*, New

York: Schenkman.

Harsch, E. (2004) 'Brazil Repaying its "Debt" to Africa", *Africa Recovery*, vol. 17, no. 4.

Hart-Landsberg, M. (2010) 'The U.S. Economy and China: Capitalism, Class, and Crisis', *Monthly Review*, vol. 61, no. 9.

Hart-Landsberg, M. (2013) *Capitalist Globalization: Consequences, Resistance and Alternatives*, New York: Monthly Review Press.

Hart-Landsberg, M. and Burkett, P. (2004) 'China's Economic Transformation', *Monthly Review*, vol. 56, no. 3.

Hart-Landsberg, M. and Burkett, P. (2005) *China and Socialism: Market Reforms and Class Struggle*, New Delhi: Aakar.

Harttgen, K., Klasen, S. and Vollmer, S. (2013) 'An African Growth Miracle? Or: What do Asset Indices Tell us about Trends in Economic Performance?' *Review of Income and Wealth*, vol. 59, No. S1.

Hartwick, J. (1977) 'Intergenerational Equity and the Investing of Rents from Exhaustible Resources', *American Economic Review*, vol. 67, no. 5.

Harvey, D. (2005) *A Brief History of Neoliberalism*, Oxford: Oxford University Press.

Haslam, P. and Barreto, E. (2009) 'Worlds Apart: Canadian and Brazilian Multilateralism in Comparative Perspective', *Canadian Foreign Policy*, vol. 15, no. 1.

Haté, V. (2008) 'India in Africa: Moving Beyond Oil', *South Asia Monitor*, no. 119, June.

Hattari, R. and Rajan, R. (2010) 'India as a Source of Outward Foreign Direct Investment', *Oxford Development Studies*, vol. 38, no. 4.

Herrera, R. (2005) 'Fifty Years After the Bandung Conference: Towards a Revival of the Solidarity Between the Peoples of the South? Interview with Samir Amin', *Inter-Asia Cultural Studies*, vol. 6, no. 4.

He Wenping (2007) 'China's Perspective on Contemporary China–Africa Relations', in Alden, C., Soares de Oliveira, R. and Large, D. (eds) *China Returns to Africa: A Rising Power and a Continent Embrace*, Cambridge: Cambridge University Press.

He Zuoxiu (2013) 'Chinese Nuclear Disaster "Highly Probable" by 2030', *The Ecologist*, 25 October.

Hinton, W. (1991) *The Privatization of China: The Great Reversal*, London: Earthscan.

Hoffmann, H. (1982) 'Towards Africa? Brazil and South–South Trade', in Carlsson, J. (ed.) *South–South Relations in a Changing World Order*, Uppsala: Scandinavian Institute of African Studies.

Hofmeyr, J. (2013) '"Africa Rising"? Popular Dissatisfaction with Economic Management Despite a Decade of Growth', *Afrobarometer Policy Brief*, no. 2, October.

Hone, A. (1973) 'The Primary Commodities Boom', *New Left Review*, vol. 1, no. 81.

Hong Eunsuk and Sun Laixiang (2006) 'Dynamics of Internationalization and Outward Investment: Chinese Corporations' Strategies', *China Quarterly*, vol. 187, September.

Hopewell, K. (2013) 'New Protagonists in Global Economic Governance: Brazilian Agribusiness at the WTO, *New Political Economy*, vol. 18, no. 4.

Hopkins, A. (1973) *An Economic History of West Africa*, London: Longman.

Hsueh, R. (2011) *China's Regulatory State: A New Strategy for Globalization*, Ithaca, NY: Cornell University Press.

Huang Yasheng (2011) 'Rethinking the Beijing Consensus', *Asia Policy*, no. 11, January.

Hughes, A. (ed.) (1992) *Marxism's Retreat from Africa*, London: Frank Cass.

Human Rights Watch (2010) 'Cancelling the UNESCO-Obiang Prize', www.hrw.org/en/news/2010/06/09/cancelling-unesco-obiang-prize (accessed 23 April 2014).

Hung, H. (2009) 'America's Head Servant? The PRC's Dilemma in the Global Crisis', *New Left Review*, vol. 60, no. 6.

Hunter, W. (2007) 'The Normalization of an Anomaly: The Workers' Party in Brazil', *World Politics*, vol. 59, no.3.

Hurrell, A. (2010) 'Brazil and the New Global Order', *Current History*, vol. 109, no. 724.

Hurrell, A. and Narlikar, A. (2006) 'A New Politics of Confrontation? Developing Countries at Cancún and Beyond', *Global Society*, vol. 20, no. 4.

Hutchison, A. (1975) *China's African Revolution*, London: Hutchinson.

India–Brazil–South Africa (IBSA) Dialogue Forum (2010) *Plan of Action*, Pretoria: Department of Foreign Affairs.

India–Brazil–South Africa Dialogue Forum (2012) 'IBSA', www.ibsa-trilateral.org (accessed 2013, no specific date available).

International Energy Agency (2012a) *IEA Statistic: Co2 Emissions from Fuel Combustion: Highlights 2012*, www.iea.org (accessed 2013, no specific date available).

International Energy Agency (2012b) *World Energy Outlook 2012*, Paris: International Energy Agency.

International Monetary Fund (2010) *World Economic Outlook Database, October 2010: Nominal GDP list of countries*, Washington, DC: IMF.

International Monetary Fund (2011) *New Growth Drivers for Low-Income Countries: The Role of BRICs*, Washington, DC: IMF.

International Monetary Fund (2013) *Sub-Saharan Africa Building Momentum in a Multi-Speed World*, Washington, DC: IMF.

Investnews (2010) 'Rich Countries will Seek Brazilian Ethanol, Says Lula', 28 September, www.istockanalyst.com/article/viewiStockNews/articleid/4539968, accessed 12 November 2013.

ITEC (2010) Ministry of External Affairs, Technical Cooperation Division, Indian Technical and Economic Cooperation Programme, www.itec.

mea.gov.in (accessed 2013, no specific date available).

Ivins, C. (2013) *Inequality Matters: BRICS Inequalities Fact Sheet*, Rio de Janeiro: BRICS Policy Center.

Jacobs, A. (2012) 'Africa's Sore Spot: regional Conflicts Across the Middle and Horn', in Möckli, D. (ed.) *Strategic Trends 2012: Key Developments in Global Affairs*, Zurich: ETH – Center for Security Studies.

Jacobs, L. and van Rossem, R. (2013) 'The BRIC Phantom: A Comparative Analysis of the BRICs as a Category of Rising Powers, *Journal of Policy Modeling*, in press.

Jerven, M. (2010a) 'Random Growth in Africa? Lessons from an Evaluation of the Growth Evidence on Botswana, Kenya, Tanzania and Zambia, 1965–1995', *Journal of Development Studies*, vol. 46, no. 2.

Jerven, M. (2010b) 'African Growth Recurring: An Economic History Perspective on African Growth Episodes, 1690–2010', *Economic History of Developing Regions*, vol. 25, no. 2.

Jerven, M. (2013) *Poor Numbers: How We are Misled by African Development Statistics and What to Do About It*, Ithaca, NY: Cornell University Press.

Jha, P. (2005) 'Withering Commitments and Weakening Progress State and Education in the Era of Neoliberal Reforms', *Economic and Political Weekly*, 13 August.

Jobelius, M. (2007) 'New Powers for Global Change? Challenges for International Development Cooperation: The Case of India', *Dialogue on Globalization* Briefing Paper no. 5, New Delhi: Friedrich Ebert Stiftung.

Jordan, P. (2010) 'A Bridge Between the Global North and Africa? Putin's Russia and G-8 Development Commitments', *African Studies Quarterly*, vol. 11, no. 4.

Jurado, E. (2008) 'Report 2008: Russia's Role in a Multi-polar World: Between Change and Stability', Berlin: Alfred Herrhausen Society.

Kanet, R. (ed.) (2011) *Russian Foreign Policy in the 21st Century*, Basingstoke: Palgrave Macmillan.

Karabell, Z. (2010) *Superfusion: How China and America Became One Economy and Why the World's Prosperity Depends on It*, New York: Simon and Schuster.

Karmwar, M. (2010) 'African Diaspora in India', *Diaspora Studies*, vol. 3, no. 1.

Karp, P. (2009) 'China's Development Experience: Key Lessons for other Developing Countries', in Beijing Forum Organizing Committee (eds) *The Global Financial Crisis: International Impacts and Responses*, Beijing: Beijing Forum.

Karumbidza, J. (2007) 'Win-win Economic Co-operation: Can China Save Zimbabwe's Economy?' in Manji, F. and Marks, S. (eds) *African Perspectives on China in Africa*, Cape Town: Fahamu.

Kay, G. (1975) *Development and Underdevelopment: A Marxist Analysis*, London: Macmillan.

Keating, J. (2010) 'Lula's Latest Dodgy Friend', *Foreign Policy*, 7 July.

Kelly, P. (1984) 'Geopolitical Themes in the Writings of General Carlos de Meira Mattos of Brazil', *Journal of Latin American Studies*, vol. 16, no. 2.

Kelsall, T. (2013) *Business, Politics, and the State in Africa: Challenging the Orthodoxies on Growth and Transformation*, London: Zed Books.

Keukeleire, S., Mattlin, M., Hooijmaaijers, B., Behr, T., Jokela, J., Wigell, M. and Kononenko, V. (2011) 'The EU Foreign Policy towards the BRICS and other Emerging Powers: Objectives and Strategies: Ad hoc Study for the Directorate-General for External Policies of the Union', Brussels: European Parliament.

Khanna, P. and Mohan, C. (2006) 'Getting India Right', *Policy Review*, no. 135.

Kimenyi, M. and Lewis, Z. (2011) 'The BRICs and the New Scramble for Africa', in Brookings Institute, *Foresight Africa: The Continent's Greatest Challenges and Opportunities for 2011*, New York: Brookings Institute.

Klom, A. (2003) 'Mercosur and Brazil: A European Perspective', *International Affairs*, vol. 79, no. 2.

Klomegah, K. (2009a) 'Russia Supplying Legal and "Illegal" Arms to Africa', *Inter Press Service*, 29 January.

Klomegah, K. (2009b) 'Trade-Africa: Russia "Could Be Left Behind"', *Inter Press Service*, 25 September.

Klomegah, K. (2010) 'Africa: Russia Outpaced by China in Continent', *All Africa*, 26 February.

Klomegah, K. (2012) 'Russia's Relations with Africa Floundering', *Business Africa*, 6 July.

Kommersant (2011) 'Russia in Africa: An Alternative to China's Investment Monopoly?' 20 December.

Kornegay, F. and Landsberg, C. (2009) 'Engaging Emerging Powers: Africa's Search for a "Common Position"', *Politikon: South African Journal of Political Studies*, vol. 36, no. 1.

Kose, M. A. and Prasad, E. S. (2010) 'Emerging markets come of age', *Finance and Development*, Vol. 47, No. 4.

Kpedekpo, G. and Arya, P. (1981) *Social and Economic Statistics for Africa: Their Sources, Collection, Uses and Reliability*, London: Allen and Unwin.

Kragelund, P. (2008) 'The Return of Non-DAC donors to Africa: New Prospects for African Development?' *Development Policy Review*, vol. 26, no. 5.

Kragelund, P. (2010) 'The Potential Role of Non-Traditional Donors' Aid in Africa', Geneva: International Centre for Trade and Sustainable Development, Issue Paper no. 11.

Kragelund, P. (2011) 'Back to BASICs? The Rejuvenation of Non-traditional Donors' Development Cooperation with Africa', *Development and Change*, vol. 42, no. 2.

Kröger, M. (2012) 'Neo-mercantilist Capitalism and Post-2008 Cleavages in Economic Decision-making Power in Brazil', *Third World Quarterly*, vol. 33, no. 5.

Kuchins, A. and Zevelev, I. (2012) 'Russia's Contested National Identity and Foreign Policy', in Nau, H. and Ollapally, D. (eds) *Worldviews of Aspiring Powers: Domestic Foreign Policy Debates in China, India, Iran, Japan, and Russia*, Oxford: Oxford University Press.

Kurečić, P. and Bandov, G. (2011) 'The Contemporary Role and Perspectives of the BRIC States in the World-Order', *Elektronik Siyaset Bilimi Arasḍtırmaları Dergisi*, vol. 2, no. 2.

Kurlantzick, J. (2006) 'China's Charm: Implications of Chinese Soft Power', Carnegie Endowment Policy Brief, no. 47.

Kuznets, S. (1971) 'Modern Economic Growth: Findings and Reflections', Nobel lecture, Oslo, 11 December, *American Economic Review*, 63, no. 3.

Kwa, A. (2010) 'The Challenges Confronting South–South Trade', *Poverty in Focus*, no. 20.

Lai, K. (2006) 'India–Brazil–South Africa: The Southern Trade Powerhouse Makes its Debut', *Panama News*, vol. 12, no. 6.

Lal, G and Vanaik, A. (2004) 'The Politics of Neoliberalism in India', interview for Alternative Regionalisms project, 1 January.

Laïdi, Z. (2012) 'BRICS: Sovereignty Power and Weakness', *International Politics*, vol. 49, no. 5.

Larson, D. and Shevchenko, A. (2010) 'Status Seekers: Chinese and Russian Responses to U.S. Primacy', *International Security*, vol. 34, no. 4.

Leamer, E. (1987) 'Paths of Development in the Three-Factor, *n*-Good General Equilibrium Model', *Journal of Political Economy*, vol. 95, no. 5.

Lechini, G. (2005) 'Is South–South Co-operation Still Possible? The Case of Brazil's Strategy and Argentina's Impulses Towards the New South Africa and Africa', in Boron, A. and Lechini, G. (eds) *Politics and Social Movements in an Hegemonic World: Lessons from Africa, Asia and Latin America*, Buenos Aires: Consejo Latinoamericano de Ciencias Sociales.

Lee, H. (2010), 'Multilateralism in Russian Foreign Policy: Some Tentative Evaluations', *International Area Studies Review*, vol. 13, no. 3.

Legro, J. (2012) 'The Politics of the New Global Architecture: The United States and India', *Strategic Analysis*, vol. 36, no. 4.

Legvold, R. (2001) 'Russia's Unformed Foreign Policy', *Foreign Affairs*, vol. 80, no. 5.

Lenin, V. (1917/1966) *Imperialism: The Highest Stage of Capitalism*, Moscow: Progress Publishers.

Lima, M. (2012) 'The Brazilian Biofuel Industry: Achievements, Challenges, and Geopolitics', *The Newsletter*, no. 62, Winter.

Lin Chun (2013) *China and Global Capitalism: Reflections on Marxism, History, and Contemporary Politics*, Basingstoke: Palgrave Macmillan.

Lin, J. and Rosenblatt, D. (2012) 'Shifting Patterns of Economic Growth and Rethinking Development', *Journal of Economic Policy Reform*, vol. 15, no. 3.

Lo, B. (2008) *Axis of Convenience: Moscow, Beijing and the New Geopolitics*, Washington, DC: Brookings Institute.

Lo, D. and Zhang, Y. (2011) 'Making Sense of China's Economic Transformation', *Review of Radical Political Economics*, vol. 43, no. 1.

Lucas, E. (2008) *The New Cold War: Putin's Russia and the Threat to the West*, Basingstoke: Palgrave Macmillan.

Lustig, R. (2010) 'Brazil Emerges as a Leading Exponent of "Soft Power"', *BBC News*, 23 March.

Lynch, A. (2001) 'The Realism of Russia's Foreign Policy', *Europe–Asia Studies*, vol. 53, no. 1.

MacFarlane, N. (2006) 'The "R" in BRICs: Is Russia an Emerging Power?' *International Affairs*, vol. 82, no. 1.

McGregor, A. (2009) 'Russia's Arms Sales to Sudan a First Step in Return to Africa: Part Two', *Eurasia Daily Monitor*, vol. 6, no. 29.

Maciel, M. (1996) 'Opening Remarks', in Guimaraes, S. (ed.) *South Africa and Brazil: Risks and Opportunities in the Turmoil of Globalisation*, Rio de Janeiro: International Relations Research Institute.

Mafeje, A. (1992) *In Search of an Alternative: A Collection of Essays on Revolutionary Theory and Politics*, Harare: SAPES.

Mahbubani, K. (2008) *The New Asian Hemisphere: The Irresistible Shift of Global Power to the East*, New York: Public Affairs.

Mahbubani, K. (2011) 'Can Asia Re-legitimize Global Governance?' *Review of International Political Economy*, vol. 18, no. 1.

Majumdar, B. (2009) 'India Plans to Triple Trade with Africa, Deepen Ties', *Reuters*, New Delhi.

Makarychev, A. and Morozov, V. (2011) 'Multilateralism, Multipolarity, and Beyond: A Menu of Russia's Policy Strategies', *Global Governance*, vol. 17, no. 3.

Mao Zedong (1961/2000) *On Guerrilla Warfare*, Champaign, IL: University of Illinois Press.

Maplecroft (2011) *Emerging Powers Integration Report*, Bath: Maplecroft.

Marcondes de Souza Neto, D. (2013) 'Contemporary Brazil–Africa Relations: Bilateral Strategies and Engagement with Other BRICS', *Global Review*, Spring.

Markovitz, I. (ed.) (1987) *Studies in Power and Class in Africa*, Oxford: Oxford University Press.

Martin, W. (2008) 'Africa's Futures: From North–South to East–South?' *Third World Quarterly*, vol. 29, no. 2.

Martynov, B. (2011) 'BRICS: Dawn of a New Era, or Business as Usual?' *Security Index: A Russian Journal on International Security*, vol. 17, no. 3.

Marx, K. (1867/1976) *Capital* vol. I, Harmondsworth: Penguin.

Marx, K. and Engels, F. (1888/2004) *Manifesto of the Communist Party*,

Beijing: Foreign Languages Press.

Matean, D. (2012) *Africa: The Ultimate Frontier Market: A Guide to the Business and Investment Opportunities in Emerging Africa*, Petersfield: Harriman House.

Mathew, G., Ganesh, J. and Dayasindhu, N. (2008) *How India Is Riding on Globalization to Become an Innovation Superpower: Innovation Geo-dynamics*, Oxford: Chandos.

Mawdsley, E. and McCann, G. (2010) 'The Elephant in the Corner? Reviewing India–Africa Relations in the New Millennium', *Geography Compass*, vol. 4, no.2.

Mazumdar, S. (2014) 'Continuity and Change in Indian Capitalism' in Becker (2014).

Mbaye, J. (2011) 'New Colonialists: The Good, the Bad and the Ugly: BRICS Relevance to the African Creative Economy', paper presented at the Arterial Network African Creative Economy Conference, Nairobi, Kenya, June.

McCormick, D. (2008) 'China and India as Africa's New Aid Donors: The Impact of Aid on Development', *Review of African Political Economy*, vol. 35 no. 1.

McKay, A. (2013) 'Growth and Poverty Reduction in Africa in the Last Two Decades: Evidence from an AERC Growth-Poverty Project and Beyond', *Journal of African Economies*, vol. 22, supplement 1.

McKinsey Global Institute (2010) *Lions on the Move: The Progress and Potential of African Economies*, London: McKinsey and Company.

McMichael, P., Petras, J. and Rhodes, R. (1974) 'Imperialism and the Contradictions of Development', *New Left Review*, vol. 1, no. 85.

McMillan, M. and Rodrik, D. (2011) *Globalization, Structural Change and Productivity Growth*, NBER Working Paper, no. 17143, June.

Mentan, T. (2010) *The State in Africa: An Analysis of Impacts of Historical Trajectories of Global Capitalist Expansion and Domination in the Continent*, Bamenda: Langaa.

Mignolo, W. (2012) 'The Role of BRICS Countries in the Becoming World Order: "Humanity", Imperial/Colonial Difference and the Racial Distribution of Capital and Knowledge', paper presented at the International Conference, Humanity and Difference in a Global Age organized by UNESCO, Tsinghua University and Universidade Candido Mendes, Beijing, 23–25 May.

Miguel, E. (2009) *Africa's Turn?* Cambridge, MA: MIT Press.

Ming Xia (2000) *The Dual Developmental State: Development Strategy and Institutional Arrangements for China's Transition*, Aldershot: Ashgate.

Ministry of Commerce and Industry, India (2011) *Export Import Data Bank*, New Delhi: Department of Commerce.

Ministry of Economic Development of the Russian Federation (2008) *Foreign Economic Strategy of the Russian Federation to 2020*, Moscow: Ministry of Economic Development.

Ministry of Foreign Affairs, China (2006) *China's African Policy*, Beijing: Ministry of Foreign Affairs.

Ministry of Foreign Affairs of the Russian Federation (1993) *Conception of the Foreign Policy of the Russian Federation*, Moscow: Ministry of Foreign Affairs of the Russian Federation.

Ministry of Foreign Affairs of the Russian Federation (2000) *The Foreign Policy Concept of the Russian Federation*, Moscow: Ministry of Foreign Affairs of the Russian Federation.

Ministry of Foreign Affairs of the Russian Federation (2008) *The Foreign Policy Concept of the Russian Federation*, Moscow: Ministry of Foreign Affairs of the Russian Federation.

Mo Ibrahim Foundation (2013) *2013 Ibrahim Index of African Governance: Data Report*, London: Mo Ibrahim Foundation.

Mohan, C. R. (2007) 'Balancing Interests and Values: India's Struggle with Democracy Promotion', *Washington Quarterly*, vol. 30, no. 3.

Mohan, G. and Power, M. (2009) 'Africa, China and the "New" Economic Geography of Development', *Singapore Journal of Tropical Geography*, vol. 30, no. 1.

Mukherjee, P. (2008) 'Opening Address by Shri Pranab Mukherjee, External Affairs at the India Africa Forum Summit, New Delhi', 7 April.

Mundkur, B. (2011) 'Incredible India: The Inconvenient Truth', *Asian Affairs*, vol. 42, no. 1.

Mutenyo, J. (2011) 'Driving Africa's Growth Through Expanding Exports', in *Foresight Africa: The Continent's Greatest Challenges and Opportunities for 2011*, New York: Brookings Institute.

Nabudere, D. (2011) *Archie Mafeje: Scholar, Activist and Thinker*, Pretoria: Africa Institute.

Naidu, S. (2007) *India's African Relations: Playing Catch Up with the Dragon*, Los Angeles: Globalization Research Center: African Studies Center, UCLA.

Naidu, S. (2008) 'India's Growing African Strategy', *Review of African Political Economy*, vol. 35, no.115.

Naidu, S., Corkin, L. and Herman, H. (2009) 'Introduction', *Politikon: South African Journal of Political Studies*, vol. 36, no. 1.

Naidu, S. and Davies, M. (2006) 'China Fuels its Future with Africa's Riches', *South African Journal of International Affairs*, vol. 13, no. 2.

Nanda, P. (ed.) (2008) *Rising India: Friends and Foes*, New Delhi: Lancer Publishers.

Narayan, S. (2005) *Trade Policy Making in India*, Singapore: Institute of South Asian Studies, National University of Singapore.

Nayar, B. and T. Paul (2003) *India in the World Order: Searching for Major Power Status*, Cambridge: Cambridge University Press.

Nel, P. and Taylor, I. (2013) 'Bugger Thy Neighbour? IBSA and South–South Solidarity', *Third World Quarterly*, vol. 34, no. 6.

Nederveen Pieterse, J. (2012) 'Asia Rising: Just Growth or Emancipation?'

paper presented at the Open University, Milton Keynes symposium on Asia Rising: A New Oriental Globalization? – and at Humboldt University, Berlin, June.

Nieto, W. (2012) 'Brazil's Grand Design for Combining Global South Solidarity and National Interests: A Discussion of Peacekeeping Operations in Haiti and Timor', *Globalizations*, vol. 9, no. 1.

Nkrumah, K. (1970) *Class Struggle in Africa*, London: Panaf Books.

Norbrook, N. and van Valen, M. (2011) 'Friend or Foe?' *Africa Report*, no. 31, June.

Nyerere, J. (1979) 'Unity for a New Economic Order', address to the Ministerial Conference of the Group of 77, Arusha, Tanzania, 12 February 1979, in Nyerere, J. (2011) *Freedom and a New World Economic Order*, Dar es Salaam: Oxford University Press.

OECD (2011) 'Africa Fact Sheet: Main Economic Indicators', Paris: OECD.

Ogunbadejo, O (1980) 'Soviet Policies in Africa', *African Affairs*, vol. 79, no. 316.

Ollapally, D. and Rajagopalan, R. (2012) 'India: Foreign Policy Perspectives of an Ambiguous Power', in Nau, H. and Ollapally, D. (eds) *Worldviews of Aspiring Powers: Domestic Foreign Policy Debates in China, India, Iran, Japan and Russia*, Oxford: Oxford University Press.

O'Neill, J. (2001) *Building Better Global Economic BRICs*, Goldman Sachs, Global Economics Paper no: 66, London: Goldman Sachs.

Otero-Iglesias, M. (2009) 'EU–Brazil *Transformismo* in the Reconfiguration of the Global Financial Order', *Austrian Journal of Development Studies*, vol. 25, no. 1.

Otero-Iglesias, M. (2012) 'The EU–Brazil Strategic Partnership in Times of Crisis: What Crisis? What Partner? What Strategy?' paper presented at the workshop The Global Economic Crisis and EU Strategic Partnerships, European Strategic Partnership Observatory, Egmont, Brussels, 2 July.

Page, J. (2011) 'Should Africa Industrialize?' Working Paper 2011/47 Helsinki: UNU-WIDER.

Page, John (2012) 'Can Africa Industrialize?' *Journal of African Economies*, vol. 21, Supplement 2.

Park, R. (1965) 'Indian–African Relations', *Asian Survey*, vol. 5 no. 7.

Patman, R. (1995) 'Russia's New Agenda in Sub-Saharan Africa', in Shearman, P. (ed.) *Russian Foreign Policy Since 1990*, Oxford: Westview Press.

Pecequilo, C. (2009) 'South America and the Challenges of South–South and North–South Cooperation: The Case of Brazil', paper prepared for the Congress of the Latin America Studies Association, Rio de Janeiro, Brazil, 11–14 June.

Pereira, A. (2012) 'Continuity Is Not Lack of Change', *Critical Sociology*, vol. 38, no. 6.

Petithomme, M. (2013) 'Much Ado About Nothing? The Limited Effects of Structural Adjustment Programmes and the Highly Indebted Poor

Countries Initiative on the Reduction of External Debts in Sub-Saharan Africa: An Empirical Analysis', *African Journal of Political Science and International Relations*, vol. 7, no. 2.

Petrobras (2006) 'Petrobras' Business Plan Foresees Doubling Investments Abroad between 2007 and 2011', press release, 7 September.

Petrobras (2011) *2012 – 2016 Business Plan*, www.investidorpetrobras. com.br/en/business-management-plan/2012-2016-business-plan.htm (accessed 2013, no specific date available).

Poddar, T. and Yi, E. (2007) 'India's Rising Growth Potential', *Goldman Sachs Global Economic Paper*, no.152.

Prasad, P. (2003) *Foreign Trade and Commerce in Ancient India*, New Delhi: Abhinav Publications.

Prashad, V. (2011) 'Quid Pro Quo? The Question of India's Subordination to the "American Narrative"', *Monthly Review*, vol. 63, no. 5.

Prates, D. and Paulani, L. (2007) 'The Financial Globalization of Brazil under Lula', *Monthly Review*, vol. 58, no. 9.

Price, G. (2011) *For the Global Good: India's Developing International Role*, Chatham House Report, London: Royal Institute of International Affairs.

Prichard, W. (2009) 'The Mining Boom in Sub-Saharan Africa: Continuity, Change and Policy Implications', in Southall, R. and Melber, H. (eds) *A New Scramble for Africa? Imperialism, Investment and Development*, Scottsville: University of KwaZulu-Natal Press.

Qian Qichen (2005) *Ten Episodes in China's Diplomacy*, New York: HarperCollins.

Quist-Adade, C. (2007) '"Friendship of Peoples" after the Fall: Violence and Pan-African Community in Post-Soviet Moscow', in Matusevich, M. (ed.) *Africa in Russia, Russia in Africa: Three Centuries of Encounters*, Trenton, NJ: Africa World Press.

Radelet, S. (2010) *Emerging Africa: How 17 Countries are Leading the Way*, Washington, DC: Center for Global Development.

Rajadhyaksha, N. (2012) 'India's New Industrial Policy', *Wall Street Journal*, 17 February.

Ramachandran, S. (2007) 'India Pushes People Power in Africa,' *Asia Times*, 13 July.

Ramo, J. (2004) *The Beijing Consensus*, London: The Foreign Policy Centre.

Ramos, J. and Sunkel, O. (1993) 'Towards a Neostructuralist Synthesis', in Sunkel, O. (ed.) *Development from Within: Toward a Neostructuralist Approach for Latin America*, London: Lynn Rienner.

Rampa, F., Sanoussi, B. and Sidiropoulos, E. (2012) 'Leveraging South–South Cooperation for Africa's Development', *South African Journal of International Affairs*, vol. 19, no. 2.

Research Unit for Political Economy (2005) 'Why the US Promotes India's Great-Power Ambitions', *Aspects of India's Economy*, no. 41, December.

Rickett, O. (2013) 'Is This the Century of Africa's Rise?' 22 January, www. vice.com/read/is-this-the-century-of-africas-rise-1 (accessed 23 April 2014).

Roberts, C. (2010) 'Russia's BRICs Diplomacy: Rising Outsider with Dreams of an Insider', *Polity*, vol. 42, no. 1.

Robertson, C. (2012) *The Fastest Billion: The Story Behind Africa's Economic Revolution*, London: Renaissance Capital.

Rocha, A. (2009) 'Lula Wants Partnerships for Investing in Africa, *Brazil–Arab News Agency*, 30 June.

Rodney, W. (2012) *How Europe Underdeveloped Africa*, Oxford: Pambazuka Press.

Rodrigues, J. (1965) *Brazil and Africa*, Berkeley, CA: University of California Press.

Rodrik, D. (2007) 'Normalizing Industrial Policy', Commission of Growth and Development Working Paper no. 3.

Rose, G. and Tepperman, J. (2014) 'The Shape of Things to Come: Hot Markets to Watch', *Foreign Affairs*, January/February.

Rotberg, R. (2013) *Africa Emerges*, Cambridge: Polity Press.

Rotunno, L., Vézina, P. and Zheng Wang (2012) 'The Rise and Fall of (Chinese) African Apparel Exports', Oxford: Centre for the Study of African Economies, Working Paper 2012-12.

Rowden, R. (2013) 'The Myth of Africa's Rise', *Foreign Policy*, 4 January.

Rowlands, D. (2012) 'Individual BRICS or a Collective Bloc? Convergence and Divergence Amongst "Emerging Donor" Nations', *Cambridge Review of International Affairs*, vol. 25, no. 4.

Roxburgh, A. (2011) *The Strongman: Vladimir Putin and the Struggle for Russia*, London: I.B. Tauris.

Roy, A. (1999) *The Third World in the Age of Globalisation: Requiem or New Agenda?* Delhi: Madhyam Books.

Rucki, S. (2011) 'Global Economic Crisis and China's Challenge to Global Hegemony: A Neo-Gramscian Approach', *New Political Science*, vol. 33, no. 3.

Russia Today (2009) '"Africa is Waiting for Our Support" – Dmitry Medvedev', 28 June.

Russia Today (2012) 'Russia Slashes African Debt and Increases Aid', 18 October.

Rutland, P. (2012) 'Neoliberalism and the Russian Transition', *Review of International Political Economy*, vol. 20, no. 2.

Sahni, V. (2007) 'India's Foreign Policy: Key Drivers', *South African Journal of International Affairs*, vol. 14, no. 2.

Sanyal, S. (2008) *An Indian Renaissance: How India Is Rising After a Thousand Years of Decline*, New Delhi: World Scientific Publishing.

Sauvant, K. (2005) 'New Sources of FDI: The BRICs – Outward FDI from Brazil, Russia, India and China', *Journal of World Investment & Trade*, vol. 6, no. 5.

Schoeman, M. (2011) 'Of BRICs and Mortar: The Growing Relations between Africa and the Global South', *The International Spectator*, vol. 46, no. 1.

Scott, D. (2007) *China Stands Up: The PRC and the International System*, London: Routledge.

Seeber, G. (2001) 'Understanding the Brazilian Market: Doing Business in Brazil, an Introductory Guide', Canberra: Department of Foreign Affairs and Trade/Austrade.

Seibert, G. (2011) 'Brazil in Africa: Ambitions and Achievements of an Emerging Regional Power in the Political and Economic Sector', Lisbon: Instituto Universitário de Lisboa, Centro de Estudos Africanos.

Senona, J. (2010) *BRIC and IBSA Forums: Neoliberals in Disguise or Champions of the South?* Braamfontein: South African Institute of International Affairs, Policy Briefing no. 24.

Severino, J-M. and Ray, O. (trans. Fernbach, D.) (2011) *Africa's Moment*, Cambridge: Polity Press.

Shambaugh, D. and Ren Xiao (2012) 'China: The Conflicted Rising Power' in Nau, H. and Ollapally, D. (eds) *Worldviews of Aspiring Powers: Domestic Foreign Policy Debates in China, India, Iran, Japan and Russia*, Oxford: Oxford University Press.

Sharma, A. (2007) 'India and Africa: Partnership in the 21st Century', *South African Journal of International Affairs*, vol. 14, no. 2.

Sharma, D. (2008) 'India Cultivates Africa', *Mail Today*, New Delhi, 25 June.

Sharma, D. and Mahajan, D. (2007) 'Energising Ties: The Politics of Oil', *South African Journal of International Affairs*, vol. 14, no. 2.

Sharma, R. (2012) 'Broken BRICs: Why the Rest Stopped Rising', *Foreign Affairs*, vol. 91, no. 6.

Sharma, R. (2014) 'The Ever-emerging Markets: Why Economic Forecasts Fail', *Foreign Affairs*, vol. 93, no. 1.

Shastri, V. (1997) 'The Politics of Economic Liberalization in India', *Contemporary South Asia*, vol. 6, no. 1.

Shaw, T. (1985) *Towards a Political Economy for Africa: The Dialectics of Dependence*, London: Macmillan.

Shen Xiaofang (2013) *Private Chinese Investment in Africa: Myths and Realities*, Policy Research Working Paper 6311, Washington, DC: World Bank.

Sherr, J. (2013) *Hard Diplomacy and Soft Coercion: Russia's Influence Abroad*, London: Chatham House.

Shevtsova, L. (2007) *Russia Lost in Transition: The Yeltsin and Putin Legacies*, Washington, DC: Carnegie Endowment for International Peace.

Shivji, I. (1980) 'The State in the Dominated Social Formations of Africa: Some Theoretical Issues', *International Social Science Journal*, vol. 32, no. 4.

Shivji, I. (2009) *Accumulation in an African Periphery: A Theoretical Framework*, Dar es Salaam: Mkuki na Nyota.

Shubin, V. (1999) *ANC: A View From Moscow*, Bellville: Mayibuye Books.

Shubin, V. (2004) 'Russia and Africa: Moving in the Right Direction?' in Taylor, I. and Williams, P. (eds) *Africa in International Politics: External Involvement on the Continent*, London: Routledge.

Shubin, V. (2008) *The Hot 'Cold War': The USSR in Southern Africa*, London: Pluto Press.

Shubin, V. (2010) 'Russia and Africa: Coming Back?' *Russian Analytical Digest*, no. 83, September.

Shubin, V. (2011) 'BRIC or BRICS?' paper presented at AEGIS Fourth European Conference on African Studies, Uppsala, Sweden, 15–18 June.

Sindzingre, A. (2013) 'The Ambivalent Impact of Commodities: Structural Change or Status Quo in Sub-Saharan Africa?' *South African Journal of International Affairs*, vol. 20, no. 1.

Singh, R. (2006) 'India, Africa Ready to Embrace Global Destiny', interview, 25 January, New Delhi: Ministry of External Affairs.

Sinha, A. and Dorschner, J. (2010) 'India: Rising Power or a Mere Revolution of Rising Expectations?' *Polity*, vol. 42, no. 1.

Sinha, P. (2010) 'Indian Development Cooperation with Africa', in Cheru, F. and Obi, C. (eds) *The Rise of China and India in Africa*, London: Zed Books.

Skidmore, T. (2010) *Brazil, Five Centuries of Change*, 2nd edition, New York: Oxford University Press.

Smith, N. (1990) *Uneven Development: Nature, Capital, and the Production of Space*, Oxford: Blackwell.

Söderbaum, F. and Taylor, I. (eds) (2003) *Regionalism and Uneven Development in Southern Africa: The Case of The Maputo Development Corridor*, Aldershot: Ashgate.

Solow, R. (1974) 'Intergenerational Equity and Exhaustible Resources', *Review of Economic Studies*, vol. 41, no. 5.

Sorbara, M. (2007) 'India and Africa: It's Old Friends, New Game and Rules', *Daily Nation*, Nairobi, 9 February.

Sotero, P. and Armijo, L. (2007) 'Brazil: To Be or Not to Be a BRIC', *Asian Perspective*, vol. 31, no. 4.

Southall, R. (2008) 'The "New Scramble" and Labour in Africa', *Labour, Capital and Society*, vol. 41, no. 2.

Southall, R. (2009) 'Scrambling for Africa? Continuities and Discontinuities with Formal Imperialism', in Southall and Melber (2009).

Southall, R. and Comninos, A. (2009) 'The Scramble for Africa and the Marginalisation of African Capitalism', in Southall and Melber (2009).

Southall, R. and Melber, H. (2009) (eds) *A New Scramble for Africa? Imperialism, Investment and Development*, Scottsville: University of KwaZulu-Natal Press.

South Bulletin (2003) 'G-20: A Powerful Tool for Convergence in Negotiations', November, 2003.

South Centre (2005) *Problems and Policy-related Challenges Faced by Commodity-Dependent Developing Countries*, Geneva: South Centre.

Standard Chartered (2012) 'Africa–India Trade and Investment: Playing to Strengths', Standard Chartered, On the Ground, Global Research, 8 August.

Stent, A. (2008) 'Restoration and Revolution in Putin's Foreign Policy', *Europe–Asia Studies*, vol. 60, no. 6.

Stolte, C. (2012) 'Brazil in Africa: Just Another BRICS Country Seeking Resources?' Chatham House Briefing Paper, London: Royal Institute of International Affairs.

Straffo, P. and Dobb, M. (eds) (1986/1817) *On the Principles of Political Economy and Taxation*, vol. 1 of *The Works and Correspondence of David Ricardo*, Cambridge: Cambridge University Press.

Strange, G. (2011) 'China's Post-Listian Rise: Beyond Radical Globalisation Theory and the Political Economy of Neoliberal Hegemony', *New Political Economy*, vol. 16, no. 5.

Stuermer, M. (2009) *Putin and the Rise of Russia: The Country that Came in from the Cold*, New York: Pegasus/Norton.

Suri, N. (2008) 'India and Africa: A Contemporary Perspective', in Sheth, V. (ed.) *India–Africa Relations: Emerging Policy and Development Perspectives*, Delhi: Academic Excellence.

Sutter, R. (2008) *Chinese Foreign Relations: Power and Policy Since the Cold War*, Lanham, MD: Rowman & Littlefield.

Sweig, J. (2010) 'A New Global Player: Brazil's Far-Flung Agenda', *Foreign Affairs*, vol. 89, no. 6.

Szentes, T. (1971) *The Political Economy of Underdevelopment*, Budapest: Akadémiai Kiadó.

Tang Jiaxuan (2011) *Heavy Storm and Gentle Breeze: Tang Jiaxuan's Diplomatic Memoir*, Beijing: Foreign Languages Press.

Tata Group (2008) 'About Us: Tata Group Profile', www.tata.com (accessed 2013, no specific date available).

Taylor, I. (1997) 'China's Foreign Policy Towards Southern Africa in the "Socialist Modernisation" Period', East Asia Project Working Paper 18, Dept. of International Relations, University of the Witwatersrand.

Taylor, I. (1998) 'China's Foreign Policy Towards Africa in the 1990s', *Journal of Modern African Studies*, vol. 36, no. 3.

Taylor, I. (2001) *Stuck in Middle GEAR: South Africa's Post-Apartheid Foreign Relations*, Westport, CT: Praeger.

Taylor, I. (2002) 'Taiwan's Foreign Policy and Africa: The Limitations of Dollar Diplomacy', *Journal of Contemporary China*, vol. 11, no. 30.

Taylor, I. (2003) 'As Good as it Gets? Botswana's "Democratic Development"', *Journal of Contemporary African Studies*, vol. 21, no. 2.

Taylor, I. (2004) 'The "All-weather Friend"? Sino–African Interaction in the Twenty-first Century', in Taylor, I. and Williams, P. (eds) *Africa in International Politics: External Involvement on the Continent*, London: Routledge.

Taylor, I. (2005) *NEPAD: Towards Africa's Development or Another False Start?* Boulder, CO: Lynne Rienner.

Taylor, I. (2006a) *China and Africa: Engagement and Compromise*, London: Routledge.

Taylor, I. (2006b) 'China's Oil Diplomacy in Africa', *International Affairs*, vol. 82, no. 5.

Taylor, I. (2008) 'Beyond the New "Two Whateverisms": China's Ties in Africa', *Journal of Current Chinese Affairs*, no. 3.

Taylor, I. (2009a) *China's New Role in Africa*, Boulder, CO: Lynne Rienner.

Taylor, I. (2009b) '"The South Will Rise Again"? New Alliances and Global Governance: The India–Brazil–South Africa Dialogue Forum', *Politikon: South African Journal of Political Studies*, vol. 36, no. 1.

Taylor, I. (2010) *The International Relations of Sub-Saharan Africa*, New York: Continuum.

Taylor, I. (2011a) 'South African "Imperialism" in a Region Lacking Regionalism: A Critique', *Third World Quarterly*, vol. 32, no. 7.

Taylor, I. (2011b) *The Forum on China–Africa Cooperation (FOCAC)*, London: Routledge.

Taylor, I. (2012) 'India's Rise in Africa', *International Affairs*, vol. 88, no. 4.

Taylor, I. and Williams, P. (2004) 'Understanding Africa's Place in World Politics', in Taylor, I. and Williams, P. (eds) *Africa in International Politics: External Involvement on the Continent*, London: Routledge.

Taylor, S. (2012) *Globalization and the Cultures of Business in Africa: From Patrimonialism to Profit*, Bloomington, IN: Indiana University Press.

Thussu, D. (2012) 'A Million Media Now! The Rise of India on the Global Scene', *Round Table*, vol. 101, no. 5.

TRALAC (2013) 'Africa–China Trading Relationship', Stellenbosch: TRALAC.

Treisman, D. (2011) *The Return: Russia's Journey from Gorbachev to Medvedev*, New York: Free Press.

Truscott, P. (1997) *Russia First: Breaking with the West*, London: I.B. Taurus.

Tschannerl, G. (1976) 'Periphery Capitalist Development: A Case Study of the Tanzanian Economy', *Utafiti: Journal of the Faculty of Arts and Social Sciences*, vol. 1, no. 1.

Tsygankov, A. (2012a) *Russia and the West from Alexander to Putin: Honor in International Relations*, Cambridge: Cambridge University Press.

Tsygankov, A. (2012b) 'Russia and Global Governance in the Post-Western World', *Russian Analytical Digest*, no. 114.

Tudoroiu, T. (2012) 'Conceptualizing BRICS: OPEC as a Mirror', *Asian Journal of Political Science*, vol. 20, no. 1.

Uchoa, P. (2010) 'World Cup Handover puts Spotlight on Africa–Brazil Ties', *BBC News*, 10 July.

UNCTAD (2011) *The Economic Development in Africa Report 2011: Fostering Industrial Development in Africa in the New Global Envi-*

ronment, Geneva: United Nations Conference on Trade and Development.

UNCTAD (2012a) *The State of Commodity Dependence 2012*, Geneva: United Nations Conference on Trade and Development.

UNCTAD (2012b) *Economic Development in Africa Report 2012: Structural Transformation and Sustainable Development in Africa*, Geneva: United Nations Conference on Trade and Development.

UNCTAD (2013) *UNCTAD Stat*, http://unctadstat.unctad.org (accessed 2013, no specific date available).

UNDESA (2013) *World Economic Situation and Prospects 2013: Global Outlook*, New York: United Nations.

UNDP (2011) *Towards Human Resilience: Sustaining MDG Progress in an Age of Economic Uncertainty*, New York: UNDP.

UNECA (2007) *Economic Report on Africa 2007: Accelerating Africa's Development through Diversification*, Addis Ababa: United Nations Economic Commission for Africa.

UNECA (2012a) 'Assessing Regional Integration in Africa V: Towards an African Continental Free Trade Area', Addis Ababa: United Nations Economic Commission for Africa.

UNECA (2012b) *Economic Report on Africa 2012: Unleashing Africa's Potential as a Pole of Global Growth*, Addis Ababa: United Nations Economic Commission for Africa.

UNECA (2013a) *Africa–BRICS Cooperation: Implications for Growth, Employment and Structural Transformation*, Addis Ababa: United Nations Economic Commission for Africa.

UNECA (2013b) *Economic Report on Africa 2013 Making the Most of Africa's Commodities: Industrializing for Growth, Jobs and Economic Transformation – Economic Report on Africa*, Addis Ababa: United Nations Economic Commission for Africa.

UNICA (2010) 'Statistics on Brazil's Ethanol Production', UNICA (Brazilian Sugarcane Industry Association) www.english.unica.com.br/dadosCotacao/estatistica (accessed 2013, no specific date available).

UNIDO (2009) *Industrial Development Report, 2009 Breaking in and Moving Up: New Industrial Challenges for the Bottom Billion and the Middle Income Countries*, Vienna: United Nations Industrial Development Organization.

UNSD (2013) *2012 International Trade Statistics Yearbook, Volume II: Trade by Commodity*, New York, NY: United Nations Statistics Division.

van de Walle, N. (2001) *African Economies and the Politics of Permanent Crisis, 1979–1999*, Cambridge: Cambridge University Press.

Vasilenko, S. (2012) 'Russia Writes off $20 billion for African Countries', *Pravda* (English version), 19 October.

Vasileva, A. (2014) 'Continuity and Change in Russian Capitalism' in Becker (2014).

Vermeiren, M. and Dierckx, S. (2012) 'Challenging Global Neoliberalism?

The Global Political Economy of China's Capital Controls', *Third World Quarterly*, vol. 33, no. 9.

Vezirgiannidou, S. (2013) 'The United States and Rising Powers in a Post-hegemonic Global Order', *International Affairs*, vol. 89, no. 3.

Vieira, M., Alden, C. and Morphet, S. (2010) *The South in World Politics*, Basingstoke: Palgrave Macmillan.

Vigevani, T. and Cepaluni, G. (2007) 'Lula's Foreign Policy and the Quest for Autonomy through Diversification', *Third World Quarterly*, vol. 28, no. 7.

Vigevani, S. and Cepaluni, G. (2009*) Brazilian Foreign Policy in Changing Times: The Quest for Autonomy from Sarney to Lula*, Lanham, MD: Lexington.

Vilela, M. (2002) 'Reflections on Language Policy in African Countries with Portuguese as an Official Language', *Current Issues in Language Planning*, vol. 3, no. 3.

Vines, A. and Oruitemeka, B. (2007) 'Engagement with the African Indian Ocean Rim States', *South African Journal of International Affairs*, vol. 14, no. 2.

Vines, A. and Sidiropoulos, E. (2008) 'India and Africa: India Calling', *The World Today*, vol. 64, no. 4.

Visentini, P. (2009) 'Prestige Diplomacy, Southern Solidarity or "Soft Imperialism"? Lula's Brazil–Africa Relations (2003 Onwards)', paper presented at the African Studies Centre, Leiden, April 7, www.ascleiden.nl/Pdf/seminarvisentini.pdf (accessed 23 April 2014).

Visentini, P. and Pereira, A. (2007) *The African Policy of Lula's Government*, Porto Alegre: NERINT.

Vlcek, W. (2013) 'From Road Town to Shanghai: Situating the Caribbean in Global Capital Flows to China', *British Journal of Politics and International Relations*, (forthcoming).

Wade, R. (2003) 'What Strategies are Viable for Developing Countries Today? The World Trade Organization and the Shrinking of "Development Space"', *Review of International Political Economy*, vol. 10, no. 4.

Walter, A. (2009) 'Chinese Attitudes towards Global Financial Regulatory Cooperation: Revisionist or Status Quo?' in Helleiner, E., Pagliari, S. and Zimmerman, H. (eds) *Global Finance in Crisis: The Politics of International Regulatory Change*, London: Routledge.

Wang Chaohua (ed.) (2003) *One China, Many Paths*, London: Verso.

Wang Hui (2003) *China's New Order: Society, Politics and Economy in Transition*, Cambridge, MA: Harvard University Press.

Wang Jianye (2007) *What Drives China's Growing Role in Africa?* IMF Working Paper WP/07/211, Washington, DC: International Monetary Fund.

Warmerdam, W. (2012) 'Is China a Liberal Internationalist?' *Chinese Journal of International Politics*, vol. 5, no. 3.

Warren, B. (1973) 'Imperialism and Capitalist Industrialization', *New Left*

Review, vol. 1, no. 81.

Webber, M. (1992) 'Soviet Policy in Sub-Saharan Africa: The Final Phase', *Journal of Modern African Studies,* vol. 30, no. 1.

Weeks, J. (2010) 'A Study for Trade and Development Report 2010: Employment, Productivity and Growth in Africa South of the Sahara', unpublished paper, Centre for Development Policy and Research, School of Oriental and African Studies, University of London.

Westra, R. (2012) *The Evil Axis of Finance: The US–Japan–China Stranglehold on the Global Future,* Atlanta, GA: Clarity Press.

White, L. (2010) 'Understanding Brazil's New Drive for Africa', *South African Journal of International Affairs,* vol. 17, no. 2.

White, L. (2013) 'Emerging Powers in Africa: Is Brazil Any Different?' *South African Journal of International Affairs,* vol. 20, no. 1.

Whitfield, L. (2012) 'How Countries Become Rich and Reduce Poverty: A Review of Heterodox Explanations of Economic Development', *Development Policy Review,* vol. 30, no. 3.

Wikileaks (2011) 'Brazil: Ambassador's Second Meeting with Presidential Chief of Staff', Cable, 16 November 2006.

Williams, G. (1980) *State and Society in Nigeria,* Idanre: Afrografika Publishers.

Woods, N. (2008) 'Whose Aid? Whose Influence? China, Emerging Donors and the Silent Revolution in Development Assistance', *International Affairs,* vol. 84, no. 6.

World Bank (2006) 'Where is the Wealth of Nations?' Washington, DC: World Bank.

World Bank (2011) 'Africa's Future and the World Bank's Support to It', Washington, DC: World Bank.

World Bank (2013) *Data,* http://data.worldbank.org (accessed 2013, no specific date available). Washington, DC: World Bank.

World Economic Forum, the World Bank and the African Development Bank (2011) *The Africa Competitiveness Report 2011,* Geneva: World Economic Forum.

WTO (2012) *International Trade Statistics 2012,* Washington, DC: World Trade Organization.

Wu Yanrui (2003) *China's Economic Growth: A Miracle with Chinese Characteristics,* London: Routledge Curzon.

Yan Xuetong (2006) 'The Rise of China and its Power Status', *Chinese Journal of International Politics,* vol. 1, no. 1.

Yao, Y. (2010) 'The End of the Beijing Consensus', *Foreign Affairs Snapshot,* 2 February.

Young, A. (2012) 'The African Growth Miracle', *Journal of Political Economy,* vol. 120, no. 4.

Zha Daojiong (2005) 'Comment: Can China Rise?' *Review of International Studies,* vol. 31, no. 4.

Zuma, J. (2010) 'Address by President JG Zuma to the South Africa–Russia Business Forum on the Occasion of the Official Visit to the Russian

Federation', Pretoria: Office of the Presidency, 6 August.

Zuma, J. (2011) '"Broad Vision, Shared Prosperity", address by President Jacob Zuma to the Plenary of the Third BRICS Leaders Meeting, Sanya, Hainan Island, People's Republic of China', Pretoria: Office of the Presidency, 14 April.

Zweig, D. and Bi Jianhai (2005) 'China's Global Hunt for Energy', *Foreign Affairs*, vol. 84, no. 5.

INDEX

Printed and bound by CPI Group (UK) Ltd, Croydon, CR0 4YY

13/04/2025